THE PRACTICE OF PSYCHOLOGY:

The Battle for Professionalism

Psyche THE NICHOLAS & DOROTHY
CUMMINGS FOUNDATION

THE PRACTICE OF PSYCHOLOGY:

The Battle for Professionalism

Edited by

Rogers Wright & Nicholas Cummings

Zeig, Tucker & Theisen, Inc.
Phoenix, Arizona

Library of Congress Cataloging-in-Publication Data

The practice of psychology : the battle for professionalism / edited by Rogers
Wright & Nicholas Cummings.

    p. cm.

Includes index.

ISBN: 1-891944-73-8 (alk. paper)

    1. American Psychological Association—History.   I. Wright, Rogers.
II. Cummings, Nicholas A.

BF11.P73 2001

150'.6'073—dc21   2001022249

Published by

ZEIG, TUCKER & THEISEN, INC.
3614 North 24th Street
Phoenix, Arizona 85016

Manufactured in the United States of America

10 9 8 7 6 5 4 3 2 1

Dedication

This book was inspired by the saga of psychology's Dirty Dozen. Once scorned, and facing insurmountable odds, this small band of professional psychologists changed the American Psychological Association (APA) forever. Their history was chronicled in both the *APA Monitor* and the *National Psychologist* in 1999, and these articles appear in the Appendix. That same year, during the APA Convention in Boston, which was the occasion of their 30th anniversary, the surviving members of the Dirty Dozen were honored in separate ceremonies by three practitioner organizations within the APA. The citations that were presented are also included in the Appendix.

This book is dedicated not only to them, but also to their scores of supporters throughout the years, without whom the struggle to professionalize the APA could not have been won. It is also intended to memorialize for future generations of psychologists how an ostensibly impossible feat was accomplished through dedicated activism, and to encourage those who come after them to triumph over the new, seemingly insurmountable challenges that are currently threatening the very survival of professional psychology.

Contents

Preface

To the degree that such things can ever be, the publication of this volume is a product of chance.

The book owes its origin to a whimsical comment to this writer in the winter of 1999 by two members of psychology's Dirty Dozen, Marvin Metsky and Eugene Shapiro. Recalling that the group known as the Dirty Dozen would be celebrating either its 30th or 40th anniversary (depending upon who did the counting and dating from what was considered to be the initial actions), they mused that this small informal group of individuals came to be one of the most influential groups in the last 50 years of American psychology. Three members of the group are deceased and the rest, if not retired, at least have curtailed their professional activities.

Metsky and Shapiro suggested that the ending of the century was an appropriate time to have a celebratory meeting of the group; and the surviving members agreed. The "anniversary" was celebrated at the August 1999 meeting of the American Psychological Association (APA) where the Dirty Dozen were honored by three of the group's more or less direct progeny: APA's caucus group, known as the Association of Practicing Psychologists; APA's Division of Psychologists in Independent Practice (Division 42); and the Association for the Advancement of Psychology, psychology's national public policy and political action group.

As a direct consequence of these meetings, two things became apparent: (1) with the passage of time and the enormous growth in the number of psychologists committed to professional service delivery, much of the history of how clinical practice in psycholo-

gy came to be defined has been forgotten; and/or (2) that history
was never part of the lore and knowledge base of younger psychologists training for professional practice. From the perspective
of the Dirty Dozen, it is fair to say that the lack of information
about the struggles surrounding the rise of professionalism in
American psychology reflects a range of efforts ranging from, at
best, attempts to treat "highly loaded" material in a scholarly
fashion to, at worst, outright denial or attempts to suppress an accounting of the actual events.

To this writer's knowledge, the only publication that attempts
to treat comprehensively the history of organized American psychology is that of Evans, Sexton, and Cadwallader (1992).[1] It also
chronicles the extended, and often bitter, battles within psychology between academic/scientific elements and those psychologists
who primarily define their identity in terms of the delivery of psychological services.

As noted, this scholarly volume (Evans, Sexton, & Cadwallader, 1992) does treat in comprehensive detail the early skirmishes
between the scientific/academic and professional wings, conflicts
that became widely apparent in the middle to late 1930s and early
1940s. Unfortunately, although their book is detailed, it lacks the
zest, color, and firsthand knowledge of those psychologists who
were leading participants in the making of that history. In fact,
the chapters dealing with APA history after 1945 are notably lacking in the kind of personal detail that characterize the first six
chapters of the volume. Thus, the present book fills that gap,
building on the additional detail as recalled by some of the leaders
of the professional revolution, that is, those psychologists who
truly have been there, done that!

In the mid 1930s the concerns around the lack of commitment
to professionalism within the existent American Psychological
Association led to the establishment of several external groups,
one of the larger ones being the American Association for Ap-

---

[1] Evans, R.B., Sexton, V.S., & Cadwallader, T.C. (1992), *100 years of the American Psychological Association: A historical perspective*. Washington, DC: APA Books.

plied Psychology (AAAP), an organization devoted to the advancement of applied psychology. The APA governance/establishment proceeding at what, in the association's history, was "blazing speed," and motivated by the knowledge that the organization's scientist/philosopher/academic wing was already outnumbered, moved to accommodate the rising "professional wing" by reincorporating the leadership (and membership) of the AAAP and other disaffected groups into the organizational structure of the APA, efforts that were accelerated by the outbreak of World War II and the role psychology played in that combat. Such attempts at "reincorporation," however, had the covert agenda of ensuring that the "scientists" would retain control of the APA's governance.

These efforts led, in 1943, to the convening of a somewhat grandiosely titled "Intersociety Constitutional Convention" (modeled on the American Constitutional Convention of 1787), which culminated in a plan to "reorganize" (apparently only the first of a long series of such reorganization proposals) the parent organization. However, despite its grandiosity and high-flown rhetoric, the proposal did find some acceptance, and provided an APA organizational umbrella for such disparate groups as the AAAP, the Psychometric Society, and the Society for the Psychological Study for Social Issues (SPSSI). The subsequent adoption of this plan allowed the disparate interests to interact with one another within the APA in relative ease for another decade to decade and a half.

A subsequent and more far-reaching development emerging from the nexus of the discussions around "reorganization" was the recognition that some modification in the education and training of "applied psychologists" was a necessary component of the rapprochement among the various interests. Under the prodding and leadership of David Shakow, these concerns culminated, in August of 1949, in the lauded and reviled "Boulder Conference on Graduate Education in Psychology." That conference produced an establishment model for training in the applied field, a model that continued to give preeminence to science and, in effect, "tacked on" training in the applied areas. By assuaging the highly irrational fears of this group that somehow they would be seen as similar to medical practitioners, the Boulder compromise (scientist/practitioner) found broad acceptance in the APA's scientific/academic community (few of whom had any real knowledge of, or experience in providing, free-standing, professional, psychological services.

What the general mythology and the *100 Years of the American Psychological Association* volume do not record is that the Shakow/Boulder compromise (scientist/practitioner) found little acceptance among younger psychologists primarily committed to psychological service delivery. Nor does psychological lore record the emergence of a competing model at Boulder for training in applied psychology, a model that gave preeminence to practice as conceptualized in the term "practitioner/scientist" (or, preferably, "practitioner/scholar"). However, the APA academic establishment quickly adopted the Boulder concept and the accreditation of APA training programs was effected along the lines of the concept, despite the fact that large numbers of psychologists across the country rejected the Boulder training model on the basis that it inadequately prepared members of their profession for the delivery of quality psychological services.

The APA establishment's widespread adoption of the scientist/practitioner model (1) ensured that there would be additional conferences struggling with the issue of training for practitioners and (2) institutionalized the strife between the controlling scientist/academic wing and practitioners (determined to reorganize the "APA" so as to give institutional prominence to the needs and concerns of applied psychologists). Thus, the core conflict within American psychology had been joined, a conflict that, in spite of all its accompanying rhetoric, basically concerned the issue of which group (academic/scientist or practitioner) would play the dominant role in shaping psychology's future and in determining how the APA's policies and operations would interact therewith.

Former APA Executive Officer Michael Pallak and current APA Executive Officer Ray Fowler (a member of the Dirty Dozen) chronicled the events of the ensuing period (1972–1979) in

Evans, Sexton & Cadwallader (1992; see chapters 8 and 9). These treatments, although comprehensive, are viewed from the perspective of the APA's Executive Office, a perspective that necessarily is somewhat circumspect and specifically omits details of the upheaval that make most segments of the association appear less than scholarly, scientific, or well-mannered.

As noted earlier, the present book was undertaken in answer to numerous requests for a "history" of the activities of the Dirty Dozen. It soon became apparent, however, that such an "overview" would necessarily omit, or treat superficially, specific areas or activities that played a major role in the rise of professionalism in psychology. Consequently, Drs. Cummings and Wright committed to the development of a treatise that would delineate the major areas of conflict in the rise of professionalism and provide the detail this enterprise deserves. A number of colleagues, some of whom were members of the Dirty Dozen, and others of whom were supporters and/or comrades in arms, were invited to submit their recollections of these events detailing their specific areas of involvement in what has been described as efforts that "forever changed the face of American psychology."

As a postscript, this writer, in preparing this preface, reviewed a number of publications, particularly the February 2000 issue of the *American Psychologist.* If there had remained any doubt whatsoever of the importance of memorializing these recollections, this four-part issue would have dispelled them. The publications's masthead lists four section editors, one for the History of Psychology and Obituary, two for "Science Watch," and one for Psychology in the Public Forum. Ironically, there is no identification of a section editor for, or the existence of, a section on Practice—although practitioners represent by far the greatest number of members of the APA. It is also striking that the associate editors are, with one exception, academics who have little visibility or credibility, whereas many psychologists identify with the concept of "practitioner/scholar."

Finally, the centerpiece of that February issue is the "History of Psychology: The Boulder Conference." The section on history includes contributions from five academic psychologists, led by former APA President George W. Albee, the only contributor to find a "fatal flaw" in the Boulder model. Not only is it the case that not one of the five contributors played a major role in the rise of professionalism in psychology; but there is a conspicuous absence of those who did. One of the more important developments in the training for applied psychology was the rejection of the scientist/practitioner model, the widespread endorsement of the practitioner/scholar model by applied psychologists, and the attendant rise and growth of the professional schools as a major source of training. It is reasonable to expect that if the impact or history of the Boulder scientist/practitioner model for training is to be evaluated, there would be significant representation of the views of those applied psychologists who considered the model to be "dead on arrival."

The foregoing suggests that the battle between academics and practitioners has by no means been resolved; it is just being fought on a different turf. If these collected reflections and musings help today's professional psychologists understand how we got to this point and place in time, then the purpose of this book will have been realized.

ROGERS H. WRIGHT

The Practice of

Psychology:

The Battle for Professionalism

CHAPTER 1

The Rise of Professionalism Within American Psychology and How It Came to Be:

A Brief History of the Dirty Dozen

Prelude

In the annals of virtually any social institution, a relatively small group of individuals will be found to have been at the center of the development, to have nurtured and shaped the growth of that institution. One might be tempted to think that with their expertise in human motivation and behavior, psychologists and their institutions would be immune to such trends. In the writer's experience, this is not so, as the same rules apply to professional psychology.

The decades between 1955 and 1995 saw the emergence and empowerment of an entire professional cadre among mental health service providers, "the professional psychologist." As in other social institutions, a relatively small number of individual psychologists not only were at the forefront of those responsible for defining the professional psychologists, but took leading roles in the restructuring of the American Psychological Association (APA) to accommodate this new entity. In the vanguard of those relatively few individuals was a small, informal group of psychologists known as the Dirty Dozen, signifying the group's willingness to engage in all sorts of "psychologically unseemly acts," such as political action both within and outside of the formal structure of American psychology.

Although actually 14 in number (leading to charges that the group couldn't count either), the name "Dirty Dozen" accurately reflected the participating membership at any given time, and/or the number of participating members involved in any given activity. The adoption of the name stemmed from the discovery by the group that the academics in the APA were utilizing their faculty emoluments to control the organization, and "The Dozen" committed to being just as "Dirty." The same individuals, Theodore F. Blau, Nicholas A. Cummings, Raymond D. Fowler, Melvin A. Gravitz, Ernest Lawrence, Marvin Metsky, C.J. Rosecrans, Jr.,† S. Don Schultz,† Eugene Shapiro, Max Siegel,† Robert Weitz, Jack G. Wiggins, Rogers H. Wright, Francis A. Young, were involved in the Dirty Dozen's activities over the decades of the rise of professional psychology, bound together by their commitment to the betterment of psychology. There were never any rules, bylaws, or procedures governing the group, or any dues. Such formalities were unnecessary. You got a phone call; and if you could, you pitched in whatever the action might be. With equal informality, I got "tagged" to chair the group; and from the perspective of both the pleasure and the demands, I've never had another job that even came close.

We debated, we fought, and we argued; but ultimately we coalesced, and then we acted. This is my personal recollection of our story.

§

The independent provision of psychological services was virtually nonexistent prior to and during World War II, and the independent practitioners of psychiatry, although significantly more abundant, were found primarily in major urban centers. In fact, it was during this era that psychiatry finally began to emerge from the shadow of neurology as an independent specialty (i.e., psychiatrists previously were known as neuropsychiatrists and the psychiatric component of this residency constituted approximately one sixth of the budding practitioner's specialty training).

World War II, with its diverse needs for psychological classification and its numerous mental health casualties, demanded mental health providers with the competencies required to address the multitude of problems occasioned by the conflict. These needs, perhaps as much as any other single factor, were the primary determinants of the rise of clinical psychology as a recognizable discipline in the medical field. The varied demands for mental health services manifested in World War II became very much a part of the mental health care scene in the post war years of the late 1940s and 1950s. Inpatient and outpatient Veteran's Administration (VA) facilities were both awash with service-connected mental health disabilities, and there were severe shortages of competent personnel trained to address them.

Consequently, the VA, as an agency of the federal government, became a major source of funding for the training of psychologists and psychiatrists. In short order, psychology training programs at the college and university level (which had previously suffered from a severe lack of financial support and student interest) now found an abundance of both. Training programs expanded; more faculty members were employed; and, for the first time, practitioners were produced who were more or less well trained to provide independent mental health services.

Yet despite the fact that much of their financial support came from sources interested in the training of clinical psychologists, most psychology departments tended to look down on applied practitioners, feeling that the "true psychologist" was the one functioning in an academic setting. Academic psychology took an even more disparaging view of psychological practitioners with any interest in independent practice. In fact, the writer recalls a long-ago predoctoral conversation with a graduate assistant colleague in which he indicated that he ultimately planned to enter independent practice. The statement was greeted with the shocked admonition: "Don't say that out loud around here or you'll *never* get your doctorate."

These attitudes were, understandably, also reflected in psychology's professional organizations. The APA, psychology's preeminent national organization, was little more than an academic debating society whose governance and professional staff were singularly lacking in any representation of professional practitioner interests. It is also noteworthy that the academic curriculum for the training of clinical psychologists was equally impoverished as far as educational and training content relevant to the delivery of psychological services was concerned. The prevailing attitude seemingly was, "Oh well, if you have to do it to make a living, okay! But we're really training scientists and academicians." In fact, mythology has it that in the late 1930s a small organization of practitioners was founded, one that eventually (through amalgamation with the APA) was swallowed up in the APA structure, APA's avowed purpose being to ensure that "practitioners would never be the tail that wagged the APA dog."[1]

State psychological associations were few in number, poorly funded, and generally were dominated by the academic community in a given state. Specialty organizations were essentially nonexistent. This situation continued through the 1950s and into the early years of the 1960s, but change was now very close at hand because the "devil's deal" that academic psychology had struck to procure clinical psychology training funds (funds that supported many psychology departments) was producing a younger, more aggressive body of psychologists for whom the progression from academic training to independent psychological service delivery seemed the penultimate step in professionalism. This younger group rejected the concept that the scientist was the sole role model for the clinician, along with the concept that an institutional setting was the only appropriate context for the provision of psychologi-

---

[1] For a highly sanitized account of these transactions, see Evans, Sexton, and Cadwaller (1992).

cal services. The emergence of large numbers of psychologists with a different conceptual model and different commitments had enormous implications for the profession, implications that were either ignored or denied by our national organization.

The APA establishment could well afford to be somewhat complacent; in the context of its earlier "amalgamation," the organization had so structured itself that once any given group gained control of the "establishment," it would be extremely difficult to change. For example, although the bylaws identified the APA's Council of Representatives as the "governing body" of the organization, it was dominated by a 12-member Board of Directors exclusively scientist/academic in its orientation. Furthermore, despite bylaws that recognized the Board as an agency of the Council, the reality was the reverse, because it ran the organization. The council met for one day per year (concurrent with the annual convention), thereby ensuring even fewer participants. The meetings were the epitome of boredom and an exercise in rubber stamping, except in those rare instances where some matter of concern to the scientific/academic community (such as tenure or program recognition) was on the agenda. The rest of the APA's governance structure was composed of the Boards of Scientific Affairs, Professional Affairs, and Publications, whose members were elected by and from the sitting Council of Representatives. The Board of Professional Affairs included one psychologist and meager support staff.

Nomination to these boards and committees was controlled by a small and select group of members of the Board of Directors, approved by the rest of the Board and submitted to the Council for concurrence. Given the additional fact of the 2½-to-1 voting edge in the Council of the scientific/academic divisions over the state associations, it is apparent that a relatively small group of academics could, with relative ease, dominate psychology nationally. In that context, it is also noteworthy that, even today, after revolutions, study commissions, and so on, much of the process remains the same; for example, candidates for the APA's Board of Directors are limited to nominations by and from the APA's Council of Representatives, must have served on the prior Council, and are elected by the Council. Thus, as few as 39 members of the APA's sitting Council (approximately 150 members) elect a candidate to the Board of Directors and its board and committees —39 in an organization of over 100,000 members. So much for the democratic process!

Conversely, especially after the Kovacs-Wright reworking of the APA constitution, the nominations and election process for other standing boards and committees did "open up" because the constitutional revision mandated (1) that such nominations be open to the entire APA membership and (2) that the final slate of candidates (for any given opening) be "representative of the organizations as a whole." However, even these drastic measures failed to democratize the process completely; as a follow-up study by Wright indicated: over 80% of the candidates for the board and committee positions were generated by their parent board committees.

This state of affairs might have continued indefinitely had it not been for the availability of training funds for the production of professional psychologists and the consequent training of psychologists less tolerant of establishment fussiness. This "new" group did not identify predominately with science and academia. Rather, its members began to go into full and part-time independent practice, a movement that brought into an archaic APA a range of issues rarely, if ever, considered by the APA establishment. Perhaps the most trenchant example is symbolized by the fact that as late as the early 1960s all members of the APA's Board of Professional Affairs were academic psychologists, most of whom had little "hands on" experience in independent professional service delivery. The major issues then impinging on psychology at both the state and national levels would shape the profession for decades to come, including: (1) the need to protect both the public interest and the profession by the enactment of mandatory credentialing legislation; (2) the emergence of prepaid or third-party-paid health insurance as a significant factor in health care delivery; (3) a demand for training that was not impoverished by an over emphasis on scientific/academic skills, but heavily emphasized the delivery of psychodiagnostic and psychotherapeutic services in all professional settings; and (4), perhaps most important of all, psychology's participation at both the state and national level in public policy and political action.

The Revolution Begins

The ferment for change in psychology was most apparent at the state level, particularly in the more populous states, such as California and New York, perhaps because more psychologists in those areas were committing to full or part-time practice. However, as a parenthetical historical note, it was Connecticut, one of the smaller states (in the sense of population), that enacted the first mandatory regulation of psychologists. Like the APA, the state associations in both California and New York were also dominated by academic/institutional interests, which, in turn, gave rise to the organization of clinical "specialty groups," such as the New York Society of Clinical Psychologists (NYSCP) and the Los Angeles Society of Clinical Psychologists (LASCP). These groups tended to be composed primarily of practitioners and, over time, played a major role in the development of strong state associations, certainly in California and New York.

California actually had two constituted "state psychological associations," the California State Psychological Association (CSPA) and the Southern California Psychological Association (SCPA), competing for state leadership. The CSPA was dominated by the three psychology training facilities in the state, the University of California at Berkeley, UCLA, and Stanford University, and the governance of the organization rotated among the faculties of the three institutions. Although a little more inclusive in its leadership, the SCPA still primarily reflected academic/institutional psychology.

Driven by all these concerns; and particularly by the need for licensure, members of the smaller specialty groups began concerted moves to gain increased representation in their respective state associations. In New York, members of the NYSCP, such as Lenny Small and Max Siegel, won election to its Board of Directors, where they became very effective voices for the concerns of professional psychology. In California, leaders of the specialty groups recognized that there could be only one state organizations speaking for psychology. Consequently, practitioner members of the SCPA, LACPA, and LASCP were successful in winning the CSPA presidency and seats on the board (thus ultimately making SCPA redundant).

The mid- and late-1950s and early 1960s were boom times for professional psychology and, in fact, for all of mental health. The government's commitment to funding training programs was underscored in the private sector by increasing demands for mental health services. Thus, the VA, state, and local mental health programs, as well as community mental health centers, offered employment opportunities to all mental health care providers, including psychologists. Ever larger numbers of psychologists were trained; and the increasing popularity of mental health services made it easy, particularly in such states as California, to establish a successful full-time (and/or part-time) independent practice.

During this same time, various health insurers began to provide coverage for mental health services. Unbelievable though it may seem, many of their claims managers were so uninformed as to what benefits they were providing and of the difference between psychologists and psychiatrists that they paid the claims of both. Unfortunately, the scene changed rapidly, becoming one of universal denial of reimbursement for the professional services of psychologists. Broadly speaking, insurance companies took the position that without state-mandated credentialing, there was no means by which their claims department could discern whether a given claim for psychological services was from a charlatan or from a fully qualified psychological practitioner. This complaint had considerable validity, given that the increasing popularity of the field and the ease of establishing a practice not only inspired outright frauds to begin practicing as "psychologists," but also encouraged many undertrained and/or marginally qualified psychologists (including those trained in areas of psychology other than clinical) to establish practices. Although these problems in many ways were national in scope, they were most acutely felt at the state level, particularly in heavily populated states such as California and New York. Arguably, the pressures were most severe in California because:

1. There were more psychologists in full-time independent practice in that state.
2. The major employers were aircraft companies, which used extensive health (including mental health) benefits as a personnel recruiting tool.
3. Limited facilities for training professional psychologists created significant shortages of competent personnel (e.g., an early study indicated that only six of the approximately 100 postdoctoral students in three APA-approved training programs in the state [Stanford, UCLA, and Berkeley] were being trained as clinical psychologists).
4. The flagrancy of abuse was most apparent (e.g., in one California city, the same individual advertised himself in one place in the Yellow Pages as a shoe repair facility and in another as a consulting psychologist).

These factors dictated that, in the mid-1950s, California's psychological practitioners begin to coalesce around the public-policy issue of mandatory credentialing, a recognition of the fact that this would be an initial step toward addressing the multitudinous problems facing a rising profession. Although representatives of practicing psychologists in New York expressed many of the same concerns, there seemed less urgency in their approach; and practitioner groups in New York were markedly less successful than their California colleagues in achieving domination of the state association.

In any event, as a result of these pressures in 1957, the state association in California sought and passed a mandatory credentialing act. It would be almost a decade before New York would follow suit, and, shortly thereafter, New Jersey.

Public Policy, Political Action, and Psychology

Concerns about protecting the public from incompetence and the urgent need to identify legitimate psychological practitioners initially resulted in action at a local level. The Long Beach (California) Psychological Association (LBPA) succeeded in procuring passage of a local ordinance identifying those who could offer psychological services within the Long Beach city limits, an action soon followed by a similar action by the San Diego Academy of Consulting Psychologists.

It quickly became apparent, however, that local action was not a viable solution to the problem (the unqualified simply moved beyond the city limits). Still, the experience was valuable in that (1) it pointed out the necessity to seek state-level mandatory credentialing, and (2) it showed that psychologists, working in concert, could have a favorable impact upon both public policy and the political process. California psychologists quickly began pressuring the state association (CSPA) to commit to a statewide effort to pass the needed legislation.

At the request of the lobbyist retained by the CSPA to direct the legislative effort, Rogers Wright, then president of the LBPA, helped to persuade a Long Beach Assemblyman (familiar with the city's ordinance regulating psychologists) to "carry" the credentialing legislation at the state level. Wright also proposed to the CSPA board that a statewide program of *political giving* be instituted to support the Assemblyman. This recommendation engendered such great trepidation among the academic/institutional members of the CSPA's Board of Directors that the organization conditioned its approval of the proposal on an outright denial of any CSPA involvement in the effort. Nevertheless, with the support of several of the practitioner members of the CSPA board, Wright organized and carried out what was apparently the first such program on behalf of psychologists.

The legislative effort was further remarkable on three additional counts: the timidity (and intellectual arrogance) of the CSPA Board of Directors led the board (1) to opt for a "certification act" restricting the title "psychologist" (a forlorn effort to allay the "ire" and reduce the opposition of psychiatry and medicine to psychology's credentialing effort—a gesture that succeeded in doing neither); while (2) attempting to limit the practice of psychology by an elaborate "definition of psychological practice" that in all its verbal erudition (and circumlocution) failed to incorporate the word "psychodiagnosis" or "psychotherapy" (see below); and while (3) maintaining the doctoral level as the standard for the independent practice of psychology.

In passing, we should note that the local and county societies, and later the state associations themselves, provided an excellent training ground for future national leadership for psychology. Southern California organizations produced leaders like Hal Bessell, Arthur Kovacs, Ernie Lawrence, Bill Morley, Rogers Wright, and Maury Zemlick, and Northern California provided a power base for Nick Cummings, Don Schultz, and Maury Rogers. This same pattern is apparent in many of the other states, for example: NYSPA's Max Siegel, Lenny Small, and Milt Theaman in New York; Marv Metsky, Eugene Shapiro, Bob Weitz, Stanley Moldawsky, and Jules Barron in New Jersey; and in the Southeast, Florida's Ted Blau and Alabama's Ray Fowler and C. J. Rosecrans. Numerous other psychologists who became highly visible and effective national leaders in the development of professional psychology served their political apprenticeships in state and specialty organizations.

Several things became clear as a result of mandatory credentialing efforts. First, psychology needed to make a strong, effective, and lasting commitment to participation in public policy and political action at both state and national levels. Second, the APA's political structure had to be modified to accommodate the emerging concerns of applied psychology. Third, the APA's maximal effectiveness in public policy and political action would rest on providing leadership to, and coordinating the concerted efforts of, the state associations. Consequently, led by state association representatives from California and New York, increasing pressure was applied to the APA to (1) change the more odious provisions in the rules of the Council that gave divisions 2½-to-1 voting advantage over the state associations; (2) develop such "practitioner friendly" items as a "model licensure law"; and (3) develop structures by which the APA could become more involved in public policy at the federal level.

These early efforts to democratize the APA attracted the attention (and, ultimately, the allegiance and support) of a most unlikely recruit to professional psychology's cause, Francis A. Young, Ph.D. Young's credentials as a scientist and academic were on a par with those of any of his colleagues in Division 3 (the then dominant division in APA affairs); and his original research on myopia had brought him national and international recognition, not only in psychology, but in related fields (such as health and medicine). His interest in practitioner causes occasioned heavy censure by his scientist/academic colleagues, who could not fathom a "real scientist's" involvement with practitioners. However, Frank Young's "real world" experience with the pathology and remediation of vision had convinced him that both scientific and applied psychology's only hope for making its contributions broadly available lay in breaking organized medicine's stranglehold on health-care delivery. For Young, the realization of that goal rested on the development of applied psychology as a strong effective professional and political presence (at both the state and national level) in the nation's health-care delivery system.

As the internal pressures increased, the APA establishment took heed of the rising "insurrection" in the way that psychology frequently responds to crises. It established a "Council Commission" chaired by George Albee. The Albee Commission, as it came to be known, had only one member who was strongly identified with state associations. Yet the commission was charged with studying the "state association problem." Albee and his commission, not surprisingly, recommended to their academic cronies the abolition of all *direct* state association participation in APA Council of Representative affairs, substituting a "Division of State Psychological Associations." Concurrently, an informal State Association Coordinating Committee (SACC) composed of NYSPA's Al Williams, Justin Cary, and Bud Orgel; California's Don Schultz and Rogers Wright; and Washington State's Frank Young had been monitoring the work of the Albee Commission from its inception, seeing its proposals as a means of broadening, rather than diminishing, state association influence. Accordingly, Council representatives of both the practice and the state associations supported the Albee Commission's proposal to charter the proposed Division of State Associations (APA's Division 31). In the political process of persuading the Council of Representatives to establish Division 31, this same group (led by the Dirty Dozen) opposed and defeated the Albee Commission proposals for ending direct state association representation.

Meanwhile, SACC members had beguiled the Albee Commission with a proposal to introduce a "political dynamic" into the election of Council members; that is, each APA member would allocate 10 votes to the divisions/state associations of the individual member's choice, with said allocations to determine the number of representatives to which each division or state association would be entitled on the APA's Council. The members of both the Albee Commission and the APA establishment apparently expected that this "political dynamic" would ensure the continued domination of the APA by scientific/academic groups. However, what was overlooked was the fact that the creation of Division 31 (SPA) gave the state associations an "in-house" and formal structure within the APA establishment by which state associations and practice divisions could coordinate their agendas and thereby process professional concerns. The state associations and "practice" divisions took full advantage of the "dynamic," and begin to elect more and more Council members (at the expense of the scientific/academic members) whose primary commitment was to the advancement of professional psychology. In the judgment of this writer, this series of events became one of the major factors in the conversion of the APA into a professional, as well as scientific/academic, organization.

Shortly thereafter, Division 31 charged Art Kovacs and Rogers Wright with reviewing the APA bylaws and the rules of the Council in order to propose changes that would maximize professional participation in APA affairs. Division 31 adopted the Kovacs/Wright proposals in total, and with the ongoing changes that were occurring in Council membership, many of the Division 31/Kovacs/Wright recommendations were accepted by the Council itself. Among these changes were (1) the mandating of two annual Council meetings, one of them for three days (a step that truly made the Council of Representatives responsible, as the by-laws intended, for APA affairs); and (2) mandating that membership on all boards and committees be representative of the APA membership *as a whole*, resulting, for example, in the election of more practitioners to APA's governance structure. Unfortunately, concurrent demands for APA involvement in public policy and political action (in order to address such issues as model licensure laws and the inclusion of psychologists as providers in health insurance plans) continued to be largely unheard by the Council.

As a historical aside and in this same context, California's bitterly fought battle for "certification" was rendered moot within less than five years of its enactment by the California Attorney General, who, after reading the "scope of practice" incorporated in the psychology certification act, ruled that psychologists performed neither psychodiagnosis nor psychotherapy. This was a profound blow to a state psychological association that was just getting established and integrated. Fortunately, the CSPA had, in the intervening years, successfully incorporated professional concerns into its corporate identity and had become an adroit operator in both the public-policy and political-action arenas. Thus, it was able, under the leadership of President Tom Gordon, to pass a new and true "licensure law" that clearly recognized both psychodiagnosis and psychotherapy as appropriate functions of a psychologist. Simultaneously, another action program, directed by President-elect Rogers Wright, persuaded the California Attorney General to take the unprecedented action of withdrawing his own formally established option. The CSPA's newly found effectiveness was measured by the fact that both the new licensure law and the withdrawal of Attorney General's were accomplished in the same calendar year.

Regrettably, it would be almost two decades before the APA finally developed a "model licensure law" one that, in several aspects, duplicated the initial mistakes made by the CSPA Board in that it was, in effect, legislation attempting to restrict a title, but without an adequate definition of the "scope of practice." As was the case in California, this oversight did, and still is occasioning substantial mischief in a number of states, many of whom followed the APA model. The states now find themselves facing much the same dilemma as the CSPA faced in the early 1960s, namely, in several regions of the country, the legal system has called into question the efficacy of psychology's licensing legislation.

Insurance Reimbursement for Psychological Services

With the 1959 passage of the California "Certification Act," the state's psychologists were ready to turn to other pressing matters affecting the independent delivery of psychological services. At that time, prepaid health insurance offering liberal mental health benefits was becoming very popular, particularly in California and New York. Inasmuch as psychologists were increasingly being excluded from participation by the insurance claims process, a major problem was becoming apparent. In California, Arthur Kovacs, then president of the Los Angeles Society (LASCP), with his frequently prescient view of the future, persuaded the LASCP and the county association (LACPA) to establish an insurance committee chaired by Rogers Wright, the primary purpose of which was to set up insurance programs for psychologists. It was an incidental afterthought that the governing boards of the sponsoring organizations added to the charge, "By the way, see what can be done about insurance reimbursement."

In the 1960s, the APA had formed an "insurance trust" (APAIT) to create and operate national insurance programs for psychologists. At that time (the mid-1960s), the "trust" offered only national programs covering a limited professional liability and a very limited disability program for psychologists (i.e., a monthly benefit of $200). Furthermore, the APAIT, dominated by academic/institutional psychologists whose insurance needs were covered by their employing institutions, was deaf to the possibility of any new "benefit" programs or of playing any role in the "psychology reimbursement" issue.

To the newly formed LASCP-LACPA insurance committee, it soon became apparent that given the "newness" of the profession, the "distributed" nature of its practice, and the "smallness" of numbers (relative to both actuarial prediction and economy of scale), any new benefit programs would have to be on a statewide basis, and probably should be on a national basis. Furthermore, it also became evident that any addressing of the insurance reimbursement issue had to be done at both a state and a national level. Accordingly, the leadership of the LASCP and LACPA, with help from the remnants of the Southern California Psychological Association, the San Francisco Psychological Association, and the San Diego Academy, persuaded the CSPA to establish a "standing" insurance committee charged with the responsibility of (1) developing an association member benefit program, while (2) pressuring APAIT to broaden its limited malpractice and disability coverage, and (3) simultaneously addressing the issue of insurance reimbursement for psychologists.

At about the same time (but independently), the New York State Psychological Association, goaded by Len Small, Max Siegel, and Milt Theaman, addressed the "reimbursement" issue by establishing an insurance committee charged specifically with attempting to procure insurance reimbursement for New York psychologists. The NYSPA group took a somewhat different approach (from the California group) by retaining professional legal help in an attempt to bring direct legal pressure to bear on mental health insurance programs that excluded psychologists. But, this initial approach also proved to be only minimally effective. Also in the early 1960s (1963), the Maryland Psychological Association, with the assistance of Mel Gravitz, established an insurance committee to consider the "reimbursement" problem.

The CSPA Insurance Committee, with its immediate focus on developing programs for its membership, and bedazzled by the intriguing (but erroneous) concept that some quid pro quo between membership benefit programs and formal recognition of psychologists for reimbursement was possible, proceeded to develop a membership office overhead insurance program. It also formed a statewide retirement trust through which member psychologists could shelter income.

Concurrently, the CSPA committee was concerned about another major threat to independent practice, the lack of health-insurance coverage for practitioners. The CSPA Insurance Committee immediately began to look at this need. At this point, the APAIT indicated some interest in establishing a national health insurance program for psychologists and asked the CSPA to delay implementation while it "studied the problem." Given that the APA's academic/institutional psychologists (as noted earlier) generally had health insurance available through their employers, the APAIT seemed to be in no hurry to move. After months of no apparent progress, the CSPA put the APAIT on notice that unless a health benefit program for psychologists was immediately forthcoming, the CSPA would unilaterally establish a state plan.

In short order, this produced APA's first national health benefit plan for psychologists, but one without a mental health benefit. After more intense discourse, the APA plan was modified to include the mental health benefit, but with reimbursement for professional mental health services limited to psychiatrists. It was infuriating to professional psychologists in California, Maryland, New York, New Jersey, and other states who were attempting to persuade insurance companies to recognize psychologists for reimbursement to be confronted with the fact that our own national health plan developed by our own national organization failed to do so. During this same time, the CSPA Insurance Committee attempted to persuade the APAIT to increase its $200-per-month disability benefit. (This "benefit" was so penurious that a California psychologist could insure, under the CSPA's office overhead program, six times the amount of the disability benefit offered by the APAIT.) These efforts were unavailing until the CSPA's Insurance Committee conducted a statewide survey (demonstrating that psychologists needed to be indemnified for at least $2,000 per month in disability), accompanied by the threat to establish its own plan. The APAIT then broadened its disability coverage to a realistic level.

All of the foregoing activities (e.g., concerns about licensure, member benefits, reimbursement of psychologists by health plans) took place in a context of great distress about the type, quality, and quantity of training. While California was badgering the APA Office of Professional Affairs and its insurance trust to enlarge member insurance benefit programs, New York's Lenny Small had developed a newsletter that began to address widespread concerns about professional training, as well as health insurance issues. Small and the New York group and Wright and the California group made common cause, forming the National Clinical Liaison Committee. Wright then purchased a used hectograph and the two groups began national mailings on subjects of interest to professional psychologists. Obviously, the *NCLC Newsletter* also provided a vehicle whereby the APA could be systematically reminded to consider those matters.

After months of badgering, the APA's Board of Professional Affairs (BPA) (still absent the participation of a practicing professional psychologist) invited Small and Wright, as representatives of their respective state groups, to address the BPA on the "insurance problem." This meeting began with the startling comment by one of the BPA's leading academic members, "I'm not going to do a damn thing to put another dollar in the pocket of private practitioners."

Despite the apparent hostility of several members of the BPA (and the latent apprehension of the rest of the group), and with substantial lobbying by a number of psychologists on both coasts, the BPA finally recommended the establishment of an ad hoc committee to study the implications of third-party reimbursement. However, even in taking this small step, the group refused to face the question of independent practice, as signified by the fact that there was no reference to independent service delivery in the "study" committee's title, "Ad Hoc Committee on Insurance and Related Social Developments" ("developments" referring to such things as community mental health programs and state and national governmental mental health programs). The acronym for the proposed study group thus became AHCIRSD (pronounced accursed); an acronym that the committee members ultimately would bear as a badge of honor.

Then the APA's Board of Directors rejected the BPA's recommendation for the formation of the ad hoc committee, and the next battle began. Small and Wright, again using the network of the National Clinical Liaison Committee (now a very visible and active group), organized a campaign to convince the APA's Board and Executive Officer of the urgency of establishing the committee, and after many, many weeks, the Board of Directors capitulated.

The establishment of AHCIRSD set other precedents within the APA; specifically, for the first time, the committee included psychologists devoted to independent practice. Health problems forced Lenny Small to curtail his professional activities and he was replaced by Milt Theaman, an independent practitioner who had previously chaired the NYSPA's Insurance Committee. Theaman, named to chair AHCIRSD, was joined by Rogers Wright, a full-time practitioner and chair of California's Insurance Committee, and Mel Gravitz, an independent practitioner and longtime stalwart in the Washington, DC, and Maryland psychological associations. The other members of the committee were academics with little knowledge of, or interest in, third-party coverage of mental health, a situation that changed rapidly as members George Coppel and William Smith became strong supporters of APA action. After nearly two more years of "study," the AHCIRSD membership recommended to the APA that AHCIRSD be made a continuing committee and address the full spectrum of problems inherent in third-party reimbursement.

Meanwhile, the writer, still involved in setting up benefit programs for California psychologists, was doing a "road show" to familiarize psychologists in the San Francisco area with the CSPA's new retirement program, one that continued for many years to be unique in the country. At the end of that presentation, a young psychologist introduced himself and asked, "If a study demonstrating that psychotherapy offset some of its cost by reducing the utilization of other medical services, would that be helpful to the APA's AHCIRSD?" That young psychologist was Nicholas Cummings and the research to which his question referred was the initial Cummings-Follette study, the first of several landmark studies unequivocally demonstrating that providing a mental health benefit had a very positive consequence, namely, that patient exposure to psychotherapy resulted in a significant reduction in the utilization of other medical and hospital services, thereby occasioning a significant reduction in overall costs.

But we precede history. The APA's AHCIRSD, just approved for continuance on an ad hoc basis, had already uncovered a number of issues that, if not directly related to the extension of reimbursable status to psychologists, were at least being used by the health insurance industry as a reason for not recognizing psychologists as reimbursable providers. In addition to the complaint that in the absence of mandatory credentialing, the industry had no readily available way to determine which psychologists were entitled to reimbursement under the mental health benefit, another health insurance industry concern was that of increased cost, presumably occasioned by the recognition of yet another provider group. The inclusion of independent practitioners in AHCIRSD made available a rather substantial, although informal, database of providers across the country that suggested that the cost of recognizing another provider group was probably offset by the reduced utilization of other medical benefits. Still, AHCIRSD lacked any formal research data demonstrating the validity of such claims. Health-industry officialdom could also point to the fact that major federal governmental health insurance programs, such as Medicare and the Federal Government Employees Program, did not recognize psychologists as mental-health providers eligible for reimbursement. Such arguments made AHCIRSD even more aware of the importance of psychology's having direct input into the development of national and state political-action and public-policy programs, especially those involving a mental health benefit. Not only could psychology contribute needed expertise in the design of such benefits, but its role as a new mental health provider group could only be ensured by its participation as one of the provider groups recognized by such programs as eligible for reimbursement.

Thus, the San Francisco meeting between Cummings and Wright was most propitious in view of Cummings' research experience with the mental health "offset" of medical costs. Furthermore, his experience in delivering mental health service derived from a private-sector institutional base, and so expanded the experience of other AHCIRSD members whose service-delivery experience was primarily in independent practice.

By this time, the workload occasioned by the APA's Board of Directors' decision to support AHCIRSD's continued existence as an ad hoc committee, and the committee's assumption of other commitments relating to the insurance problem, had grown exponentially, and the resulting conflict of commitments compelled several of the academic members of AHCIRSD to resign. In this context, Wright proposed, and the AHCIRSD members agreed, that two more practitioners would be recommended to APA's Board for AHCIRSD membership. Nicholas Cummings was an obvious choice, as was the choice of Melvin Gravitz, another Dirty Dozen member, because AHCIRSD was aware of both the APA's and the committee's lack of information about, and input into, governmental activities affecting psychology. Gravitz was a well-known psychologist in the Washington, DC area, and had been extremely active when serving as president of the Washington Society of Clinical Psychologists. His knowledge of the federal government and its agencies was encyclopedic, and his many contacts within the government proved extremely valuable as AHCIRSD began to implement its action program. Later, he was able to persuade one of the federal employer health groups to include qualified psychologists as *independent* providers of mental health benefits (i.e., without medical supervision).

It is important to note that, at this point in history, key APA power bases (Division 29 and 31 and AHCIRSD) were well established, staffed by revolutionaries with considerable knowledge and experience and a commitment to a wholesale reorganization of the

APA. Dirty Dozen members Don Schultz, C. J. Rosecrans, Rogers Wright, and Frank Young were ensconced in the Division 31 leadership, while Nick Cummings and Mel Gravitz, as well as Rogers Wright, were driving AHCIRSD. Blau, Cummings, Gravitz, Lawrence, Metsky, Shapiro, Siegel, and Wiggins were also highly visible members of the Divisions 12 and 29 "leadership." And "Dirty Dozeners" also continued to maintain important positions in their state associations Alabama, California, Florida, Illinois, New Jersey, New York, Washington State, and Washington, DC/Maryland. In this way, pressure from numerous constituencies could be applied to persuade the APA to change its organizational structure so as to better process practitioner concerns.

With the input and concurrence of the states associations and relevant APA divisions, AHCIRSD initiated an action program designed to achieve the recognition of psychologists in all forms of prepaid mental health programs. To reach this goal, AHCIRSD addressed the revamping of the APA and began to define professionalism in psychology as well. Specifically, AHCIRSD and its supporters asked the APA:

1. To support mandatory credentialing in the states through the development of a "model licensing law," and, in the interim, to adopt as policy "a definition of psychologists" for purposes of insurance reimbursement.

2. To develop a capability in the central office for interacting with the Health Insurance Association of America (HIAA) and individual insurance companies to promulgate health insurance programs offering mental health benefits.

3. To sponsor and implement a national conference on the broad issue of the appropriate training for the delivery of psychological services in all settings.

4. To develop a periodical, to be published at least monthly, whose primary function would be to present national news of interest to professional psychologists. The periodical also would focus on the actions of government, industry, and the public-policy sector with

implications for the delivery of psychological health services.

5. To develop a capability for participating actively in the public-policy and political arenas.

Nationally, in ever-increasing numbers, professional psychologists began to coalesce around the action program. The pressures brought to bear on the APA establishment were intense; one of the first to feel that pressure was the APA Executive Officer, traditionally a member of the academic/scientific wing of psychology. The APA's CEOs, because of both their own predilections and the priority they gave to the interests of the academic/scientific groups in the APA, tended to heighten organizational tensions. In fact, about the kindest thing that can be said about those CEOs, from the standpoint of professional psychology, is that they lacked insight into and an understanding of the issues besetting that discipline. Consequently, the Dirty Dozen (and professional interests generally) committed significant resources to facilitating the departure of a sequence of APA Executive Officers.

Next, the Dirty Dozen, by virtue of their involvement with a number of the major power bases within the APA organizational structure, were able to help generate sufficient pressure to persuade the APA's Board of Directors (and subsequently its Council) to adopt a "definition of psychologists for insurance purposes." However, the group was markedly less successful in persuading the APA governance to act on the issue of a model licensing law.

In that context, the recent national hubbub over prescriptive privileges for psychologists is familiar because the objections currently raised by the APA to the promulgation of a model *licensure* law reflects many of the same conceptions. For example, it is argued, "we'll anger psychiatry; we don't want to be junior psychiatrists after the almighty dollar; we will unduly limit the freedom of psychology by defining it so narrowly in the legal sense; we are not really trained to function as independent practitioners." It is also true that in many of those long-ago deliberations, many of our academic and scientific colleagues felt the need to oppose statutory credentialing in state legislatures. Fortunately with respect to statutory control, the state associations, responding to grass-root's pressures, tended to ignore the APA and individually went about the business of enacting legislation. The consequence, of course, is history in that we still have many varieties of credentialing at the state level and continue to expend scarce resources on attempts to deal with those variations.

The "definition of psychologists" served a useful but short-lived purpose in that some insurance companies were persuaded to adopt the verbiage as a basis for recognizing psychologists for reimbursement under the mental health provisions of larger health plans. However, the rapid enactment of mandatory credentialing by many states, and a massive class-action suit against the U.S. Civil Service Commission, essentially made moot the usefulness of the definition.

As a parenthetical aside and in the context of efforts to persuade APA to adopt officially a "definition of psychologists for insurance purposes," Dirty Dozener Jack Wiggins (who has more ideas than 10 people could possibly implement) proposed an adjunct that was designed (1) to mitigate to some degree the APA's reluctance to take action on the insurance issue and (2) to address the slowness with which state associations were procuring statutory definitions through licensing and/or certification laws. Jack Wiggins, a member of CAPPS (see below) EX-COMM, proposed in its early days that CAPPS should establish a National Register of Qualified Psychologists to which insurance companies could refer to aid in their claims processing. Although the idea was a significant contribution and CAPPS EX-COMM explored it thoroughly, it also posed potential legal and management questions that seemed unsolvable. Specifically, it was the opinion of CAPPS's legal counsel that such a quasi-regulatory activity raised serious antitrust issues for an organization chartered for activities in the area of public policy and advocacy. CAPPS EX-COMM then referred the concept to the appropriate structures in the APA (such as Divisions 29 and 31), along with a cautionary note about the possible antitrust implications. Subsequently, divisional study of the concept of a "national register" also found it to pose major threats to the APA's legal position and tax status with the consequence that an independent group composed of some of the leadership of Division 29 and a former APA employee founded an independent organization now bearing the name of *The National Register of Health Service Providers in Psychology*. Dirty Dozener Bob Weitz, CAPPS liaison to the organizing committee for the Register, had supported the efforts from its outset and was one of the psychologists present when the "organizing" group committed to its establishment.

The demand for additional staff support to assist in the processing of practitioner concerns at the BPA level was also somewhat successful. Existing staff members were replaced and the staff expanded so that the BPA now had two full-time professional staff positions along with clerical support. Although the new staff members were somewhat naive with respect to pressing clinical issues (one having come from academia, the other from a government agency), they both had an identification with professional psychology and were willing to learn. This writer still recalls overhearing one of the new BPA staff members say (at the staffer's first convention as an APA employee), "You know, I'm amazed! Those guys really know the literature. They're in there [an adjacent meeting room] talking about stuff I haven't even had to think about."

Through the efforts of these staff member and the active participation of members of AHCIRSD, the APA quickly developed considerable visibility at the level of HIAA and in the executive rooms of a number of health insurance agencies. But it continued to be highly problematic and symbolically distressing that the Federal Government Employees Program (which then had a very substantial mental health benefit) and the APA's own health insurance program (developed under pressure from the California group) failed to recognize psychologists as providers eligible for reimbursement. However, the crowning, and most egregious, blow was that the APA governance lacked both preparedness and sensitivity to the criticality of the issue, resulting (in the mid-1960s) in the passage of Medicare and Medicaid health legislation that failed to recognize psychologists as reimbursable providers of mental health services.

With respect to the need for consistent, up-to-date internal communication, the professional interests did much better. The APA Board of Directors and Council recognized that if they wanted to get full value for organizational resources expended in supporting AHCIRSD, it was mandatory that the group be kept informed. At this point, the only national publication for psychologists was the *American Psychologist*, a somewhat fusty periodical that printed no article that did not include a "test of significance" in its content. At the strong insistence of ACHIRSD, the APA Central Office began the publication and distribution of a mimeographed monthly called *The Washington Report*, which was specifically designed to inform the professional community of issues of relevant concern, particularly with respect to governmental and industry actions in the health-care area. The periodical became successful far beyond anyone's anticipation. It is currently known to virtually every U.S. psychologist by its derivative name, *The APA Monitor*. One of the reasons for its success was that segments of psychology other than professional community began to appreciate the necessity and convenience of up-to-date information concerning the broad world of government and civilian action, arenas in which psychology, in all its dimensions, increasingly operated. It was *slowly* becoming apparent that all of psychology was in the same boat!

In the training area, the professional action program initially fared little better than had efforts to develop model licensure, etc. However, the APA establishment, in a gesture meant to quiet the restless practitioners, hurriedly initiated and implemented the so-called "Miami Training Conference," a conference that only further inflamed the APA's professionals because its participants were almost exclusively academic and institutional psychologists. The Miami Conference was additionally problematic in that it was conducted almost in secrecy (apparently in an effort to minimize the intrusion of professional interests) and culminated in yet another endorsement of the status quo.

No sooner had the conference closed, then professional interests within the APA began to complain volubly and extensively about its makeup and the conclusions (or lack thereof) reached. The APA response to the new and intensified complaints was to summon yet another conference informally called the "Boulder Conference" (a play on the title of the 1940s Boulder Conference that originally established the scientist/practitioner paradigm governing APA clinical training). This convocation in 1968 was known as the Vail Conference and was publicized as a summit conference on training "for all of psychology." The conference was more inclusive of practitioner interests than was the unfortunate Miami Conference, although the agenda and the preponderance of participants were somewhat biased toward a reaffirmation of the so-called scientist/practitioner model, giving precedence to "science" rather than to service delivery. However, the greater numbers of "professional representatives" refused to go along with this exercise, insisting that there had to be a training model giving professional service delivery preeminence, that is, practitioner/scholar. But, this produced little change in the APA-approved training programs.

In retrospect, the value of the Vail "Boulder" Conference is probably best memorialized by the fact that even though it was a secondary consideration, the roster of conference participants, by their consideration of the practitioner/scholar model, gave legitimacy to practitioner interests and concerns about participation in the training enterprises. It also served to convince many of the clinicians and professional psychologists who had worked for a change in the APA's role in training to recognize that again their best resource would be themselves.

Almost immediately thereafter, following a tradition that began in the 1964 rise to power of professional interests within the California Psychological Association that "old CSPA presidents don't just fade away," Nick Cummings chose as his post-presidential project the development of a training program in professional psychology. Thus was the "secondary" Vail model for training, the practitioner/scholar model, given its initial imple-

mentation. With the unflagging support of Californians Don
Schultz, Ernie Lawrence, and Rogers Wright, along with the members of Divisions 29, 31, and 12, and led by Dirty Dozeners Blau,
Fowler, Gravitz, Metsky, Rosecrans, Shapiro, Wiggins, Weitz, and
Young, Cummings began to plan for a "plug-in program" in professional psychology that could fit within the defined limits of any
existing university-based psychology program. However, Cummings' training program would also have the unique input and
participation of professional psychologists; input incorporating
the clinical knowledge gained from "real life" experience in the
independent delivery of a broad range of psychological services.
The program was also uncommon in maintaining its autonomy in
the makeup of its training program and its commitment to training for practice—rather than experimental research and/or academic pursuits. After nearly two years of fruitless negotiations
with numerous academic institutions, all of which wanted to
modify the program and/or limit it autonomy, Cummings and his
supports made a bold decision. The only way in which there
could be a true clinician-directed and operated training program in
professional psychology would be if such a program were freestanding, an independent *professional school* outside the constraints
of a "parental department or institution.

Accordingly, and with the active support of the Dirty Dozen,
the California State Psychological Association and Divisions 29,
31, and others, Cummings launched a historic movement in psychology by establishing not one but two independent professional
schools (based in Los Angeles and San Francisco). The initial programs were very successful, and were quickly followed by two
additional campuses, in San Diego and in Fresno. In passing, it is
worthy of note that the Fresno campus, located in the heart of
California's predominately agricultural Central Valley, was the
first psychology program to focus on the unique mental health
needs of rural and agricultural America. The whole effort of establishing the California professional schools was extraordinary in
that, for the first time in the history of psychological training, it
demonstrated that professional psychologists could both develop

and operate a high-quality doctoral-level training program. The California Schools of Professional Psychology (CSPP) were also unique in that there were no full-time faculty positions; that is, all faculty members were required to maintain, at a minimum, a continuing half-time commitment to independent service delivery.

With Cummings as the president and Schultz as the dean, the CSPP program was quite successful and encouraged psychologists across the country to emulate the California experience. New Jersey psychologists, led by Dirty Dozen Bob Weitz as founding executive vice president and acting dean, and joined by Marv Metsky and Gene Shapiro, as well as by NJPA leaders Stanley Moldawsky, Jules Barron, Bert Schwartz, Sam Kutash, and others, culminated a six-year battle by establishing the Graduate School of Applied and Professional Psychology affiliated with Rutgers University. The New Jersey experience was also unique in that it showed, for the first time, that independent psychology practitioners could develop and implement a professional training program operating as a "college" within the confines of an established university. The success of both the California and the New Jersey programs demonstrated unequivocally to those in "higher education" that there were both a body of knowledge and a training discipline that could serve a broad educational need. The academic and economic success of these pioneering programs played a major role in helping to persuade the APA's academic/scientific community (never slow to appreciated economic opportunity) that changes in the education and training of professional psychologists were at hand. The phenomenal rise of the professional school as a preferred training modality in psychology has been documented elsewhere and is included here only as in the sense of its important role in the shaping of the APA and as an indication of the breadth of interest and activities of the small group known as the "Dirty Dozen."

In passing, it should also be noted that within a very short time, Southern California psychologists, incensed about the severe restrictions limiting psychoanalytic training for psychologists (to which psychologists had made major contributions), founded a complete training program designed and operated by psychologists for psychologists. One of the leaders in that movement, as he had been in the founding of the California Schools of Professional Psychologists, was the Dirty Dozener Ernest Lawrence.

Finally, the insurance issue in both the private and governmental sector (particularly the passage of Medicare and Medicaid, neither of which included psychologists as reimbursable providers of mental health services), and the establishment of the Federal Government Employees Health Insurance Plan (which also then excluded reimbursement for psychological services) made it abundantly clear to all but certain die-hard members of the APA's establishment and governance that an active and effective public-policy and political-action program was a critical and immediate necessity. Furthermore, the unwillingness of the APA establishment to revise its structure to incorporate representatives of clinical and professional interests into its highest echelons strongly suggested that an important concomitant of any political-action program required major political action within the APA itself.

Throughout this entire time, up to and including the late 1960s the APA's AHCIRSD was still an ad hoc committee and, therefore, tenuous. At that time, only the "safest" and most timid professional psychologists were allowed to advance beyond "token" visual leadership positions (as chairs of low-level ad hoc committees, commissions, and the like). In particular, professional psychologists were excluded from committee membership/leadership of standing boards and/or other policy-making structures in the APA governance structure.

ACHIRSD, joined by some of the leadership of Division 12 and the full leadership of Divisions 29 and 31, began to press for the creation of a national-level political lobbying group established and operated by the APA. This so alarmed the APA establishment that it provided very little, if any, support for such a course of action. The ostensible reason given was the threat of such activities to APA's cherished C(3) tax status, a tax status of whose primary importance was in terms of protecting cash flow from the APA's numerous journals and publishing and real estate businesses. However, the Dirty Dozen had, through independently obtained legal opinion and independent consultation with the Internal Revenue Service, learned that the threat to APA's tax status at that time was minimal and well within the organization's manageable economic limits.

The Dirty Dozen decided, erroneously in this writer's opinion, that the APA establishment's commitment to the 501(c)(3) charitable/scientific tax status was so great that it would strategically forgo efforts to change its status to a 501(c)(6) business and professional tax status. Had the Dirty Dozen forced the issue, many of the limitations under which the APA continues to operate would have been alleviated. (The American Psychiatric Association [APA], also owners and operators of a publishing empire under a 501 (c)(3) tax status, recently opted to remove all but its publication business from the (c)(3) designation to a 501(c)(6) tax status in order to allow it greater freedom in the pursuit of political-action initiatives and public policy.) Furthermore, the APA establishment's opposition to action in the public policy and political arenas was manifestly broader in scope than its fears about the claimed threat of such action to its 501(c)(3) tax status. For example, a former secretary of the APA's Board of Directors acknowledged in a letter to Rogers Wright that he had great concerns with participating in public policy and political action because "psychology's representatives might someday be seen leaving a Congressional Hearing Room in the company of chiropractic representatives."

Tension between the academic and professional wings of psychology concerning all these issues continued to mount, and ultimately came to a head over the discovery that the APA's Insurance Trust (APAIT), dominated as it was by academics and some APA members who were also employees of insurance companies, had written a health contract that excluded psychologists as reimbursable providers of mental health services. In this context, AHCIRSD developed an action program to be presented at the next meeting of the Council. As an aside, none of the members of AHCIRSD were APA Council members at that time, and so, as an economic means both of conducting their business and of lobbying the Council (about times little understood by the full Council), AHCIRSD regularly scheduled committee meeting to coincide with the extended January midyear Council meeting.

When it became apparent that AHCIRSD was planning to raise highly controversial issues at the winter meeting, the chair of the BPA (of which AHCIRSD was a subordinate committee) forbade AHCIRSD to meet. Recognizing that acceptance of such control by a BPA chair would make it impossible for the Council to hear from its own experts on insurance, and would, over time, eviscerate AHCIRSD's work, the group informed the BPA chair of its intention to meet despite his directive. The BPA chair then told AHCIRSD that he would not approve any travel or committee expenses for the meeting. AHCIRSD responded that it felt it to be so critical that the Council hear from its own experts that AHCIRSD members would pay their own expenses.

AHCIRSD met; the Council met, and after considering more than 30 resolutions forwarded by AHCIRSD, passed not a single one. In fact, when one Council member expressed some concern about the content of one of the resolutions, he was assured publicly by a Division 3 Council representative: "There is no need to worry because we (the representatives) aren't going to pass any of the recommendations anyway."

Recognizing that defying the BPA chair's prohibition on meeting, would diminish, or end, AHCIRSD's usefulness, the group, long concerned about the vulnerability of its "ad hoc" status, decided to exploit the Council representatives' collective guilt concerning their obstreperous behavior. Accordingly, AHCIRSD persuaded other Dirty Dozen members who were also Council members to propose the dissolution of AHCIRSD, and its replacement by a standing committee to be called to the Committee on Health Insurance (COHI).

The Council approved, and in doing so made its first unequivocal commitment to addressing the insurance reimbursement problem, while creating and funding what would ultimately become one of the association's most powerful committees: the COHI. The change also rid the committee of the irrelevant euphemism "related social developments" while ensuring that it would never again function under overzealous constraints. The unseemly sequence of events beginning with the BPA chair's attempt to control the committee, and capped by the evident arrogance of the scientific/academic wing of the Council, also gave birth to two verities: (1) professional interests had to take a more active political role in determining the structure of the APA governance, and (2) it was absolutely necessary that psychology as a whole have, at a national level, an independent and viable public-policy and political-action component. Meanwhile, the COHI, now chaired by Nick Cummings and numbering Dirty Dozeners Mel Gravitz, Gene Shapiro, and Jack Wiggins among its membership, continued and expanded the activist mode established by its predecessor AHCIRSD.

In a letter to this writer, Cummings admonished that this "remembrance" must include the single most important accomplishment of the COHI.

> If you recall, with the tutelage of Red Halverson of Occidental Life, we devised the legislative thrust that Jack Wiggins later named the "Freedom-of-Choice Legislation." You introduced me to Red, who then introduced me to Paul Brandes, the deputy chief counsel of the California Insurance Commission. We prepared a do-it-yourself legislative kit, gathered all of the state insurance chairs in San Francisco, and did a two-day workshop, with Red and Paul participating. California and New Jersey both passed bills, but Governor Pat Brown pocket vetoed the California bill, so New Jersey was the first state to pass freedom-of-choice legislation. California got it passed and signed by the governor the very next year. Within three years, six states had passed such laws, and the APA finally (after several years of requests from the COHI) made freedom-of-choice APA policy. Jack Wiggins succeeded me as chair of the COHI, and he continued the fight. When the law passed in 29 states, the issue became moot, as indemnity carriers voluntarily fell in line in the remaining states. To this date, this form of

legislation has been passed in far fewer than 50 states as it became unnecessary. But there was the resistance of Blue Cross/Blue Shield, which claimed exemption from insurance laws because the Blues had special status as "medical service corporations." This led to the Virginia Blues suit, which in time ended that objection.

The initial legislation devised by Halverson and Brandes and championed by the COHI was amazingly simple. To the definition of physician, it added three words parenthetically ("which includes psychologist"). Thus, insurers did not have to provide mental health benefits, but, if they did, and reimbursed psychiatrists, they would have to reimburse psychologists as well. Soon it was obvious that the language would have to be more extensive to cover the Blues, policies written out of state, and so forth. But overall it was a relatively simple and highly effective strategy, and one that the individual state psychological associations had the capacity and resources to undertake. The do-it-yourself legislative kit assembled by the COHI with the help of Halverson and Brandes was used universally, and Division 31 added its support. When six states had adopted the legislation, the APA made this effort to amend the state insurance codes to mandate the inclusion of psychologists for reimbursement on official APA policy. At this point, Cummings resigned as the first COHI chair to found the professional school movement, and he was succeeded by Wiggins, who gave the legislation its name, "Freedom of Choice." Not merely a catchy phrase, its emphasis on patient choice enabled state legislators to espouse it as a consumer issue, rather than one of special interest to psychology.

With the continued refusal of the APA to take an advocacy stance on the questions so important to professional practice, the Dirty Dozen determined that the time had come to form their own advocacy organization. This would be a bold undertaking, and it was not clear how such an organization would be financed. Thus, it was imperative that it be accepted by the rank-and-file practitioners who would have to pay for it out-of-pocket. Wright, Cummings, and Lawrence took on the responsibility of solving these problems, and with the goal of establishing an advocacy organization immediately, on a Friday noon they locked themselves in a room, vowing not to emerge until details of the organization's structure and bylaws were complete.

As an aside, the degree of trust exhibited by the Division 31 Board is noteworthy. One of the compelling things that made the Dirty Dozen so successful was the knowledge that each of the individuals involved had a primary commitment to the emergence of a strong professional body within our national organization. It is further noteworthy that, within the group, personal ambitions took a back seat to the successful pursuit of the group's goal. It is also significant that everyone in the Dirty Dozen brought to the task (and their relationship with one another) a broad background of experience and knowledge as successful professionals, managers, and directors of numerous enterprises, as well as substantial political knowledge and experience. At that time, Cummings, Lawrence, and Wright had all been board members and presidents of the CSPA, arguably one of the more aggressive and successful state associations, and Don Schultz had been executive officer of the CSPA. Max Siegel had been both a board member and president of the NYSCP and NYSPA; Rosecrans and Fowler had both been presidents of their state associations and a major regional association (as had Ted Blau), and had served as creators and members of their state licensing boards. Metsky, Shapiro, and Weitz had been board members and active governance figures in the New Jersey State Association; Bob Weitz had served as president of the organizing committee for Division 42 and the precursor of Division 29; and Jack Wiggins, a relative newcomer to the group, had been active in Ohio, particularly regarding the insurance problem. Blau, Cummings, Fowler, Gravitz, Lawrence, Rosecrans, Shapiro, Siegel, Weitz, Wiggins, Wright, and Young had also been presidents of one or more of APA's major divisions.

The Cummings/Lawrence/Wright committee met, and after some 40 hours of work, had a plan ready for implementation. It was submitted to and approved by the Division 31 board, which in turn, asked the originators of the plan to implement it. Thus was born one of psychology's most controversial and, in many

ways, successful entities, the Council for the Advancement of the
Psychological Professions and Science (CAPPS, as differentiated
from CAPP, which came much later).

From the outset, CAPPS was a highly active public-policy group,
broadly representative of the various regions of the country, the
logic being that whereas the APA divisions do not vote in national elections and are prohibited by APA's tax status from election-
eering, members of state associations are the direct constituents of
federal legislators and do electioneer. Although the original three
were all from California, the Division 31 board felt that whereas
such representation might do some disservice to geographic representation, it was justified by the expertise that Cummings, Lawrence, and Wright brought to the task. In addition to the original
group, Max Siegel from New York, Ted Blau from Florida, Jack
Wiggins from Ohio, Helen Sunukian from Illinois, and James
McCall from Texas accepted invitations to become CAPPS Executive Committee members. The members of the organizing group
each signed notes for $1,000 to generate organizing capital. While
recruiting an executive officer and legal counsel, CAPPS Executive Committee (EX-COMM) conducted a national fund-raising
campaign that generated well over $100,000 in less than 30 days,
an incredible sum for that time and place. At that point, Bob Weitz
joined CAPPS as chief fund raiser and, in the context of implementing CAPPS's plan to sue the federal government for excluding psychologists as providers under the Federal Employees Health
Plan, funded the class action by raising an additional $89,000.

Now securely funded, EX-COMM continued seeking an executive officer and a legal counsel with substantial Washington experience. After a couple of false starts, EX-COMM retained the services of Jack Donahue, who, although trained as a pharmacist, for
several years had been leading staff member of the American Op-
tometric Association's extremely effective political lobbying organization. Donahue served CAPPS so well that most people
thought he was a psychologist. With the ultimate dissolution of
CAPPS, Donahue became a very highly regarded Associate Executive Officer of the APA. To the writer's knowledge, the only

other nonpsychologist to rise to such a position was the APA's Chief Financial Officer, Jack McKay, a CPA with an unusual background who has also been of great service to all of psychology, including professional psychology. CAPPS's choice of legal counsel was propitious from the outset in that we retained Joseph Nellis, a senior member of a highly regarded Washington law firm. He had served on the Hill as counsel for Senator Estes Kefauver's Senate Committee on Racketeering, and subsequently as chief counsel to Representative Peter Rodino's House Committee on Crime. Nellis had a long-standing interest in psychology stemming from the pioneering work of his wife, Muriel, on psychotherapy with women (which, at the time, had just won an APA award). Although the EX-COMM members were all experienced political operators in their own right, the experience was primarily at the state level and it was the wise counsel of Jack Donahue and Joe Nellis that helped harness it and make CAPPS the efficacious political organization that it became.

The group also undertook the task of negotiating with the U.S. Civil Service Commission to recognize psychologists in the Federal Government Employees Health Program, while preparing a legislative program designed to include psychologists in 1964's recently passed Social Security Medicare Program. EX-COMM's efforts were supported by Don Schultz and Herbert Dorken of California and Logan Wright of Oklahoma.

EX-COMM quickly learned that efforts to negotiate psychologists into the Federal Government Employees Health Insurance Program as providers would be unsuccessful. On the advice of counsel, the group filed a class-action lawsuit against the U.S. Civil Service Commission for excluding psychologists as recognized providers under the Federal Government Employees Health Program. As an aside, it is noteworthy that most of the more than $100,000 raised went for employee salaries and to support the class-action suit against the Civil Service Commission (the oversight group for the Federal Government Employees Health Program, a harbinger of the fact that CAPPS would struggle for financial support throughout its existence.

In addition to the foregoing activities, in its first active year, CAPPS developed some extremely valuable contacts on the Hill, and within a short time had established itself as a national presence in the advocacy for psychology. Concurrently with its fund raising, its negotiations with the Civil Service Commission, and the mounting of the class-action suit, CAPPS was also engaged in a series of negotiations with both the Congress and the Social Security Administration (SSA) regarding the inclusion of psychologists under Medicare.

Unfortunately, these exhaustive, time-consuming, and expensive negotiations with the SSA were fruitless because both our contacts in the Congress and the bureaucracy operating the Social Security system were unwilling, or unable, to make such a change on an administrative basis. CAPPS was told that the only way that psychologists could gain recognition as mental health providers under Medicare was to change the law itself. Our legislative contacts advised CAPPS that Medicare was already "in trouble" from an economic standpoint, and that the probabilities of opening the Act for legislative change was seen as entailing a significant risk of additional economic loss. Thus, the probabilities of "opening" up Medicare to include additional providers were zero. However, sources both on the Hill and within the SSA indicated an interest in conducting a study designed to evaluate the feasibility of including psychologists in the Medicare program. CAPPS was quick to seize the opportunity and, in conjunction with the Colorado Psychological Association, began to develop such a study. Thus was born the well-known Colorado study on the feasibility of including psychologists in Medicare, a study that subsequently demonstrated that such inclusion was feasible and cost-effective.

The implementation of the Colorado study, however, was complicated by the appearance of yet another lobbying organization—one set up by the APA. The establishment of a second political advocacy organization for psychology reflected the political turmoil in the APA itself, and posed the potential for serious damage to the success of *any* effort in public policy and advocacy. This second lobbying organization not only cut heavily into CAPPS fund-raising potential, but competition on the part of the staff of the new organization resulted in a number of uncoordinated and destructive actions. The writer has commented elsewhere on the irony of the fact that the APA, which for years had had no organized political-action group now had two competing with each other for scarce resources, and for visibility and stature in representing psychology in the forum of national public policy.

The sad story of how such a state of affairs came to be cries out for study and analysis by a competent psychologist. How could a well-educated group of people succeed again and again in shooting themselves in the foot? For example, Nick Cummings tells the unchallenged story that when the then-current Executive Officer of the APA (at the time Medicare was passed) was queried by friendly contacts on the Hill as to whether or not psychology should be incorporated as a reimbursable provider under the mental health provisions of Medicare, he told them that "psychology was not interested." The failure of psychology to be incorporated initially as a recognized provider set in motion a battle that required over a quarter of a century to be resolved, and that has never been completely won.

A few years later, yet another APA CEO (who also taught clinical psychology) approached the zenith of insensitivity when he stated, in a public document that there should be no conflict between psychology and psychiatry about psychotherapy . . ." because psychology did not (treat) the seriously mentally ill, whereas psychiatry did." One might imagine that in virtually *any* organization such a statement by an executive officer would lead to immediate dismissal. Not so in psychology! The errant CEO in each instance continued in office. One might also wonder how such a state of affairs could possibly come about. For this writer, the explanation lies in the makeup of the APA at that time: its insularity, the need of its academic/scientific wing to control the organization at all costs, and its failure to recognize that without an "opening to the marketplace" (i.e., an employment market for psychological providers), psychology would forever remain nothing more than an underfunded academic "science." And, there still remains among some academic psychologists a failure to recognize that that which affects part of psychology affects all of it.

With the establishment of CAPPS and the creation of the new "practice" divisions, practitioners had new hope for, and renewed vigor in supporting, the proposition that the APA could and would speak for all of psychology. The state associations (collectively through Division 31, and individually through their newly broadened individual representation on the APA's Council of Representatives) were making ever more tenuous the academic/scientific control of the APA. For example, virtually all of the members of CAPPS EX-COMM were also state or divisional Council representatives and/or members of their state or divisional board of directors. Those same divisions and state associations had much broader representation on the APA Council of Representatives (obviously, to some degree at the expense of the domination of that Council by representatives from the "scientific/academic" divisions). The success of the CAPPS's class-action suit against the Civil Service Commission, even though ultimately found to be "moot" in judgments at the federal, district, and appellate levels, had pressured the Civil Service Commission into recognizing psychologists as mental health providers in the Federal Government Employees Health Program (which was, after all, the point of the original legal action). Meanwhile, at the national level, Richard Nixon was elected and began to serve his first term as president, triggering a sequence of events that had enormous potential consequences for psychology. It is also ironic that CAPPS, as public-policy advocates for liberal organizations such as psychology had very productive contacts with the Nixon administration.

As its January (continued) 1973 meeting, the APA Council was informed that the Nixon administration aimed to propose heavy slashes in federal budgets that would have an impact on training and research funds. Such actions, if implemented, would have had a devastating effect on research and training efforts in psychology. Although dire prophecies for the future of psychology were extant, the Council ultimately adjourned, having accepted the APA staff position that nothing could be done about this state of affairs. In those days, the January meeting of the Council adjourned at noon on Sunday. However, CAPPS EX-COMM members (also Council members) Cummings, Gravitz, Lawrence, Schultz, Wiggins, and Wright decided to prolong their Washington stay (at their own expense) to see if something could be done through the intervention of CAPPS' friends in the administration.

Despite the fact that it was Sunday, the group was successful in reaching some key figures in the Nixon administration and the Congress; and were told that if formal representations were made by the APA, they would be carefully reviewed as to their impact on proposed budget allocations. What then followed constitutes the ultimate irony. Despite the demonstration that, at last, psychology had an effective presence in public policy and voice for political action, yet another APA CEO decided to "do nothing" because it was ". . . an inappropriate action for the APA, and when the government wants to hear from the APA, they will invite us to consult."

The Dirty Dozen Council members refused to accept the APA CEO's position and immediately set about to reverse it. Employing an obscure (and heretofore unused) provision in the APA Council rules, the dissident members called for an unprecedented special meeting of the representatives a month later—a special meeting that not only formally protested the proposed federal budget cuts for training and research, but also passed a number of previously rejected proposals for professional psychology. The special meeting was also fruitful in that, after receiving the representatives protests, the administration withdrew its proposed budget cuts in research and training.

At the close of the special Council meeting, one of the more prominent spokespersons for the academic/scientific coalition made a most trenchant and, for him, prescient observation: "You have just seen the power balance in this room shift from the front rows to the back of the room" . . . a reference to the fact that Council members were seated by division number from the front to the back of the Council chamber, an arrangement that gave the "younger" professional and state association divisions a higher divisional number, and thus a seat in the "back benches" of the room.

Despite the success of the special Council session; and the fact
that it was called by legitimate members and procedures, the establishment maintained that the calling of the meeting had, in some
way, represented an improper action by CAPPS and the Dirty
Dozen, and began an effort to reverse their own representatives'
prophecy. The APA attack charged CAPPS with being an undemocratic organization controlled by a small group whose only
interest was in advancing the concerns of professional psychologists. This convenient sophistry overlooked the fact that the EX-
COMM membership had been elected by its founding Division 31
Board of Directors. Furthermore, CAPPS's bylaws called for
subsequent Executive Committee membership to be chosen
through election of the total CAPPS membership. This charge is
especially humorous in light of the fact that the APA membership, to this day, only gets to vote for one member of its Board of
Directors (the president). The second charge, that CAPPS was interested only in clinical issues, not academic/scientific or public
social issues, was even more sophistical in light of the fact that the
very action that had precipitated the attack on CAPPS was the re-
versal of devastating funding for training and research in the
federal budget.

The APA Board of Directors recommended, and the Council
hurriedly established, a committee "to investigate CAPPS," the
"Committee on Relations between APA and CAPPS"—a name
yielding the prophetic acronym CRAPACAPPS. The arrogance
of the committee was incredible. For example, CRAPACAPPS
demanded that CAPPS provide a whole series of documents, including the CAPPS's constitution, its bylaws, its articles of incorporation, and the minutes of EX-COMM meetings, although most
of the documents were already available to the public in CAPPS's
Articles of Incorporation in the Washington Office of Corporations. CAPPS EX-COMM took the position that, at the insistence
of the APA's Board of Directors, CAPPS had been established as
a separate and independent corporation with its own bylaws and
articles of incorporation; and that, as such, it not only was inap-

propriate for CRAPACAPPS to demand such documents from an independent organization, but for EX-COMM to comply. However, EX-COMM did invite members of the CRAPACAPPS committee to visit the CAPPS's Washington offices, where they would be free to study any document they wished (all requested documents being also publicly available in accordance with D.C. corporate law). CRAPACAPPS members have yet to avail themselves of the invitation. CRAPACAPPS chair Wiltse Webb was, from CAPPS's perspective, surprisingly sympathetic and even-handed, but it seemed to CAPPS EX-COMM that the rest of the committee, led by lifelong academic Norman Garmazy, was determinedly "out to get CAPPS."

It is important that an additional bit of history, extant at that time, be made explicit here. Given the growth in political strength, the power structure of the APA then reflected two major groups and one minor group, the major groups (in terms of numbers and clout) being the academic/scientists and the professionals. A smaller group, although composed in part of some members of both major groups, was made up of psychologists who saw their primary identification in terms of "social action." For several years, whenever the major groups presented competing candidates for the APA presidency and/or for a Board of Directors' or Council of Representatives' position, election to the position required that one of the major groups gain the support of the "social action" psychologists. This state of affairs was further compounded by the fact that votes for election to APA offices are "counted" by something that only can be described as a somewhat psychotic version of the Hare system (a system that can best be described as very complicated). Thus, as is the case in many such situations, where two essentially equal forces interact with a third and smaller group, the outcome is determined by which major group succeeds in enlisting the support of the small group (the "swing" vote).

As for the "investigation of CAPPS" by the Committee on Relations of the APA with CAPPS (CRAPACAPPS, dubbed by practitioners as "crap-on-capps"), the committee was notable for its lack of representation of professional interests, so predictably it found that CAPPS was underdemocratic and did not speak for the broad scientific, academic, and social interests in the APA. The solution to the problem, as proposed by CRAPACAPPS, was that APA undertake the establishment of a truly "representative" advocacy group to be called the Association for the Advancement of Psychology (AAP). The new organization, whose governance would feature a 24-member Board of Directors, would be composed of members to be "equally representative of the three major interests within the APA." Thus, we have the further irony that the establishment, which three years earlier, had refused to establish an advocacy organization "because of the danger to its 501(c)(3) tax status," now assumed direct leadership in founding a competing political-action group. Furthermore, it was to be "housed" in the APA building, staffed by APA employees ("rented out" to the new organization), and financially supported by this very establishment. This is how the Association for the Advancement of Psychology (AAP) was brought into being.

From day one, AAP appeared to be doomed to minimal effectiveness, both because of the structure of its governance and because of the passivity and competitiveness of its staff. After several misadventures in which CAPPS and the AAP staff presented different positions to important governmental agencies (one of which threatened the success of the Colorado Social Security project), CAPPS EX-COMM decided that there could not be two organizations claiming to speak for psychology at the federal level. CAPPS was also aware of the excruciating financial and emotional choices being forced on individual psychologists as to which organization to support. Accordingly, CAPPS proposed, and the AAP accepted, a plan for consolidating the two groups in which some members of CAPPS EX-COMM and its staff would join the AAP— thus ensuring that much of CAPPS's expertise and its resources for advocacy would be available to the AAP. Furthermore, the criticality of an independent advocacy organization was, at least arguably, somewhat diminished by surprising, rapid changes within the APA governance structure. In spite of some attempted last-ditch finagling by the established power structure (see "Political Action within the APA"), Rogers Wright was elected to the APA Board of Directors, soon followed by Blau, Cummings, Schultz, and Siegel.

However, this by no means was the end of the matter. Upon learning of Wright's election to the APA Board of Directors, the existing Board quickly adopted, and the APA Council approved, an APA policy denying a seat on APA's Board to anyone who "concurrently held a seat on the Board of Directors of a national political advocacy organization." The APA Board then attempted to apply the newly passed action retroactively to include Wright. Furthermore, inasmuch as CAPPS was already amalgamating with AAP, and Wright was one of several CAPPS Board members who had declined to seek membership on the CAPPS/AAP combined board, the APA establishment's hasty action would not have applied. Nevertheless, the APA Board then contemplated interpreting the new action to preclude participation for those *who had been* members of the board of a "national political advocacy organization" at the time of their election. Wright assured APA's Board of Directors that his legal advice was that there could be no *retroactive* application of the new policy; and that he had every intention of making an all-out legal fight, should the APA pursue such a course. Wisdom prevailed, the Board of Directors withdrew its opposition, and the rigid control of the APA governance by academic/scientific interests was about to be splintered.

Meanwhile, what about the AAP as an independent public-policy body and a vehicle for political action? From this writer's perspective, it can be said that only a group of psychologists could create such a governing structure and political dynamic as was incorporated in the AAP's founding bylaws. Furthermore, it's this writer's judgment that the establishment of the governance structure of the AAP was a major step in legitimizing what was to become (and is) the "Balkanization" of the power structures within the APA. But, there also was no finite requirement that members of AAP's Board of Trustees have any knowledge, experience, or sophistication in the art of political action. Consequently, with three groups equally represented in its governance, few of which initially had qualifying public-policy or political-action expertise, the AAP's activities were problematic from the outset.

Fortunately for psychology, the Colorado Social Security

study had been well structured and well established and was underway prior to the amalgamation of CAPPS and the AAP and continued to its successful conclusion. Ironically, the AAP then received psychology's recognition of a program that had been conceived and implemented (by CAPPS) before the AAP ever became a functional body. Furthermore, the AAP's lack of coherent direction failed to provide for an evaluation of staff performance and accountability, with the consequence that its potential as an effective political advocacy organization for psychology was never realized.

Earlier on, in this context, a psychologist/political expert, Pat DeLeon, became increasingly visible as a member of Senator Inouye's Washington staff. From the time he arrived he was a strong supporter of political action, public policy, and advocacy for psychology. As DeLeon rose to prominence within the APA governance structure, he guided such political advocacy as was permissible through formal structures that he caused to be created within the APA's Washington establishment. The creation of these public-policy structures under his direction gave psychology the only really effective political advocacy it enjoyed through the closing years of the 1970s and most of the 1980s.

Meanwhile, the AAP continued its senescent decline, and may well have gone out of existence altogether had it not been for the creation of the APA's Practice Directorate, which meant that professional psychology finally had a structure, staff, and resources (paid for by an added dues levied on practitioners). The Practice Directorate's planned action programs—especially the ultimately successful attempt to amend the Medicare Act to incorporate psychologists as recognized providers—made apparent the urgent necessity for a well-structured, energetic, and well-resourced political-action group completely outside the APA establishment.

Such an advocacy group had to be independent of the APA in order to be able to engage in the kind of public policy and political advocacy required to support the initiatives of the Practice Directorate. Over the years, the unwieldiness of the AAP's large Board of Trustees (and its cost) dictated the replacement of that 24-member Board of Trustees with a smaller number (six), while maintaining the unfortunately mandated "equal" representation of the three groups within the APA. This structure not only ensured internal competition within the AAP's Board of Trustees, but overlooked the fact that by the mid to late 1980s the three designated and equally represented groups (academic/science, professional, and social action) were no longer truly representative of the body politic of American psychology. It also overlooked the fact, as it had from the outset, that the academic/scientific and social action groups did not match their highly vocal demands for equal representation in the AAP's governance and action programs with an equal responsibility for financial support and membership participation. Specifically, AAP members who named either academic/science or social action as their primary identification constituted less than 5% of the AAP's membership and financial support base (academic/scientific, approximately 2.6%, social action, approximately 1.4%).

At this point, the AAP was also in dire financial straits. Its membership had shrunk to the minuscule. Staff action was almost nonexistent, and the supporting membership was largely uninformed. Only the economic tolerance of its parent APA allowed the organization to continue. In other words, the organization was bankrupt economically. Only the tolerance of the APA, and the life support provided by a few dedicated psychologists maintained its existence.

At this point, yet another of those incredible ironies occurred that have characterized the rise of professionalism within the APA: the AAP's Board of Trustees invited this writer (Rogers Wright) to become Executive Director of the organization on a part-time (two days a week) basis. It was a challenging offer in that (1) the Practice Directorate was ready to make its move to seek amendment of the Medicare Act to include psychologists; (2) money had to be raised for operations and staff salaries; and (3) arrangements had to be made to pay the AAP's substantial debt to the APA. The organization also had to be revitalized. The AAP's Board of Trustees accepted staff recommendations that the AAP bylaws be changed to make the Board of Trustees elective positions dependent on the number of members and the contributions by such members identifying themselves with one of the AAP's founding groups. The AAP's members overwhelmingly approved the proposed changes to the AAP constitution. Under the direction of its new leadership, the AAP developed an aggressive action program and was highly visible in the successful legislative effort to amend Social Security. Within approximately five years, the AAP became one of the top 10 PACs nationally among health-care public-policy and advocacy groups.

Political Action Within the APA

Throughout this personal recollection of the rise of the professionalism of the APA, much has been made of the fact that psychologists whose primary identification was with professionalism were blocked out of responsible positions in the APA governance. As noted earlier, this was relatively easy to achieve given that the election process was controlled at the Board of Directors' level. Typically, in those times, the APA Secretary and Executive Officer, and one or more members of its Board of Directors would generate a slate of nominees to fill upcoming vacancies on all of APA's boards and committees. Indeed, where professional psychology had any input at all, it was typically through academic institutional psychologists who were (1) only marginally identified with applied psychology and (2) had little, if any, "hands on" experience in the direct provision of psychological services. Next, in the APA system, the slate of nominees went to the Board of Directors for approval and then was presented to the Council for election, a system that, with some modification, still prevails in APA affairs.

Spokespersons for professional psychology were essentially limited to "offices" in the governance of the divisions they had created and/or state associations largely controlled by professional interests. The rise of the APA's professional divisions, and the increasing importance of the state associations in psychology's affairs, along with the ever-increasing number of providers (who identified primarily with applied psychology), argued for political action within the APA, action that would ensure the elevation of applied psychologists to positions of power within the APA governance. Concurrent with some of the other projects previously discussed, the Dirty Dozen, an informal group centered on CAPPS, Divisions 12, 29, and 31, and the APA's Committee on Health Insurance, turned their attention to the election of professional psychologists to positions of responsibility within the organization.

Some organizational structure was necessary to offset the so-called "dean's network," an informal arrangement among the academics whereby their departmental resources, including long-distance telephone lines, were being systematically (and successfully) used to influence the APA election process. Accordingly, New Jersey's Marv Metsky and Gene Shapiro called a Dirty Dozen meeting, attended by Cummings, Gravitz, Siegel, Schultz, Wright, and Young, with the stated purpose of electing a practicing psychologist to the APA presidency. That meeting was held in conjunction with the APA convention in Hawaii in 1972. Previously, the only practicing psychologists to gain any stature within the APA establishment had been Ted Blau, who did, and does, epitomize what the Vail conference called the practitioner/scholar (although he himself would probably opt to be identified as a scientist/practitioner). Dr. Blau pioneered the delivery of a wide range of psychological services from the base of full-time independent psychological service delivery, while maintaining a high level of scholarliness in both research and service delivery efforts. His erudition and the quality of his service delivery efforts led to leadership positions in Divisions 12 and 29, to the chair of the APA's Board of Professional Affairs, and to continuing participation as a highly visible and articulate member of the APA's Council. Despite such achievements by a full-time independent practitioner, and the unstinting support of the professional community (and many academic colleagues), the political dynamic of the APA structure (two strong groups of essentially equal strength competing in a system with a third, and less numerous, group) and the vagaries of the APA's version of the Hare system, repeatedly frustrated Blau's presidential candidacy. In fact, Blau's candidacy was caught up in the struggle between the "scientific" and professional interests, resulting in a political standoff with the establishment candidate, Wilbert McKeachie. Consequently, "third party" candidates (social-action representatives) had, for several years, been elected to the APA presidency.

This situation not only saddled the APA with well-meaning, but weak, leadership, but also ensured the frustration of professional psychologists within the APA framework. Metsky and Shapiro proposed a change in tactics in that the Dirty Dozen should build a support group in the hope that Nick Cummings' national visibility, engendered by his "utilization-economic offset studies" and his chairship of the COHI, might be able to bypass the existing standoff between professional and academic/scientific psychology. After intense discussion, the group decided that whereas the election of one or a series of APA presidents would be an important step, it would be primarily a symbolic victory in that it would *not* address the establishment's hold on the APA election process, nor would it bring significant numbers of professional psychologists into the power structure. Consequently, the group decided to organize a political-action group within the APA structure with the specific intent of nominating and electing professional psychologists to positions of authority on all boards and committees in the APA governance structure. Second, the group decided to continue to support Blau for APA president and to seek the election of Cummings and Schultz to the APA's Board of Directors. Marv Metsky took responsibility for the operation of the program, a commitment that would last for over a quarter of a century. The Dirty Dozen immediately procured a listing of all APA boards and committees with vacancies and called a public meeting of all APA Council members representing the practice divisions and state associations, to be held concurrently with the next APA Council meeting. At that meeting, nominations for every APA elective office were solicited from the attendees, with particular attention to candidates for the APA's Board of Directors and other significant boards and committees, such as the Board of Professional Affairs. Given the now substantial political sophistication of the Dirty Dozen about the APA's elective process, a political strategy was evolved whereby there would be primary and secondary candidates for key APA positions. This stratagem of a "stalking horse" was devised to address the APA elective process by attracting second-place and third-place votes to a second candidate, thereby strengthening the "first place" vote of the primary candidate. This strategy had the additional advantage of gaining visibility and organizing support for the secondary candidate, whom, it was presumed, would be the primary candidate in the next election cycle.

Those readers knowledgeable about the APA's history and election process will recognize that this political-action group, organized by the Dirty Dozen, was the direct progenitor of the APA's current political caucus system—brought about by the decided successes of the Dirty Dozen's initial operations. In short order, state association representatives, whose structural relationship to the APA was, and is, different from that of the divisions, recognized the value of an independent caucus group whose primary commitment would be to the concerns of the states. Consequently, the first caucus also spawned a state association caucus (as well as the professional psychology caucus), soon to be followed by many caucuses representative of the major (and frequently minor) interest groups within the APA family.

To return to the early history, the group's initial efforts focused on electing members to the APA's Board of Directors. Initial candidates were Don Schultz in the primary position and Rogers Wright in the secondary position. These political efforts were successful from the outset, but the vagaries of the APA-modified Hare system elected Rogers Wright, the first full-time practitioner, to the APA's Board of Directors. The APA establishment's worst dreams were now reality because one of the most highly visible and rabid of the APA's professional psychologist foxes was squarely ensconced in the APA hen house. Negotiations were instigated between representatives of the establishment's perpetual presidential candidate, Wilbert McKeachie, and representatives of the Dirty Dozen. An agreement was reached that allowed for the uncontested election of McKeachie to the APA presidency, with the quid pro quo that the academic establishment would drop its opposition to Blau's candidacy. Blau was then elected to the APA presidency and Cummings to the Board of Directors. Another part of the agreement was that Wright (and subsequently Cummings) would also become members of the Board of Directors "Search Committee" for a new APA CEO. In short order, Don Schultz, and Max Siegel were also elected to the Board of Directors. With five card-carrying members of the Dirty Dozen now ensconced on the APA's Board of Directors, the absolute control by the academic/scientist wing of the APA, if not at an end, was clearly on life support.

One of the major problems for professional psychology from 1960 through 1974 lay in the personage of a series of APA executive officers. Although undoubtedly well intentioned, those holding the APA CEO position were, without exception, (1) monumentally insensitive to the needs of professional psychology, and (2) essentially unaware of both the growing power and mounting frustration of that group. In fact, five successive CEOs had their tenure successfully challenged by the Dirty Dozen's leaders, who made widely known professional psychology's disaffection with the operation of the APA's Executive Office.

At the time of Cummings' and Wrights' election to the APA Board of Directors, the organization was about to launch yet another recruiting effort to fill the CEO position. As previously agreed, Wright and Cummings were members of the Search Committee. Predictably, the 40 candidates (for the APA CEO position) were, without exception, from the academic/scientific wing of the APA. Although those on the list were outstanding psychologists, they shared the common shortcoming of being relatively uninformed about the needs of professional psychology. The adamant opposition of Cummings and Wright exhausted the initial list of 40 candidates and a second list also of 40 prospects was generated. Despite the urgency of the need to resolve the CEO vacancy, the Practice Contingent on the Board "hung tough" through the review of an additional 38 candidates; and it was not until candidates 39 and 40 on the second list (actually candidates 79 and 80) were interviewed that the Board's Practice Contingent agreed on the two candidates, both of whom could offer the broad range of capabilities demanded by the Practice Contingent.

Chuck Kiesler entered the APA executive structure as a young, dynamic psychologists without substantial prior involvement in APA politics. He was open to new ideas and willing to work with all dimensions of the APA family, a quality not previously seen in the personage of the APA's Executive Officer. He recruited new and younger staff, especially in the practice areas. Kiesler also recruited Jack Donahue, former Executive Officer of the original CAPPS group as an Associate Executive Officer of the APA, a move that, for the first time, brought directly into APA's central office the substantial knowledge and expertise of someone familiar with advocacy and public-policy action for psychology. It was also during Kiesler's tenure that the caucus structure (informal political groups initially organized by the Dirty Dozen) was expanded to include virtually every interest group within the APA; and was incorporated into the formal structure of the organization.

The "breaking open" of the APA power structure symbolized by the election of Wright, followed by that of Blau, Cummings, Schultz, and Siegel to the APA Board of Directors, continued and was enhanced by the successes of the Dirty Dozen-organized practitioner and state association caucuses. In a short time, it became axiomatic that whereas it was not always the case that a member of the practitioner caucus would necessarily be elected APA president, without the endorsement of that group a person would *not* be elected to APA's presidency. In this same time frame, both Blau and Cummings served their terms as APA presidents, to be followed by the presidency of Max Siegel, and then, somewhat later, by the presidencies of Ray Fowler and Jack Wiggins. Over this same span of time, eight members of the original Dirty Dozen (Blau, Cummings, Fowler, Schultz, Shapiro, Siegel, Wiggins, and Wright) also served on the APA Board of Directors.

Shortly thereafter, scientists and academics in the APA began to complain that their interests were being summarily treated and that their opportunities for participation in the membership of the APA's governing hierarchy (including the presidency) were extremely limited or nonexistent. Thus began their litany of emotional blackmail, including overt threats (that had previously been muted) to bolt from the APA and start their own organization.

Practitioners had once (in the late 1960s) also threatened to leave the APA, a movement that died for lack of support when it failed to gain the endorsement of leading state associations, such as California and New York. This separatist movement was also actively opposed by a number of highly visible psychologists in the professional movement (including the members of the Dirty Dozen). The writer, regrettably, failed, in subsequent years, to avail himself of opportunities to discuss this action with colleagues Max Siegel and Lenny Small, but did discuss the issue of a separate professional organization with a number of the Dirty Dozen members, including Cummings, Gravitz, Lawrence, Rosecrans, and Schultz, all of whom shared to some degree the feeling that the interests of professional psychology would have been better advanced through the auspices of a purely professional organization. Psychology is virtually unique among the major professions in that it has not formally developed separate specialty groups devoted to the needs of clearly defined specialties within the overall profession. This writer is now of the opinion that there are so many competing groups within the APA, each with its attendant political action group, that the strength and resources of a major interest group are dissipated by supporting the myriad "minority" groups within the organization. In this writer's judgment, the dues paid by professional psychologists to support the APA *and* the Practice Directorate would be more efficiently expended by supporting an independent organization, such as an "Association of Professional Psychology."

In the late 1980s and 1990s, the APA—in spite of the sour-grapes content of the academic scientists' complaint (after almost 40 years of totally dominating the organization)—decided to "talk" with its dissidents despite the clearly irrational demands of some of the APA's scientific/academic colleagues. This temporizing (as it virtually always does) only served to encourage the dissident interests, who ultimately confronted the APA establishment with a proposal for "confederation," a proposal that envisioned three essentially independent organizations linked only by a common name and an impotent central governance (shades of the AAP troika).

After uncountable hours of association time and the expenditure of thousands and thousands of association dollars, a number of the surviving members of the Dirty Dozen were in the forefront of the movement opposing the "confederation proposition," and with the support of other prominent members of the APA governance, such as Charlie Spielberger, led the successful fight to defeat the proposed reorganization of the APA.

Subsequently, a fairly small number from the APA's academic/scientific wing defected and started a competing national organization, the American Psychological Society (APS). This writer's last information indicated that the APS had stagnated, with a membership of approximately 15,000 (a large number of whom were students) and a substantial proportion of whom were subdoctoral practitioners. One puzzling aspect of this movement was the behavior of former APA presidents Logan Wright and Bonnie Strickland, who, if not the driving force in the defection, certainly were strongly supportive of the academic/scientific interests, and visibly supportive of the leadership of the dissident group. In the case of Logan Wright, this support was especially puzzling because he had, for years, been a strong supporter of all of the activities of the Dirty Dozen, and, in fact, only the lateness of his arrival on the national scene (i.e., after the formation of CAPPS) precluded his membership in the Dirty Dozen. Nevertheless, Wright was a staunch supporter of the Dirty Dozen action program and was one of the advisory members (along with Bob Weitz) to the original CAPPS EX-COMM. Furthermore, both Logan Wright and Bonnie Strickland had sought, and obtained, the support of professional psychologists in their respective campaigns for the presidencies of the Division of Clinical Psychology (Division 12) and their subsequent APA presidencies. Additionally, they had been highly visible proponents of the "Flexnor commission" to address issues surrounding doctoral-level competency for the delivery of professional psychological services. When their efforts as APA presidents (to advance the interests of the scientific/academic group) were unavailing, both took very prominent roles in the formation of the APS, and especially its so-called practice wing, composed predominantly of subdoctorally trained psychologists.

A number of additional recent developments in public policy and advocacy for psychology featured some or all of the membership of the Dirty Dozen. One was in the mid-1970s, when a governmental agency denied psychologists authorization to use the terminal end nerve stimulation (TENS) technique they had developed for the treatment of chronic pain. The bureaucracy had ruled that the electronic "black box" they had invented was a medical device. Dirty Dozen members Ernie Lawrence and Rogers Wright, along with CAPPS former adviser, Logan Wright, were named to an APA Task Force charged with defining the psychologist's use of physical interventions. The work of this group, subsequently adopted in 1976 as APA policy, set forth a variety of physical interventions covered by psychology's training, including the use of medication (prescriptive privilege).

A few years later, when the APA's poorly conceived venture into peer review resulted in a major lawsuit against the APA by some of its own members, Dirty Dozeners Cummings, Rosecrans, Shapiro, and Wright again served on a task force charged with the redesign of the program; an action that eventuated in the development of the only extent research-based Professional Service Review program. A few years later, Dirty Dozeners Fowler, Gravitz, Metsky, Rosecrans, Shapiro, and Wright played a prominent role among those professional psychologists involved in the formation of the Practice Directorate.

Summary

The Dirty Dozen, composed of, at any given time, from 12 to 14 participants, was involved, in part or completely, in virtually all of the major developments in professional psychology in the past

30 years. This group was unique in the degree to which highly individual members came to trust in and cooperate with each other in the pursuit of common goals. Those involved, coming from substantially different backgrounds, brought a variety of experience and knowledge to the group, and although each had a private agenda, they were united in their subscription to the principle that those personal agendas had to take second place to the interests of professional psychology. Each felt that any of the others in the group would do equally well in handling whatever issue was at hand, whether it was seeking the APA presidency or acting on some conceptual matter confronting the profession. This in no way implies that those involved were always of a like mind about anything. In fact, any particular to issue was likely to have a dozen or more different perspectives, and long and vigorous were the debates and arguments by which those individual perspectives became married to a common conception and common goals.

Interestingly enough, although the Dirty Dozen created organization after organization, structure after structure, with attendant bylaws, procedures, and so on, there was never a written document (other than the minutes of our meetings) that structured the actions of those involved. Whether it was signing notes to establish credit for the financial foundation of CAPPS or a decision as a group to hold a meeting (because some urgent matter demanded attention) regardless of reimbursement for expenses, a verbal commitment was all it took.

Obviously, no dozen, dirty, miscounted, or otherwise, could single-handedly produce the monumental changes that have occurred in the many years of the Dirty Dozen's operation. The group could only evoke, propose, provoke, and provide leadership. It was joined in its crusades by hundreds, and then thousands, of psychologists across the country, people who themselves have become major figures in psychology's march toward respected professional stature. Many of these supporters would have been welcome contributing members of the Dirty Dozen; their failure to be included was an accident of time in that most of us were older and/or simply got there first. It would be impossible to list all the individuals who joined us in the development of a profession, but a few names stand out because of their major contributions. The Dirty Dozen could not have existed without the support and help of Pat DeLeon, Ron Fox, Stanley Moldawsky, Arthur Kovacs, Bud Orgel, Diane Willis, Ken Schenkel, Laura Toomey, Jay Benedict, Jules Barron, Herbert Dorken, Suzanne Sobel, and on and on and on.

To the writer, participation in the work of the Dirty Dozen was a unique experience; he otherwise would never have known, or been privileged to work with, individuals such as those identified. Nick Cummings tells a story that in the writer's early days as the chair of CAPPS, he was the only person who had the chutzpah to set up a conference call of the group on Super Bowl Sunday, and to have enjoyed 100% participation in the call to which this writer can only add that his courage probably rested on the knowledge that the commitment of these individuals exceeded his own, and that they would, in fact, *all* find a way to participate. Aside from my personal pleasure in setting down this series of recollections, the documentation of the efforts of this group is valuable because it recognizes the many and valuable contributions of unique human beings.

Ernie Lawrence, in a recent communication to the whole group, perhaps says it extraordinarily well when he notes: "If we could [now] accomplish one thing: the demonstration of what a handful of dedicated psychologists could do in the face of overwhelming odds—that one does not have to submit or compromise, or even be political. If clinical psychology is to survive, it has to learn how to fight uncompromisingly, and bitterly, if necessary (although we did have plenty of laughs). We made the APA take a 180-degree turn. And that is the job of today's clinical psychologists. It doesn't take an army or a fortune, although they can be useful. What it takes are will and guts and smarts and leadership! That is what is necessary!"

Addendum

A Look to the Future

Some funny things happened on the way to the 30th anniversary of the Dirty Dozen.

The history of the Dirty Dozen was prepared in anticipation of an anniversary meeting of the group in conjunction with the 1999 Boston convention of the American Psychological Association. In planning our 30th (40th, depending on who does the counting) anniversary meeting, the group considered writing a history of the group, and what with the group's involvement in so many of the developments in professional psychology across the past 30–40 years, also considered generating a section on "Recommendations for the Future." As the "Dozener" around the longest, this writer, with the help of Nick Cummings, was selected to do the "History," while other Dozeners volunteered to summarize some "Recommendations." However, a majority of the group, decided that it might seem presumptuous to address our younger colleagues in such a fashion. This objection became more and more popular as the countdown toward the anniversary date advanced, notably among some of those who had initially agreed to produce such a document. In any event, the sentiment was persuasive and the group decided that we would forgo any prognostication.

Concurrently, and to the delight of the Dirty Dozen, three of the organizations spawned by members of the Dirty Dozen decided to honor the group at the 1999 APA Convention (the APP Caucus, the Division 42 Board of Directors, and the Association for the Advancement of Psychology, psychology's national advocacy organization).

At the conclusion of the prepared presentation, the group was asked to comment on what it perceived to be the major issues confronting professional psychology: and what, if any, actions organized psychology should take to address such issues. Additionally, individual psychologists repeatedly asked the individuals who made up the "Dozen" to prepare some kind of formal statement in the name of the group.

A number of ideas were expressed by Dirty Dozen members at the various presentations and at the group's formal dinner meeting following the APP presentation. Further informal discussions among group members generated additional ideas about the directions that organized psychology might choose to pursue.

This addendum is an attempt to capture some of the most relevant ideas of the Dirty Dozen about the future. The writer made notes on these ideas as he heard them expressed, and submitted a draft document to the members of the Dozen, along with a ballot for the expression of individual members' opinions. This addendum is an attempt to report the group's thinking, although that effort is obviously biased by the writer's point of view. This will be especially apparent in the summaries of the discussion. It should be noted that, as was so frequently the case in the past, unanimity did not characterize our thought processes. Unfortunately, this time the Dozen did not have a formal opportunity to interact, as was the case in the past, so there is no "Dozen" position on any of the reported matters. Rather, the report reflects the position of the majority of those voting.

The issues will be stated in the order of importance as perceived by the group, followed by a brief summary of our thinking. It is important to note that the Dirty Dozen agrees that there is a very short time in which to implement any meaningful action program, certainly no more than a maximum of 5 to 15 years. Otherwise, meaningful mental health care becomes a memory.

I. Health-Care Economics

The group was unanimous in considering that the primary problem confronting providers of health care (including mental services) is its cost. Any effort to address the nation's health-care needs (and psychology's role therein) must begin with knowledge about and sensitivity to the impact of health-care economics. It almost goes without saying that this is a topic on which most psychologists are naive. Consequently, many proposals advanced for addressing health-care service delivery die aborning. Some psychologists (and other health-care providers) see the solution to the problem in some form of a "single-payer" national health-care program; a solution that has proponents among psychologists. Proponents of such a federal/state plan may even be found among the Dirty Dozen. However, the majority of the Dirty Dozen voting *are not* supportive of such an approach. Proponents of a national health plan overlook the fact that such plans apparently are economically troubled (the highly touted Canadian plan included), and offer diminished quantity and quality of health care. Proponents of a national health plan also overlook the fact that, in this country, government adventures into health care, such as Medicare, Medicaid, Community Mental Health Centers, and state mental health programs, have been in economic difficulty from their outset.

Regardless of whether the future will see a universal health plan, the Dirty Dozen unanimously agree that cost will be the predominant feature in shaping a health delivery program. This is a compelling argument for psychologists at every level to be totally committed to, and participatory in advocacy for, mental health services and psychology. For most, this includes all-out support for a comprehensive federal "Patient Bill of Rights" incorporating full legal responsibility and liability for the operators and subsidizers of such plans.

II. Advocacy

There is among the Dirty Dozen unanimous support for "all-out" advocacy for psychology at all levels of government, and one that is cognizant of the economic realities of the current health-care environment. At a federal level, this translates into unequivocal support for psychology's only national advocacy organization, the Association for the Advancement of Psychology.

1. Communications with the AAP leadership reveal that despite

an outstanding record of positive accomplishment, psychologists' support for the Association for the Advancement of Psychology dropped *yet another 10%* in calendar year 1999, despite the fact that (as of this writing in early fall of 1999), federal legislation incorporating a "Patient Bill of Rights" is active in the Congress.

2. The American Psychological Association and "psychology" could, and should, have done much more over past decades to support advocacy and political action. The APA governance establishment has been immobilized by the fear that taking such steps as it might take legitimately and legally in some way would jeopardize the organization's favorable tax status, especially with respect to its publication business and real estate operations. Furthermore, the APA's political structure and the political aspirations and timidity of much of the current leadership have further immobilized the APA and precluded its taking actions to support advocacy.

III. Prescriptive Authority

The Dirty Dozen, with one exception, has long supported prescriptive privileges for psychologists. Several of the Dirty Dozen, having been trained in neuropsychology (before there was even such a recognized specialty within psychology), early recognized the importance of psychopharmacological interventions in the management of certain neurological *and* psychological disorders. In fact, Dirty Dozen members Wright and Lawrence were on an APA task force that originally recommended (in a document entitled "The Psychologists' Use of Physical Interventions") that the Council adopt as APA policy the psychologists' use of a number of physical interventions, including the prescribing of a limited formulary of medications. Psychologists have long supervised the use of a variety of physical interventions (including medication) in such areas as the treatment of neuropsychological problems and intractable pain.

Furthermore, it is the rationale of those of the Dirty Dozen supportive of prescriptive privileges for psychologists that the highest quality of mental health care demands that psychologists have prescription privileges. This position is based on the training of psychologists; which best qualifies them to evaluate and assess the impact of chemotherapeutic interventions on the patient's overall psychological functioning. This perspective also posits that it is in the patient's best interest for psychologists to be qualified to prescribe a limited formulary. Furthermore, the economics of health-care delivery will not tolerate the needless squandering of economic resources institutionalized in the current practice of employing two professionals to do a job best done by one. Finally, the Dirty Dozen has carefully reviewed the objections of those opposing prescriptive privileges for psychology in light of the above-stated rationale, and finds such objections lacking in persuasiveness.

Unfortunately, the political structure of the APA again comes into play in that needless years have been, and are being, squandered in attempting to appease, cajole, or persuade a small, but vociferous, minority who oppose the seeking of the privilege. At the outset of these remarks, we noted that it is the unanimous judgment of the Dirty Dozen that psychology has a relatively short time (probably five years or so, at best) in which to address the current crisis, one aspect of which is the gaining of prescriptive privileges. Like advocacy and political action, the APA establishment has been slow to deal with this issue, in part because of the complexity of large organizations attempting to deal with small groups and minority opinions.

IV. Political Action Within and Without the APA

The history of the Dirty Dozen documents the extreme difficulty of moving a large multiinterest group in any given direction. It would seem that the only issue that can be moved rapidly through the APA governance is a resolution that has one or more of the following characteristics: (1) it has been labeled "social interest," (2) it is being pushed by one of the APA's significant interest groups, or (3) it will have little subsequent impact on society.

As our history makes clear, psychologists as a group have long been concerned (perhaps overly) with minority interests (perhaps because underneath it all, we suspect that each of us may belong to such a group) to the degree that we allow "minority rights" to prevail too often, with the consequence that a political Balkanization of the large and diverse structure occurs. It is the judgment of the Dirty Dozen that if professional psychology is to rescue itself in the time remaining, it will do so only (1) if major changes are made in the existing APA organizational structure and/or (2) professional psychologists establish an independent (but perhaps affiliated) organization devoted to the advancement of their interests and concerns. In that context, some of the enormous resources that are siphoned off to support a broad, and often unrelated, spectrum of APA activities might be committed more effectively to the advancement of professional practice.

A. Reorganizing the APA

It is no doubt incendiary to use such a term because past efforts have been made by special interest groups to "reorganize the APA" in such a way as to favor one or more of the APA's "interest groups." However, despite these efforts, no real attempt has been made to address the primary problem with the APA governance structure; namely, the fact that the APA governance is, in and of itself, a closed corporation; that is, the members of the Board of Directors are chosen exclusively from and by the APA Council, resulting in a very undemocratic situation in which a very small number (approximately 150 APA members) are the only ones eligible to serve, and of which 39 (at last count) were required to elect. This closed system (allegedly in the interest of selecting the best qualified to serve), when combined with the Hare system, ensures an incestuous situation in which minority interests have undue impact. The solution is a petition to be signed by the requisite number of Council members or by the requisite number of APA members, mandating an election on a bylaw revision. Based on our long experience with the system, this is the only way we can perceive of getting the APA apparatus modified within the time remaining for professional psychology.

B. Independent Organization for Professional Psychology

For those who believe that our resources are too thin and that the time line too short and/or resent having to pay APA dues and the heavy additional levy required to subsidize the APA's superstructure and special-interest activities, and/or those who believe that the APA can never move with sufficient speed to address current problems, there is always the alternative of an independent organization.

Although highly controversial, such a conception is by no means new to APA history. A broadly supported effort to do precisely that was attempted in the early 1960s.

It is also historically true that in virtually every professional organization, there ultimately comes a time when specific interests or needs of major parts of the organization require the development of organizational structures independent of the parent body. The most immediate and analogous situation is, of course, medicine, where each of the specialties long ago recognized the need for an independent specialty organization (in addition to the American Medical Association). Such an independent organization for psychology could, and should, be a 501(c)(6) "Business and Professional Organization," which, under federal law and regulations would give the organization sufficient latitude to pursue the types of advocacy and/or political action necessary for the survival of professional psychology. This is in no way to be construed as a "stalking out of the APA," as the scientific/academic wing has threatened over the past three decades. Rather, it is a recognition that the economic necessity of having to support the range of endeavors of a broadly based organization limits the resources that can be specifically targeted to the amelioration of problems for particular segments of the group (i.e., professional psychology).

C. Change the Title of Professional Psychology

Although there is some tentative support among the Dirty Dozen for changing the current appellation for the professional psychologist from Ph.D. to Psy.D., sentiment with respect to this proposal ranges from ardent, to lukewarm, to outright opposition. There does seem to be a tentative consensus that such a step may ultimately be necessary, and that such a change may have genuine advantages. Reservations have to do with the concern that, at this point, such a change will not address the primary problem currently confronting psychology. Furthermore, some Dirty Dozeners expressed the concern that if we get too caught up in the "name change" issue, it may be at the expense of limited resources that would be better expended to support the other recommendations.

In general, the Dirty Dozen concurs that the Ph.D. degree is a generic title that professional psychology would probably have been better advised to discard, especially in reference to those psychologists providing mental health services. In reality, psychology has repeated opportunities to address this problem, but has not done so. Part of the motivation for not addressing the problem is our unending identification with academia. Furthermore, by clinging to the "respectable" Ph.D., the APA sets its "professors" apart from the subdoctorally trained, another issue the APA has refused to address definitively. Regrettably, many state associations have made the same error.

In recent memory, Division 12 (the Division of Clinical Psychology) attempted to address the problem by limiting the application of "clinical" psychology to those psychologists who met the traditional qualification of having undergone specialty training in clinical psychology. For a variety of reasons—the politics in the APA, the fact that the efforts were "too little" and too late—these efforts were essentially nonproductive. Thus, if there is to be a way to deal with the issues of who is competent to provide quality mental health services, those ends will probably best be pursued by (1) an organization independent from the APA and (2) a concept of training and an appellation totally different from that of the long-bankrupt "scientist/practitioner."

V. Stay on the Message

Among political gurus, it is axiomatic that political success obtains only when the candidate establishes a "political" action program incorporating a relatively small number of highly important topics, and then repeatedly calls attention to, and expends resources only on, further defining those selected issues.

Psychologists being psychologists, we have tended to pursue a wide range of issues, presumably because, as psychologists, we have a duty to "speak out" in the interest of enhancing our professional stature, when, in fact, the pursuit of such chimera has simply diverted our attention and expended our resources unproductively. One recent example is the pursuit of additional "credentials" and "specialties" in the mistaken belief that *more education and more credentials* will resolve or assist in the resolution of our current dilemma. The APA's founding of a "college" to train for these additional proficiencies seems to be one of these highly visible exercises in futility.

If one accepts the premise that the primary problem in health-care delivery (of all kinds) is economic, it is fatuous to believe that the acquisition of additional credentials, diplomas, and so on, represents a solution to the problem of adequate health care. At a time when the predominant concern of government and health-care agencies in the private sector is cost, it borders on the ridiculous to propose that the acquisition of another "certificate" makes a given practitioner a more desirable member of an HMO provider panel or allows the psychologists to participate in some under-resourced program to which admission is otherwise denied. The ever-increasing utilization of subdoctoral practitioners, whether nurse practitioners, mental health counselors, physicians' assistants, or drug, alcohol, marriage, and child-abuse counselors, makes clear that, for the present, health-care economics dictate the choice of those with less, rather than more, training. Furthermore, buying into the proposition that any provider with a "certificate" in some proficiency becomes a "specialist" competent to "treat" (1) tacitly accepts the proposition that treating the symptom is treating the causative problem; and (2) denigrates the value of doctoral training in the process. Treating a symptom may be, and often is, desirable, but symptoms are manifestations of a larger problem occurring in a total person. The value of doctoral training is that it trains the provider to deal with a functioning human being with a problem, giving rise to a distressing symptom. High blood sugar (the symptom) may need to be addressed, but such treatment must recognize that (the problem) is diabetes, and requires the intervention of physician, not a "certified" diabetes counselor.

Health-care economics, the unwillingness of some providers to commit their resources to train themselves adequately, and the economic self-interest of academics and educational institutions, have been the primary determinant of the "certified" approach to the treatment of mental health problems. It ill behooves organized psychology to participate in such a process, especially when the publicly stated purpose dictating the APA's venture into such training is that: "Psychologists can participate in governmental/ private sector programs requiring such certification." What such programs are really interested in is the symbolic address of a public policy issue at the lowest possible cost. The APA's participation as a trainer in such a process puts psychology's imprimatur *on the process*, and is, in this writer's judgment, antithetical to the long-range interest of doctoral training in psychology.

The all-encompassing yardstick, for any new venture by professional psychology in training, public policy, and so on, should be done, "Does this really contribute to the process of sufficient and high-quality mental health care delivery and psychology's role as a major participant therein?

The foregoing recommendations will be controversial for many in the field of psychology in that they puncture the balloon of a number of special interests in the field. However, it is the belief of those of us who have grown long-in-the-tooth fighting for psychology's survival that any or all of these recommendations offer the best possibility for the survival of a profession.

ROGERS H. WRIGHT, PH.D.,
FOR THE DIRTY DOZEN

Theodore F. Blau, Ph.D.

Nicholas A. Cummings, Ph.D.

Raymond D. Fowler, Ph.D.

Melvin A. Gravitz, Ph.D.

Ernest Lawrence, Ph.D.

Marvin Metsky, Ph.D.

A. Eugene Shapiro, Ph.D.

Robert D. Weitz, Ph.D.

Jack A. Wiggins, Ph.D.

Francis A. Young, Ph.D.

In Memorium

C. J. Rosecrans, Jr., Ph.D.

S. Don Schultz, Ph.D.

Max Siegel, Ph.D.

CHAPTER 2

The Professional
School Movement:

Empowerment of the Clinician
in Education and Training[1]

E very profession has a major, if not decisive, influence on its training. This is accomplished by an approvals process conducted by its professional society. Such professional approval is above and beyond the determination of academic excellencies that is the sole prerogative of the regional accrediting body in higher education. The latter restricts its accreditation to academic matters, and defers to the professional society the responsibility to determine its standards of training, as well as the subsequent standards of practice for those so trained. In the mid-1960s, this was true of every profession except clinical psychology. Whereas every

---

[1] This history reflects the personal experiences of the founder of the professional school movement, and it is presented in the same spirit as the history of the Dirty Dozen by Dr. Wright. The intent is to convey the nature of the activism, which often required gettings one's hands soiled, and earned the appellation of the Dirty Dozen for its leadership. For a more formal, expurgated delineation of events, see Stricker, G. & Cummings, N. A. (1992), The professional school movement. In D. K. Freedheim (Ed.), *History of psychotherapy: A century of change* (pp. 801–828). Washington, DC: American Psychological Association.

other profession had a truly professional society, the education and training of professional psychologists were vested in the APA, an essentially academic organization with a decidedly antiprofessional bias.

Approval of a doctoral program in clinical psychology was based on evaluations conducted by site teams under the aegis of the APA's Education and Training Board (E&T). The standard of evaluation was the Boulder model, so-called because the Boulder (Colorado) Conference on Education and Training in Clinical Psychology enunciated the following dictum: The science of psychology has not progressed sufficiently to warrant the existence of an independent professional practice. Therefore, clinical psychologists are trained first as scientists, and only secondarily as clinicians.

The evaluation of a doctoral clinical program stressed the importance of academic/scientific aspects, and glossed over the quality of clinical training. If the laboratories and other scientific necessities were firmly in place, it did not matter if field placements were mediocre, or even nonexistent. Clinical courses typically were taught by faculty members who had never been in practice, and many of whom had never worked with a patient, because clinicians did not possess the number of publications and other prerequisites for faculty appointment. Those who taught and trained us were openly disdainful of anyone in practice, and any doctoral student who planned to enter practice knew that success in the program was dependent upon this fact being hidden from the faculty. The APA approvals process had its beginnings in the late 1940s, but it was not until the mid-1970s that a program would be denied APA approval solely on the basis of slipshod clinical training. Herbert Dorken, Ph.D., was a member of a site committee and insisted that a particular program be failed on the basis of inadequate field placements, even though its laboratories and other aspects of scientific training were superb. This was a landmark that was quickly forgotten, as Dr. Dorken, and other psychologists like him who might stringently examine clinical, rather than scientific, training, were not again appointed by the E&T board to its site committees.

Academia promulgated and tolerated the emerging Boulder model doctoral programs in clinical psychology because of government funding. First the Veterans' Administration (VA), later joined by the National Institute of Mental Health (NIMH), sought to address the shortage of mental health professionals by providing training stipends for psychologists, along with those for psychiatrists. These government agencies required professional standards and an approvals procedure, and the universities acceded to these demands in spite of academia's distaste because the psychology departments used this influx of money to expand and upgrade their experimental programs and faculties.

Enter the Dirty Dozen

The members of the Dirty Dozen were aware that training in clinical psychology was inadequate to meet the challenges confronting the increasing numbers of psychologists who were entering independent practice, and they had every intention of addressing the issue. However, the escalating psychiatric opposition to insurance reimbursement for psychological services, coupled with a stiffening resistance from the APA on a number of issues, consumed all of the Dirty Dozen's time, energy, and very limited resources. The few attempts to meet with members of the E&T board were effectively rebuffed. The education and training process seemed more insulated and aloof than other functions of the APA that were beginning to feel the brunt of constant attacks from the Dirty Dozen and its followers. So although training was regarded as a paramount issue, it received little attention from the activists until fortuitous events would present an avenue whereby the E&T board might be successfully approached.

Enter the NCGEP

A group of graduate students from Washington University in St. Louis contacted me in 1965. Led by Norman Matulef, who subsequently received his doctorate in clinical psychology and entered independent practice in Missouri, they expressed gross dissatisfaction with graduate training in our profession, but as they were naive as to how they might approach the APA to express this dissatisfaction, they sought the help and advice of the Dirty Dozen. They had created a loosely formed organization they called the National Council on Graduate Education in Psychology (NCGEP), certainly a grandiose title in view of their small number. I flew to St. Louis and met with the leadership of the NCGEP, three graduate students.

At that meeting, we developed a strategy that unfolded over the next several months. Matulef and I were joined by the late Herbert Freudenberger, Ph.D., Stanley Moldawsky, Ph.D., Eugene Shapiro, Ph.D., and Don Schultz, Ph.D. Shapiro, Schultz, and I were members of the Dirty Dozen, and Freudenberger and Cummings served as the working marshals, and Matulef was proffered as the grand marshal of the NCGEP. Impressive stationary, bearing a prestigious address, was printed with Matulef as chair and Freudenberger and Cummings as co-chairs. A newsletter was widely circulated among graduate students and practitioners. We contacted the Council on Professional Approvals (COPA), which accredits the accreditors, and declared our intent that the NCGEP become the approvals body for professional psychology. A copy of our COPA application was sent to the E&T board, along with the information that the NCGEP represented psychology graduate students nationally. The NCGEP was preparing a petition in which 2,000 graduate students would attest to their dissatisfaction with the work of the E&T board in particular, and with the lack of real clinical training in general. This petition would be sent not only to the COPA, but also to what was then the U.S. Department of Health, Education, and Welfare (DHEW). Fearing that we were a powerful new organization with clout, the E&T board granted us an audience at its next meeting.

Once before the E&T board, Matulef, Freudenberger, and I demanded that the approvals process be amended to allow practicing clinicians faculty status, that all APA-approved programs have affiliations for field placement with settings that were truly clinical, and that clinical courses be taught only by clinicians. We indicated that if our demands were not met, we were prepared to expose the APA's dereliction in approving slipshod clinical training, thus jeopardizing the public these graduates one day would be treating. None of our demands were satisfied, but the E&T board began taking these demands seriously and actively engaged the NCGEP in seeking a compromise. We continued to play the game, buying valuable time in the education and training arena while the Dirty Dozen were meeting issues head-on that could not wait.

What Is a Professional School?

A professional school is an autonomous or semiautonomous (if part of a university) program that trains its future practitioners, and is administered by a person with the rank of dean or higher. We are all acquainted with dental, medical and nursing schools, but few psychologists realize that these are fairly recent in origin and that the first professional schools were in theology, for the training of the clergy. Until a few years ago, all health professionals were trained in professional schools, except for clinical psychologists, who continued to be trained in departments of psychology within colleges of art and science. Even social work, which seems to follow psychology by 10 or 15 years in licensing, insurance reimbursement and other practice issues, had professional schools beginning in the 1890s.

Why has psychology lagged behind every other profession? The main reason is that psychology as practice in the way we know it today emerged as a post-World War II phenomenon. Up until then, psychology was essentially academia and science, with a few practitioners in independent practices scattered about the country, most of whom were women with masters' degrees who saw children. Defining professional psychologists as doctoral-level practitioners has been APA policy for only the last 30 to 35 years. In fact, the Dirty Dozen and the group's practitioner/activist successors demanded, and achieved, this doctoral-level policy through the APA Council of Representatives, and it stands to this day.

By virtue of its professional schools, for which it sets the standards and curricula, a profession controls its training. It became increasingly apparent to those of us in the NCGEP who were wrestling with the APA's E&T board that we would not be a completely autonomous profession until we had our own professional schools. It is no longer clear in my memory whether the Dirty Dozen chose me to lead the charge, or whether I grabbed the bit in my teeth and ran with it. Nevertheless, in either case, before I could proceed with founding the professional school movement, I had to address priorities. First, by becoming the first chair of the APA's Committee on Health Insurance, I designed, and saw passed, the first freedom-of-choice legislation, which finally opened the door to insurance reimbursement (1965–1968). Second, I was elected president of the California Psychological Association (CPA), which had become the main power base for the Dirty Dozen's operations nationally (1968–1969). It was during my CPA presidency that events occurred that catapulted me into what came to be known as the professional school movement.

The Harvard–Stanford Phenomenon

It would seem unlikely that the launching of the Russian earth-orbiting satellite *Sputnik* would have given impetus to the creation of the professional school movement, but that is what happened. The United States was stunned when the USSR beat us by two years in orbiting the earth, even though Sputnik was "unmanned." There followed a national obsession with the reaffirmation of science in our schools and colleges, and a deemphasis on liberal arts.

In response to this concern, psychology departments began cutting back on their clinical programs, and with new government funding for science, they could afford to give up the VA and NIMH clinical stipends. Some universities, led by Harvard on the East Coast and Stanford on the West Coast, eliminated clinical/counseling psychology programs entirely. I dubbed this the "Harvard–Stanford phenomenon," as I talked about its threat to the future of professional psychology. Two other events in rapid succession also fueled the fire and drew large audiences to hear me. The first was the fact that in 1965 the largest higher education complex in the world, the University of California with nine campuses and 19 California state universities, graduated only eight doctoral clinical psychologists, and the estimate was that the following year there would only be four such graduates. Then, in 1970, the president of the APA, George Albee, Ph.D., was quoted in *Psychology Today* as predicting the death of clinical psychology in his presidential address, "The Short Unhappy Life of Clinical Psychology: Rest in Peace." I made much of these two happenings as I traveled the nation championing the need for psychology to have its own professional schools.

This idea of professional schools of psychology captured the imaginations of clinicians everywhere I went. More than anything else I said, I had inadvertently tapped the almost universal dissatisfaction on the part of professional psychologists with their graduate education and training, and, for the first time, they were able to express that dissatisfaction by supporting the professional school movement. My speeches were rewarded with standing ovations and an increasing army of adherents.

During this time, there were three friendly debates between Albee and myself, known in the literature as the Albee-Cummings debates. The first was at an APA Division 29 meeting in the Bahamas before a group of about 150, and the last was in San Diego before a psychology audience of 2,000. In that debate, I lauded Albee for alerting us to the need to have our own house in which to practice, and extended this truism by pointing out we first needed our own house in which to train. Albee, in turn, conceded that in predicting the demise of clinical psychology he had not foreseen the coming of the movement that was bringing rebirth to the profession. Subsequently, Albee and Cummings came to be known, respectively, as the mortician and the obstetrician of clinical psychology.

The Numbers

With the current overproduction of professional psychologists, it is difficult to imagine that in the mid to late 1960s there was a shortage of practitioners. The increasing demand for psychologist clinicians generated much interest on the part of prospective students. In fact, during this period, psychology became the most popular undergraduate major. The subject itself, coupled with the career opportunities it offered, was irresistible. However, of every 340 persons graduating with a bachelor's degree in psychology, only one would eventually earn a doctorate in professional psychology. Much of this had to do with the limited number of openings in clinical programs. Getting into an APA-approved doctoral program was reputed to be as difficult as getting into medical school.

So severe was the lack of available training that I used to joke, "For a profession obsessed with sex, we have not yet mastered the art of reproduction." To this I would add for California audiences, where the shortage of psychologists and the lack of training facilities seemed to be the most acute, "California's leading import is clinical psychologists trained in New York."

The present generation of practitioners, who face a glut of both doctoral-level and master's-level psychologists, tend to blame the professional school movement of the oversupply. The fact this blame is unwarranted will be addressed in the discussion of what went right and what went wrong with professional schools.

The Launching of the CSPP

The California Schools of Professional Psychology (CSPP) was founded in 1969 and classes began simultaneously on its first two campuses, San Francisco and Los Angeles, in September 1970. And this launching was accomplished with only $38,000 in cash, thanks to overwhelming support of the practitioners of psychology. First and foremost, 250 psychologists volunteered to teach at least one class each for the first 18 months of the schools existence. This constituted the CSPP's founding endowment, and earned each member of the volunteer faculty the appellation of founder. The first two campus deans, S. Don Schultz, Ph.D., in San Francisco and Arthur Kovacs, Ph.D., in Los Angeles, worked without compensation for the first six months. After that, they became the first paid administrators of the CSPP. As founding president, I did not receive a salary for the first four of the seven years of my tenure. In the fifth year, and at the insistence of the Board of Directors, I began to draw a modest salary, one that was far less than that paid to the campus deans.

This sacrifice on the part of the founding faculty and administration made it possible to offer a third of our students tuition-free scholarships—quite a feat for a school that was totally supported by tuition and one that contributed immensely to the morale, dedication, and excitement that characterized the early years of the CSPP.

The sites of the first two campuses were more than just Spartan. The Los Angeles campus was housed in a condemned Elks Club building; the San Francisco campus was over a machine shop. In Los Angeles, clumps of plaster frequently fell from the ceiling; in San Francisco, the huge machines below created a constant noise and vibration. The faculty's commitment was infectious, and neither the instructors nor the students seemed to mind the surroundings.

The Western Association of Schools and Colleges (WASC) required that the school have a formidable library before it could apply for provisional accreditations. Through the *California Psychologist*, I made an appeal to practitioners to donate books and journals, and several hundred boxes were received within just a few weeks. It fulfilled our need for a journal library and gave us a good start on psychology texts, as well as over 200 sets of the *America Psychologist*, most of which were complete sets spanning from 10 to 20 years each. Still, our libraries were woefully inadequate, and conservative estimates indicated we would need up to half a million dollars for library acquisitions before we could satisfy the WASC. It was then I discovered an obscure state regulation. This little-known provision accorded any doctoral candidate in any college in the state a courtesy library card to any campus of the University of California system. When I applied for library cards for our students, the librarians were stunned, but they were forthcoming when California's Superintendent of Public Instruction advised them that my request was valid. Thus, our library problem not only was solved, but our students and faculty had full access to one of the greatest libraries in the world. The WASC was both impressed and satisfied.

The State Charter: Meeting with Governor Reagan

California has, as most states do, a provision under which business, barber, and beauty schools, and other such institutions, are chartered and allowed to solicit students. I doubt if anyone had thought of applying this set of regulations to establishing an academic institution, and we frankly did not believe it would be a viable approach for us. Nonetheless, it was worth exploring. Our first inquiries brought the response that the University of California would never allow the chartering of a new college in this fashion. Such formidable opposition requires drastic and even brash response. Through my association with Alex Sherrifs, Ph.D., a psychologists who had been dean of students at Berkeley and now was Governor Reagan's education adviser in Sacramento, I was granted an appointment with the governor himself. As Don Schultz, who had enthusiastically joined the effort to establish the CSPP, and I drove to Sacramento, he said that he fully expected that we would be chastised and thrown out. I had been president of the CPA in 1968 and he had been the executive officer. Both of us had been outspoken, on behalf of psychology, in opposing Governor Reagan's decimation of the Department of Mental Health, and particularly the drastic reduction in the participation of psychology.

The picture was even gloomier. On the day of our scheduled meeting with the governor, S. I. Hayakawa, his newly appointed president of San Francisco State University, mounted the sound truck in the midst of a student strike and disabled the loudspeaker. The future U.S. senator was the governor's hire. Our appointment was for 9:00 A.M., but we waited most of the day, talking with Alex Sherrifs. Occasionally, the governor would poke his head in to the room and ask Dr. Sheriffs, "Shouldn't I order out the National Guard now?" With each new crisis on the campus, the question would be repeated, and each time, Sheriffs would strongly recommend against the use of such force. Finally, at about 3:30 in the afternoon the campus had quieted, and we were ushered into the governor's office with the statement that we only had 15 minutes. I began, "Your Excellency, we are here about a crisis in higher education." I had discovered in a book of political etiquette that this was the formal way to address the governor of a state. Mr. Reagan smiled, added that this seemed to be the day for crises, and asked me to continue. We explained the problems in educating professional psychologists in California, making much of the University of California's role almost eliminating such training, and then revealing its opposition to the founding of the CSPP. What was to be a 15-minute meeting stretched to 2½ hours, after which Governor Reagan pledged to facilitate the founding of the CSPP if we demonstrated a first-class faculty, a strong and appropriate curriculum, and had high admissions standards for students. He fulfilled that pledge. Within a year, the CSPP had a state charter for each of our first two campuses.

Many institutions have taken the state charter route since our initial success, and it now looks easy. It must be remembered that the CSPP was the first to venture into heretofore "uncharted" territory, but in so doing we were committed to obtaining full regional accreditation as soon as possible. A number of institutions in California today have no intention of going beyond the state charter, remanding their graduates to practice only in California, where a loophole allows them to take the licensing examination.

What About Licensing Graduates?

The state charters enabled us to operate and solicit students, but without regional accreditation, our credits were not transferable and our graduates would not be admitted to psychology licensing examinations. Later, the courts would decide that students from chartered but unaccredited programs had to be admitted to California licensing procedures, but we did not expect this to be the situation when we began. Anticipating a long procedure before final recognition by state licensing board, during the first two or three years, we accepted students who had received a license on the master's level under the "grandfather" provisions when the states had enacted these laws. Thus, we were able to upgrade to the doctorate licensed, practicing psychologists, and not have to face the idea that our graduates would not be able to practice until sometime in the future.

We gambled that we would have the appropriate recognition within three years, so from the outset we accepted beginning students in a four-year program, anticipating that by the time they graduated, they would be admitted to licensing procedures. Not only did we stake our credibility and reputations on such projections, but we were rewarded by a first wave of students who were eager, dedicated risk takers who shared our vision and would be believable interviewees during the difficult accreditation procedures that lay ahead. Half of them were women, and more than half were ethnic minorities. No school ever had better spokespersons than the CSPP's students. Every site visit report praised them as the most dedicated the accrediting examiners had ever seen.

Norton Simon, Jennifer Jones, and the CSPP's Endowment

The WASC was firm regarding the need for a sizable endowment, stressing that this was particularly important in establishing the stability of a new school that essentially depends on tuition fees. This was our most formidable hurdle, as the figure of $1 million that was frequently mentioned was the equivalent in 1970 of $3 or $4 million today. We hired a fundraiser who spent six months planning a campaign, at the end of which he presented me with research he had done on the 10 richest Californians. This research ostensibly would enable him to construct letters for my signature that would be tailored to the recipients. To my surprise, however, he had written the same letter to be sent to each of the 10. Then why all of the meticulous preparation? Receiving no answer that made sense, I fired him, lamenting the wasting of precious dollars on this man who had come to us so highly recommended.

When I examined his research, however, I found it to be excellent. I took the name at the top of the list, Norton Simon, who not only was the wealthiest man in California, but also was one of the wealthiest in the world. I then composed a letter in which, without addressing the suicide of his psychologist student son or the messy divorce from his wife, I attempted to tap his emotional needs, and to provide an outlet for them through his possible involvement with the CSPP. It was a good letter, but it had to be better. It had to bear a message that would inspire the assistants who would be screening his mail not only to make sure that he personally saw it, but also to give it priority. It was a tall order, and I wrote and tore it up dozens of drafts during the next several days. Finally, at 4:00 in the morning, I typed the newest version myself, for I knew that if I left it for my secretary to type, I would change my mind. At 5:00 in the morning, I drove to the post office and mailed the letter before I could once again lose my courage.

A month passed, and hearing nothing, I concluded that my letter had bombed. Then one morning, while I was seeing a patient, my secretary interrupted me, excitedly saying, "This is either a joke or I have *the* Norton Simon on the line." It was Mr. Simon, who had been in the Bahamas for the past month and had just returned. "Dr. Cummings, my desk is loaded with mail and work. At the top of the pile was your letter. I started to set it aside, and then I wondered why my staff earmarked it for my special attention. I read it, and I haven't been able to think of anything else since. When can we meet?" I was ready to drop everything and fly to Los Angeles the next morning, but he suggested that instead we meet in San Francisco following the University of California's Board of Regents meeting the next week. Excited and terrified, I agreed.

Early on the day we were to meet, I had my car washed and polished. But Simon had a limousine and driver to take us to the airport, where he would catch a flight home. "Dr. Cummings, you have the 20 minutes before we reach the airport to make your pitch." I made a gut-level decision to be brutally honest. He liked my approach and what I had to say. He decided that we would have dinner at the airport, and changed his reservation. As we talked over dinner, he changed his reservation three more times, finally taking the last hourly flight to Los Angeles. It did not occur to me until the next day that the midnight plane had no first-class section, and that *the* Norton Simon had flown coach just so we could continue our discussion!

At 11:00 P.M., Simon decided to really consider my invitation to join our Board of Directors, and asked his two final questions. First, he demanded to know whether it was his knowledge, expertise, and influence that I wanted, or his money. Without hesitation, I replied that I wanted both his expertise and his money. "For how long would I serve on the board?" When I replied that it would be for just one year, he looked puzzled. "Why for such a short time?" I decided then and there that I could not abandon my stance of brutal honesty. "Mr. Simon, my office did not research you for six months without our learning that you are a very difficult man, and that, in fact, you're known as a control freak. Within a year, you would be telling me how to run the school. So I am giving myself one year to pick your brains, and also get a million dollars out of you." There was dead silence. Simon reddened noticeably, but after about five minutes, he began to soften. Finally, he was both relaxed and amaible. "No one has talked to me like that in many years because they either are intimidated or want something. In fact, I wonder if anyone is really honest with me anymore. If you promise to be the one man who always tells me the truth, no matter how bad, I'll come on your board." With that, he shook my hand, saying, "I'm with you, Nick. And from now on I'm Norton." Within a short time, we became very good friends.

In spite of our relationship and his involvement in the CSPP, there was no money forthcoming. I would ask about this from time to time, and he would put me off, "Not yet, if ever." I knew he was still depressed and unhappy over the loss of his son and his divorce. I decided to play Cupid. Another friend, Jennifer Jones, was a well-known movie star during the late 1930s and 1940s. She had had three tragic marriages, all of which had ended with the death of her husbands, one by suicide. This beautiful woman was still a frightened Oklahoma farm girl looking for a strong man, one who seemed invincible, like Norton Simon. As a homely man, he often talked of his dream of meeting a lovely woman. To me, this was a marriage made in heaven, and my wife and I hosted an all-CSPP party on our campus above the machine shop. The not-so-hidden purpose was to introduce Norton to Jennifer.

It must be remembered that during the 1970s, psychologists and their students did not sit in chairs, but on pillows on the floor. So when Norton asked for a chair, it took almost 20 minutes to locate one. This prompted Jennifer to ask who the stuffed shirt was with whom I had paired her off. In turn, he asked me what he was supposed to do with that spoiled Hollywood brat. The meeting was a disaster. Six weeks later, I was awakened in the middle of the night by Norton and Jennifer calling from Paris. They had run into each other three days earlier, had hit it off, and had just been married. "Nick," said Norton, "We wanted you to be the first to know. And we want to tell you that our wedding present to each other is the gift of CSPP's endowment."

Our highest hurdle had been vaulted. But then another set of problems developed. Every idealist on campus, and the CSPP attracted some of the most ardent, wanted to spend the money on student scholarships, especially underprivileged applicants. As lofty as this intent was, it was also impractical, for spending our endowment would jeopardize the CSPP's accreditation. I found myself having to guard our endowment almost with my life.

The Struggle for Federal Stipends

At that time, the person in charge of NIMH grants was Stanley Schneider, Ph.D., an affable psychologist who enjoyed dispensing training stipends and other goodies. In fact, his position made him somewhat of a czar, with colleagues in APA-approved doctoral programs currying his favor at every opportunity. His ability to determine who would receive a grant gave him incredible power over the shaping of professional training in psychology. He favored the large, prestigious universities with rather traditional programs, and when he was approached on behalf of the CSPP, he indicated that our program was many years short of being eligible for consideration. Nonetheless, in our first year, we did apply for training stipends for both the San Francisco and Los

Angeles campuses. Schneider visited us, was amiable, and even sympathetic, but was firm in discouraging our expectations. Of course, our applications went nowhere.

The next year, the CSPP applied for two training grants in each of our two campuses: one for clinical and the other for community psychology. This time, however, Norton Simon was on our board, and he announced that he was going to monitor the progress of our applications. The following strategy was devised: At the beginning of each month, I would call Norton, who would then call his friend Robert Finch, Secretary of the Department of Health, Education and Welfare (DHEW). (At that time education had not yet been split off from DHEW into its own Cabinet, the Department of Education.) Finch would then send an inquiry as to the status of the CSPP applications through channels to Stan Schneider, who was obligated to send a thorough report back through channels. Since the inquiry bore the letterhead of the Cabinet Secretary, Schneider would have to produce a meticulous report; I later learned this would require about three days each month. In the eighth month, he notified the CSPP that two grants, one for clinical psychology at CSPP-San Francisco and one for community psychology at CSPP-Los Angeles, had been approved. We were ecstatic. The important thing, however, is that subsequently all four of the CSPP campuses regularly applied for, and received grants from NIMH. Another hurdle had been vaulted.

The CSPP's Innovative Curriculum

The initial curriculum was a dramatic departure from anything that had gone before. The calendar was a trimester year, so that the students attended all year and earned 1½ academic years annually. From entry to the doctorate, the program took six years. The first two years earned the associate of arts (AA) degree and qualified the graduate to be a psychological paraprofessional; that is, to serve as an employee of a psychologist, psychiatrist, or hospital, performing duties that had historically been part of being a psychiatrist technician. The second two years earned the master of arts (MA) degree, and qualified the graduate to work as a psycho-

logical assistant. The CSPP was active in bringing about legislation that permitted each licensed doctoral-level psychologist to
employ, supervise, and be responsible for two psychological assistants. Several other states followed California's lead and passed
similar legislation. The duties paralleled those of physician assistants (PAs), thus giving our profession a psychologist extender. In
creating these first two levels, it must be remembered this was
during a severe shortage of journey-level psychologists, and the
CSPP was responding to the recently enacted legislation that established the category of psychological assistant. The final degree,
comprising the fifth and sixth years, was the doctorate (Ph.D.) in
clinical psychology.

There was considerable discussion at the time as to whether
the CSPP should grant the Ph.D. degree or the professional degree of doctor of psychology (Psy.D.) that had been established in
the psychology program at the University of Illinois, and had
been headed by Don Peterson, Ph.D. I leaned toward the Psy.D.,
believing the profession could best be served by having a professional degree just as every other health profession had. But out-
wardly I opposed the CSPP's giving the Psy.D. because we had
enough changes to legitimize without taking on the establishing of
a new degree. Furthermore, whereas many wanted the scien-
tist/professional model replaced by the purely professional model,
I was strongly in favor of preserving within the highly trained
clinician all the essentials of the science. I called this the profes-
sional/scientist model, and was pretty much alone it its advocacy.
Nonetheless, my views prevailed, and one of the demands of our
program was a scholarly doctoral dissertation. This not only
would be a contribution, but would teach the student to conduct
research using a variety of methods, from epidemiological studies
to the field testing of delivery systems. In other words, the dissertation was not limited to a controlled experiment per se. Furthermore, the dissertation had to be completed by the end of the sixth
year, as all students move through the program in unison, or they
failed. There would be no so-called ABDs (all but dissertation),
known as psychology's most prevalent "degree." The dissertation

was always problematic on campus. There was considerable anti-intellectualism during the 1970s, and some faculty members were willing to sign off on almost any rendering, and thus, I took seriously the dictum that as long as we were conferring the Ph.D. rather than the Psy.D., the dissertation had to meet stringent scholarly standards. This contention between the president and some faculty members never subsided below a crescendo, and was instrumental in the president's ultimate demise, as will be seen in a later section.

All faculty members held the rank of instructor, because they taught only the courses that reflected their vocations. In other words, psychotherapy was taught by persons in the practice of psychotherapy, statistics by one who made a living as a statistician, and so forth. This represented a radical departure from traditional faculties, and it was made possible by the fact that during the first 18 months, all instructors were part-time unpaid volunteers. When faculty members began to be paid, we also kept most of the volunteers, who were happy to continue their careers while teaching one of two courses at the CSPP. Later, we required half-time commitments from all instructors.

Each student had to undergo personal psychotherapy every year while in the program. The school had a long list of psychotherapists in the community who had agreed to see students either free of charge, or for a very reduced fee. The student could choose a therapist, and although the school never intruded on the therapy, the psychotherapist was obligated to report that the student was keeping all appointments and was making progress. Each student was required to have two years of individual therapy, and then could either take part in group therapy, or continue in individual treatment.

Our innovative curriculum was designed by a committee chaired by the late Hedda Bolgar, Ph.D., a Hungarian by birth who was trained in the Chicago School of Psychoanalysis (Franz Alexander, M.D., et al.). She practiced psychoanalysis for many years in Southern California, and although those of us who knew her innovative thinking were not surprised, most psychologists were startled that a curriculum so radical could be produced by a psychoanalyst. She was the CSPP's first system-wide Dean of Academic Affairs, but remained for only two years, and went on to found the Los Angeles branch of the Wright Institute.

Psychopharmacology

By 1970, psychotropic and antipsychotic medications had skyrocketed in importance, and the CSPP curriculum was the first to include mandatory courses in psychopharmacology, along with the survey courses in neurology and neurophysiology that were requisite to an understanding of drug therapy. The courses were taught by a physician, usually a psychiatrist, and we had no difficulty in recruiting instructors who would teach these courses on the same basis as all our instructors. The M.D. and Ph.D. instructors were paid exactly the same. The startling aspect is that, characteristically, physicians command higher salaries than do psychologists, but the physicians who were attracted to the CSPP were as infected with the ideas of innovation and egalitarianism as all other faculty members.

The purpose of the psychopharmacology sequence was to render the psychologist knowledgeable about medication so as to be able to help the physician in prescribing. This included an awareness of which patients could benefit most from medication, as well as of which drugs would be most suitable for which patients, inasmuch as the prescribing physician would be dependent on the therapist's knowledge of the patient. Our experience with the psychopharmacology sequence during the first couple of years had such an impact that I prevailed upon the APA to appoint an ad hoc committee to study whether or not the profession of psychology should seek prescription authority. At my suggestion, the late Karl Pottharst, Ph.D., of our CSPP-Los Angeles faculty was appointed chair of this committee. After meeting for two years, the committee concluded that psychology had introduced so many effective new psychotherapies because it did not have the expediency of the prescription pad. To give the psychologist prescription authority might eliminate the one profession that was pioneering so many behavioral interventions. I was somewhat disappointed with this conclusion, but empathized with its logic, and, in looking back, am satisfied that we anticipated by two decades the APA's current drive for psychologists' prescribing authority.

The Founding of the San Diego and Fresno Campuses

Most persons affiliated with the CSPP today are unaware that the master plan called for eight campuses throughout California. This was somewhat grandiose and I used to present the plan tongue-in-check, but I was always convinced that the CSPP should have at least four campuses, one of which would be a rural campus. The four proposed campuses that never got any serious consideration were to be in Sacramento, Santa Barbara, Chico, and Monterey, whereas two additional campuses were established, in San Diego and Fresno. This happened sooner than I had originally anticipated because two aggressive potential founders petitioned the Board of Directors.

The first was Maurice J. Zemlick, Ph.D., who, after having convinced me, was encouraged to petition the Board of Directors. In 1973, CSPP-San Diego was founded. While this was in progress, I was being besieged by I. M. Abou-Ghorra, Ph.D., a well-known Fresno psychologist who was eager to establish the fourth campus. The prospect of two additional campuses was frightening to a board that was struggling to keep the first two campuses viable, but I persuaded it to approve both new campuses on the promise I would abandon all plans for campuses five through eight. Secretly, I was relieved, as I never seriously considered the eight-campus master plan produced by an overly enthusiastic planning committee and consulting group. Thus, CSPP-Fresno was established in 1974.

From the outset, each campus had decidedly different character. It was at CSPP-San Francisco that the anti-intellectualism of the 1970s reached its epitome. Graduation was conducted outdoors and barefooted, with the members of the graduating class holding hands and chanting. It was this campus that constantly petitioned for exotic courses, such as astrology, channeling, past lives, and Werner Earhart's EST, all of which were refused. But it was our most vibrant campus, and secretly my favorite, as long as S. Don Schultz, Ph.D., a very capable administrator, was its dean. He was able to allow enough of the "spirit of Aquarius" to keep things lively, while preventing them from descending into the absurd. When, after four years, he was promoted to vice president, the campus experienced a series of campus deans who were unable to control the anti-intellectualism. The first, Zalmon Garfield, Ph.D., turned on the president in order to preserve his standing on campus, and did not last a full year. His successor, Robert Morgan, Ph.D., to whom I shall always be grateful for stepping in when no one else dared, was even more laid back than our student body. And the last, Theodore Dixon, Ph.D., who ostensibly could rule with a strong hand that could bring order to the campus, barricaded himself in his office and let his subordinates deal with the daily problems. From almost his first week, he began to plot the demise of the president.

CSPP-Los Angeles, more than any of the other campuses, probably reflected what the CSPP was intended to be. Radical in its own right, it nonetheless was not engulfed by the anti-intellectualism of CSPP-San Francisco. Arthur Kovacs, Ph.D., was its first campus dean, and he continued in that role throughout my seven years as founding president. This campus was as much committed to social issues as CSPP-San Francisco, but was always aware that without accreditation any strides would be negated. Los Angeles, however, had one propensity: the clash between the faculty and the campus dean. Kovacs was a professional psychologist who reflected all of the aspirations and needs of our program, but he was just not a good administrator. Periodically, the faculty would "fire" him and, after obtaining the concurrence of the faculty, I would reinstate him. It was of constant amazement to me how we could take the most empathetic clinician, give her or him a faculty appointment, and within one week that person would become contentious. Our Los Angeles faculty was typical: fiercely dedicated to the CSPP, but always ready for a fight.

Our most stable campus was CSPP-San Diego, which had only one campus dean while I was president. Maurice Zemlick would have no slum school. He created a campus in a new industrial park where the students had access to a swimming pool and other niceties not known on the other campuses. He was a capable administrator who, with his wife, Lucille Zemlick as business manager, was very protective of the superior surroundings. He wanted no nonsense in the curriculum, or in teaching it. Because the faculty and students did not have the same liberties as the other campuses, they referred to CSPP-San Diego as the "mom-and-pop store." Twice they demanded the removal of Lucille Zemlick and twice I flew down and convinced the faculty that she was a valuable asset and that we needed her. CSPP-San Diego reflected the CSPP dream, while, at the same time, being our most solid campus.

CSPP-Fresno was always the "low man on the totem pole." It would not have survived without the fierce promotion of founding campus dean, Abou-Ghorra, a fanatic regarding excellence and a strong believer in training in rural community psychology if we were to reach underserved areas. To say he was irrepressible is an understatement. He could never hear "no" in response to his requests. I supported him throughout, especially in the constant attempts to shut down his campus. With his wife, Eva, he made that campus a success even though it was the least popular with student applicants. He fulfilled the CSPP dream without the turmoil found on other campuses. His faculty was completely loyal to him, and he is the only Egyptian I know who could introduce his Jewish deans as "three of my people." To this day, I still count Abou and Eva among my closest friends.

The Vail Conference

There is no question but that the impact that the CSPP and the professional school movement had at the time convinced the APA and NIMH to mount a new conference on the education and training of clinical psychology. Interestingly, Colorado was again chosen as the location, but in Vail rather than Boulder. We went to Vail with the greatest of expectations. It became the venue in which to discuss, debate, and advocate all of the issues that were to define psychology's new social conscience, but the real reason for the conference, the articulation of a new model of clinical training, was dwarfed in the process. There was only one small group assigned that task, and Don Peterson and I were both in it. There emerged within that committee a commitment to the strictly professional model, and we were the only voices advocating the professional/scientist model.

A side issue that is little remembered is that the National Register of Healthcare Providers in Psychology was conceived in Vail. At that time, psychologists could obtain licensing and certification in many states, but the standards varied. For example, some states required two years of internship, one predoctoral and one postdoctoral, whereas others required only one year. And there were still states that had no statutory recognition of psychologist. These factors were severely hampering the fight to obtain insurance reimbursement for psychological service. The insurers complained that the undue variability in standards was too great. In response, the National Register was conceived as a way of establishing one standard, so that anyone approved by that body would be eligible for insurance reimbursement. The American Board of Professional Psychology (ABPP) was chosen to launch this organization while all of us were at Vail. The strategy worked, and it was very critical at the time in the struggle for recognition by third-party payers.

Should the CSPP Have Been on a University Campus?

From the beginning, it was apparent that much of the difficulty in founding the first professional school of psychology could have been avoided if it had been founded as part of a university campus. I openly hoped that such an affiliation could be accomplished, but inwardly I was skeptical that a university would accept our curriculum, the lack of faculty rank and tenure, and other radical ideas without diluting them considerably. The idea of a professional school of psychology attracted a number of suitors within a few months of the school's opening its doors. One university was in New York, and the distance was an insurmountable problem from the beginning, as were a number of other suitors. The field was narrowed to two serious offers, and consideration of them was to occupy a great deal of my time for the next two years. One was from the chair of the department of psychology at the University of the Pacific (UOP) in Stockton, California. UOP had an APA-approved doctoral program, and John Preston, Ph.D., was serious about bringing the CSPP to his campus as a semiautonomous professional school. The plan was scuttled after two years of extensive negotiations by a traditional faculty that was very nervous about the curriculum. Neither Preston nor I was willing to dilute the CSPP concept, so the faculty ultimately blocked the plan for merger by open revolt.

A second offer came from the University of California at Davis, where the vice-chancellor was intensely interested in bringing the CSPP into the system. After two years of active negotiations, however, it became apparent to both of us that it would take many more years to clear the world's largest academic bureaucracy, if it could be cleared at all. I had to accept the premise that the first professional school of psychology had to be autonomous so that it could showcase its very advanced curriculum and concepts. Other schools that were to follow could then be part of an existing university.

The Proliferation of Professional Schools

Shortly after the launching of the CSPP, Robert Weitz, Ph.D., a member of the Dirty Dozen, undertook to found a professional school in New Jersey. Within the following year, Ronald Fox, Ph.D., now a former president of the APA, mounted a similar effort in Ohio. I served on the advisory boards of both of these efforts, as I did on the advisory boards of the more than a dozen professional schools that came afterward. Weitz's efforts resulted in the professional school at Rutgers University, with Don Peterson as its first dean, whereas Fox's work brought about the professional school at Wright State University, with him as the first dean. After Bob Weitz retired and moved to Florida he founded yet another professional school there.

A historical note is important here. There has been confusion in the last 25 years as to which professional school was first. The late Gordon Derner, Ph.D., for whom the Institute for Advanced Psychological Studies at Adelphi University is named, referred to the CSPP as the first autonomous professional school, and to Adelphi as the first professional school. I have remained silent because of my profound respect for, and debt to, my mentor, Gordon Derner. He founded the first professional *program* in psychology, which I attended and from which I graduated with a Ph.D. It was a remarkable program, and sowed the seeds in my head that flowered during the founding of the CSPP. But the program at Adelphi was part of the psychology department and was not a professional school. I remember Derner's coming to me during the CSPP's first year, and saying, "You have shown us the way. We should have professional schools." He then asked for my help in persuading the trustees of Adelphi University to make his program a professional school, and to elevate him to dean. I wrote an eight-page letter, and soon thereafter, the trustees granted Gordon's request. Therefore, it is more accurate to say that Adelphi was the first professional school on a university campus, whereas the CSPP was the first professional school of any kind. There is another reason why I remained silent during Derner's lifetime. He had always wanted to become president of the APA. The fourth time he ran unsuccessfully was my first run, and I was put in the uncomfortable position of defeating the mentor whom I owed such a debt. Probably it was he, in the first place, who instilled the idea in me of becoming APA president, although I had never thought of such a possibility until just before it happened.

The CSPP's Governance System: Idealism Run Amok

The 1970s were a period in which rules were to be broken, standards were to be ignored, and love would triumph over all. In this spirit, a governance systems was created for the CSPP that defied all probability of success. First, in keeping with my own strong, but displaced, belief that the profession of psychology should always evolve its own education and training, half of the CSPP's Board of Directors were elected by the Board of Directors of the California Psychological Association (CPA). In turn, the president of the CSPP was ex-officio with a vote on the CPA board. Reflecting the egalitarianism of the time, another one fourth of the CSPP board was elected by the faculty, apportioned among the four campuses. Finally, the last quarter of the board seats were elected by the students on the four campuses. This was in keeping with the tone of the times that students should have a deciding stake in the training enterprise.

From the outset, this governance system was a nightmare. At the monthly Board of Directors meetings, a frequent concern of the CPA directors would be the closing of one of the four campuses, usually identified as Fresno. The faculty and student directors often would have caucused, and would demand the raising of faculty salaries and the lowering of tuition. At best, there would be a standoff, and after hours of haggling, I would declare a presidential consensus. This meant that since the board had not come to a decision, the president would make that decision. At worst, one of a large number of possibly destructive motions would pass and I would have to argue why the president, in the best interest of the school, could not implement it.

The architects of this well-intentioned system were Hedda Bolgar, who sincerely believed it would work, and Irwin Leff, the school's attorney and board secretary, who wanted to demonstrate his pet theory of political dynamic tension. But dynamic tension is one thing; this was built-in warfare. Initially, I was as enthusiastic as they were, but when it became obvious that it was nonworkable, I begged that we reconsider it, but my pleas were rebuffed.

Fortunately, there were some wise heads on the CSPP Board of Directors, usually from the CPA, but occasionally from the faculty and the students. Among these were Dirty Dozen members Rogers Wright and Ernest Lawrence. At a time when things were really falling apart, George Hoff, Ph.D. (a CPA-elected board member) was elected chair. For the next three years, he devoted countless hours to making the potentially destructive governance system work, and so had to share with the president the angry fallout when the demands for campus autonomy were once again thwarted. Another very helpful board member was an alumnus, James Anderson, Ph.D., whose devotion to his alma mater never wavered. When things got so bad that some board members would not speak to one another, he volunteered his Lake Arrowhead mountain home for board retreats.

These were turbulent times, but in the end, reason would prevail. Two things were of immense help. The board shared an intense belief that the CSPP must survive and prosper, and the members all possessed a sense of humor. As an example, a very troublesome faculty board member who was disgruntled because the CSPP would not adopt his system of multiple therapists (two or more therapists in each individual session with one patient), came to the meeting in a bizarre costume, complete with satin breeches and jacket, plumed hat, and silk hose. He assumed a position on the floor behind the president's chair, and for the entire morning, silently performed yoga exercises. The board members ignored him, and he grew more and more agitated. When we broke for lunch, he tendered his resignation and left in a huff, never to be seen again. But, alas, this was not the strangest thing that would occur with this board, nor was it to be the last.

The Board of Overseers

The CSPP had an extensive community board, which borrowed its name, the Board of Overseers, from Harvard. Initially chaired by Charles Thomas, Ph.D. founder of the Association of Black Psychologists, he had among its members some of the top business and community leaders in California. These included Stanley Langsdorf, senior vice president and controller of the Bank of America; Bruce Woolpert, president of GranitRock; Carl Fredrick, senior vice president of FiberBoard; Judge Creed of the superior court; and Patricia Costello, president of the California

Association for Mental Health. The board participated in our Board of Directors' meetings and provided much-needed ballast. The Board of Directors would have bogged down much earlier had not the overseers, individually and collectively, captured the vision of the CSPP and became committed to its success. When the campus deans staged their "palace coup" (see below), the overseers, more than any segment of the community, felt betrayed.

Exit Nick Cummings

In retrospect, I must say that I very much enjoyed all of the currents and subcurrents that swirled around this new school, as this turmoil was also the excitement and enthusiasm that made it work. I enjoy startups, and when the new organization reaches a certain level, I lose interest because I am not an institution builder. My life has been characterized by a succession of startups, leaving the institution builders to pick up where I left off. After five years as president, I knew that the CSPP was far from mature. But I am also a realist who knew that every time I had to declare "presidential consensus," I had spent another chit in my depleting arsenal of good will. The time for me to leave was getting close, and during my last two years, I resigned every six months, four times in all. Each time, the board refused my resignation, dunning me with guilty feelings because the job had not yet been completed. So I stayed, only to be fired by that same board a month after I tendered my fourth resignation.

It is not surprising that the initial volunteers who stampeded to be a part of this new school brought with them a variety of social, political, and personal agendas, which often seemed to override the main purpose of the CSPP to redefine graduate education and training in psychology. I empathized with most of these, having been an early part of the civil rights movement, and every movement thereafter, through the feminist revolution to gay liberation. As each member of the CSPP had an ax to grind, sometimes I felt as if I were the only one who remained focused on the need for accreditation and subsequent survival. But I really was not alone in this concern, as psychologists on the board who were not faculty, and thus were not caught up in the idealism run amok, were alarmed at the poor quality of the dissertations. Among them was Rogers Wright, who headed a special commission to investigate and advise the school on dissertations. His commission concentrated on the Los Angeles campus as a start, where the preliminary report described the dissertations as "appalling." Reforms would have prevailed at that time had it not been for Campus Dean Kovacs and a prominent faculty member, Karl Pottharst, who actively undermined the work of the commission. The Wright Commission was disbanded, and the dissertations ranged from about 10% good, and even excellent, to 50% unacceptable.

Actually, the overwhelming consensus even among the faculty and student body was that the school had to achieve standing, but there were unrealistic expectations of the president and those who were helping me achieve the goal of recognition for the CSPP. The prevailing attitude was that since we had pulled so many rabbits out of the hat, we would continue to do so. WASC said we needed, among other things, an endowment, admissions standards (rather than open enrollment), doctoral-level faculty (instead of good people without higher degrees but with their hearts in the right place), and solid doctoral dissertations. Yet much of the well-intentioned CSPP community believed we could ignore these requirement and still "wiggle the system" to accredit us. After all, "Nick will do it."

I was under constant assault to declare open enrollment, spend the endowment, rehire ineligible faculty, approve slipshod dissertations, and declare each campus autonomous, free to pursue its own designs. Any one of these would prevent the school's success; together, they spelled disaster. The CSPP was coming to the end of its provisional accreditation and we had to step up to the plate. Under particular scrutiny were our dissertations, about which we had been warned: If you insist on the Ph.D. rather than the Psy.D. the dissertations must be of academic quality. I knew most were not just substandard, but were outrageously inadequate. In one, for example, the student wandered about the mountains behind Big Sur for three days without a watch and wrote about his "disorientation." Others were even worse, yet the faculty had signed off on them, justifying their behavior as in the spirit of the anti-intellectualism of the 1970s. I had to take drastic steps, and I informed the campuses that 58 of 73 doctoral dissertations would not warrant graduation. The reply was that the faculty approves dissertations, not the president, to which I responded that it is the president who signs the diplomas. At that moment, I knew I had cashed in my last chit.

Coupled with the faculty disaffection was the rebelliousness of three of the four campus deans, who knew they were on their way out because they could not maintain the necessary academic standards. Dixon could not control his campus, and Zemlick was on probation. At my last meeting with the campus deans, Kovacs announced, "There will be no cabal against the president." Then he immediately set out to lead the other rebellious campus deans in a "palace coup," except for Abou-Ghorra, who would have none of it. The strategy was simple. At the next board meeting, the three campus deans would declare that they no longer would follow the president, whereupon the school counsel and board secretary, Irwin Leff, who was also on his way out, would declare the president "incapacitated" under the bylaws. Under the tutelage of the rebellious deans, well-meaning faculty and students lobbied the board members aggressively, convincing them that getting rid of the president was the only way to save the CSPP. Actually, the campus deans firmly believed that without the president, they would be autonomous, ruling their own fiefdoms. All of this was accomplished secretly and launched within the month preceding the February 1976 board meeting.

That meeting began as a circus and concluded as a massacre. The campuses had chartered buses to bring in students by the hundreds. There were too many to be accommodated in the relatively small board room, so they were seated in the grand ballroom of the hotel, while in the board room, a student with a walkie-talkie (cellular phones had not yet been invented) described everything that occurred there. As I entered the room, I heard him say, "The president and the vice president just walked into the room. Nick has a stunned look on his face." When the meeting was called to order, in a swift progression of preplanned motions, the chair, George Hoff, was removed without thanks. I demanded time to call for a vote of thanks for his three years in that office, but was gaveled down by the newly installed puppet chair. Wright, Lawrence, Anderson, and other board members who were not privy to the plot objected loudly, and threatened to walk out. Had they done so, the meeting would have lost its quorum, a fact that was not lost on the rebellious campus deans, who quickly brought the circus atmosphere under some semblance of control. I was allowed to move to thank Dr. Hoff for his dedicated service, and the motion was passed perfunctorily without any real acknowledgment. The massacre continued as the cooler heads on the board were outvoted. They immediately resigned from the board, and I resigned the presidency effective July 1.

In large measure, I was relieved, as I was ready to move on. However, I was startled by the vehemence and treachery of persons who ostensibly had been my friends long before the founding of the CSPP. Not only was I bitterly attacked, but my family as well. The intensity of that attack left my wife and my then-teenage children, bystanders at best, with a sense of distaste for the CSPP and a disdain for the perpetrators. It was as if I had to be assassinated several times over, and be further crippled by attacks on my family, or else I would rise from the dead and retaliate. The legal counsel I consulted was adamant that Leff's fabricated "incapacitation" of the president would not hold up in court, and that I had excellent recourse. My being elected to the APA presidency just one year later convinced many at the CSPP that now I would take my revenge. But a father does not sue or destroy his own rebellious child, and I chose to withdraw quietly and forever. Furthermore, I was already convinced that I had accomplished all I could for the CSPP.

Only one task remained to conclude my work for the professional school movement, and for that reason, I demanded to keep the title of president for six more months. In exchange, I even accepted the indignity of suffering under the authority of a preselected puppet president who would actually be running the school in the interim.

The NCSPP

That last remaining task was to establish the National Council for Schools of Professional Psychology (NCSPP). I had been working on this for some time, and in mid-1976 I convened the first meeting. By this time, the professional school movement had really blossomed, and more than 20 such schools were represented at the organizational meeting. I advised them that the way had been prepared with the Council of Professional Accreditation (COPA) in Washington for the NCSPP to apply to become the accrediting body for the professional schools of psychology, and that COPA was congenial to the idea. The group then passed the bylaws and elected Gordon Derner, Ph.D., dean of the professional school at Adelphi, its first chair.

The NCSPP did not seek accrediting status, as I had hoped. The reasons were complex, but of importance was that Gordon Derner, as he explained to me years later, had just made his third unsuccessful run for the APA presidency and was interested in increasing his credibility there when he made a fourth attempt. In looking back, I am convinced that many compromises had to be made in seeking APA approval, and that the professional schools would have been farther ahead without it. In addition, the emergence of so many professional schools on university campuses dictated that many of the innovations, such as part-time faculty members who had concurrent careers doing what they taught, as well as the absence of tenure, had to be discarded in an established academic environment.

Nonetheless, many of the main thrusts of a professional program, with clinicians being eligible for faculty appointments, survived and thrived. The Psy.D. degree has become the professional degree of the professional schools, and there are probably more Psy.D.s than Ph.D.s in professional psychology graduated today.

Epilogue on CSPP: Enter John O'Neil

My successor as CSPP president, John O'Neil, was far from the pushover the campus deans had hoped for. He is an institution builder, and he set about doing just that. Through a series of lawsuits, he dismantled the unworkable governance system and divested the school from CPA "ownership." The faculty and students no longer controlled the board, and he immediately got rid of the disloyal attorney. Leff, however, refused to step down, insisting that he had been appointed by the board, not by the president. The board would have none of this, and when it fired him, he removed his shoe and pounded it on the table, as Nikita Krushchev had done years earlier at the United Nations. Then, in rapid succession, O'Neil fired the campus deans, beginning with Dixon, then Kovacs, and finally Zemlick. When he refused to leave, Zemlick was forcibly carried off the premises and the locks replaced.

We built a CSPP that was very strong, making it impossible for the four campuses to break away into fiefdoms as the rebellious campus deans had planned. They surely would not have survived competing against each other. Then John O'Neil made sure that the CSPP would endure well into the future by divesting it, through a series of lawsuits, of its well-meaning, fanciful governance system. He served for twenty-one years as president, three times as long as I had. Such was in keeping with our respective roles: I did the startup and he built the institution, for which I am grateful. And I look forward with excitement to the presidency of Judith Albino, Ph.D., who assumed that role in 1998. She shows promise of being an outstanding institutional builder as she begins expanding the CSPP as one school within a university.

What Went Right and What Went Wrong?

Once and for all, professional education was established within psychology, and even the traditional programs brought clinicians on campus as faculty. It established the Psy.D. as a legitimate professional degree, but it fell short of establishing it as *the* professional degree in the same way that the M.D., R.N., D.D.S.,

D.P.M., and other such degrees immediately define the professionals in the health-care arena.

Perhaps the greatest failing is that the profession did not solve the master's-level problem. I predicted in the *APA Monitor* in 1975 that if we did not find a place for master's-level practitioners, eventually they would form an independent profession and become our successful competitors. This has come to pass, and it is not the glut of doctorates that suppresses doctoral-level incomes, but the horde of master's-level practitioners who undercut us in the marketplace.

One of the outgrowths of seeking APA approval rather than making the NCSPP our own accrediting body is that professional schools became too closely identified with the APA, and failed, along with it, to adapt to the swiftly changing demands of the marketplace. As a result, the curricula of the professional schools are only slightly, if at all, ahead of the traditional schools in having failed to evolve education and training relevant to the industrialization of health-care. And finally, we have yet to define adequately what a professional school is and to ensure its proper place in the scheme of things. After 26 years, the Vail model still has not been articulated satisfactorily. Consequently, in too many instances, a professional school is still whatever a particular school wants it to be. The public is not protected adequately from the fly-by-night programs or even the diploma mills that masquerade as professional schools.

Finally, as has all psychology, professional schools have the obligation to inform students of the stark realities of employment in our field. But most professional school faculties are as ignorant of what is demanded by the new behavioral-health-care marketplace as are traditional programs. The current and continued decline in applications should be a warning. The programs that survive are the ones that prepare the graduate for the new health-care environment.

NICHOLAS CUMMINGS, PH.D., SC.D.

CHAPTER 3

Impact of the Dirty Dozen and Increased Practitioner Professionalism on the American Psychological Association

Introduction

The activities and influence of the Dirty Dozen greatly enhanced the development of psychological practice in the United States, and played a critical role in changing the nature and culture of the American Psychological Association (APA) as well. This chapter explores some of the changes that occurred in the APA in three broad areas: education and training, political and professional advocacy, and the organizational power structure. The changes listed are derived from personal recollections regarding events with which the author was directly involved. Others involved in the APA governance during the same time would doubtless have a different list. Despite the subjectivity, it is hoped that the ones chosen for discussion will serve to document the major impact of the Dirty Dozen on the largest psychology membership organization in the world.

Education and Training

Because of the Dirty Dozen's concerns with licensure, public access to psychological services, member benefits, and advocacy, it has been easy to overlook the group's strong influence on professional education. From the beginning, it disagreed intensely with the prevailing attitudes regarding the nature, quality, and quantity of professional education and training.

At the time, most doctoral programs adhered to the so-called scientist/professional model of education, which was intended to produce graduates who were proficient in both research and practice. But, after a number of years, it seemed clear to many observers that such programs were problematic in a number of respects. Professors often denigrated full-time practice as a career path. Only a small minority of graduates ever did any research or published a single study. Many practitioners felt so inadequately prepared for work with patients that they had to arrange for more supervision and training after graduation. These criticisms and a multitude of other issues, led to the convening of the National Conference on Levels and Patterns of Professional Training in Psychology in 1973 in Vail, Colorado. Members of the Dirty Dozen had lobbied for several years for such a conference, and some of their members were active in how the conference was organized and structured.

Among those in attendance was the Dirty Dozen's Nick Cummings, who had established, in 1969, the California School of Professional Psychology (CSPP), which by this time had four campuses. His more detailed history of the professional school movement is found elsewhere in this book. At Vail, his strong advocacy for explicitly professional education, along with Don Peterson's cogent arguments for a professional degree, struck a resonant chord with many attendees. In fact, two of only a handful of conference recommendations that were ever implemented were: (1) the recognition of professional model programs as legitimate alternatives to the traditional scientist/professional model, and (2) affirmation of the Psy.D. as an appropriate degree for graduates of professional model programs. Divisions 29 and 31, hotbeds of practitioner advocacy, quickly endorsed these recommendations. In 1974, Division 29 introduced a motion in the Council of Representatives that the APA recommend the Ph.D. as the appropriate degree for scientist/practitioner programs and the Psy.D. degree as the preferred degree for graduates of practitioner programs. Although the measure failed to win approval, the Psy.D. did come to be accepted and was incorporated into several APA policies, such as the criteria for accreditation. The next few years saw the establishment of a number of professional programs across the United States, the graduation of large numbers of new psychologists with professional degrees, and changes in the APA's accreditation criteria, all of which helped legitimize an increased emphasis on professional issues within the organization.

Few psychologists were prepared for the ensuring explosion in freestanding and university-based doctoral programs. Derogatory and unsubstantiated charges regarding poor quality were leveled at the new programs with little attention to differentiating between good and bad ones. In such discussions, it was often assumed that existing programs that were accredited by the APA were of high quality. But the Dirty Dozen members were skeptical of such claims and supported attempts to develop training that was more relevant to psychological practice. They were concerned about the deficiencies they saw, and they wanted to establish a new process for training practitioners and then socializing them into the profession. Typically, local practitioners were more heavily involved in the planning, implementation, teaching, and supervision at the new programs than they were in existing ones.

The number of new doctoral training programs grew so rapidly that Cummings convinced the APA Board of Directors to authorize him to convene a meeting of the programs' directors to help them form an organization that would keep the board apprised of developments and serve as a communication conduit between the APA and professional model programs. The group quickly established itself as the National Council of Schools of Professional Psychology (NCSPP) and elected Gordon Derner, longtime head of the professional training program at Adelphi University, its first chair.

Over the years, the NCSPP became a strong voice for the development and implementation of training standards that went beyond the minimal criteria incorporated in the APA's accreditation criteria. Further, all programs were required to meet the higher standards in order to maintain membership in the organization. To this time, the NCSPP is the only psychology training body to develop and adopt a model curriculum for professional education, which was seen by professional program leaders as one way of holding themselves accountable to the public for what psychology practitioners should know.

Members of the Dirty Dozen were centrally involved in the development of the four campuses of the CSPP in California (with the strong support of the California Psychological Association), and of one professional school at Rutgers University in New Jersey and another in Florida. Psychologists in other states quickly followed suit. Representatives from the California and New Jersey schools, along with Jack Wiggins and Ron Fox from Ohio, were heavily involved in the successful effort to establish a program in that state. To ensure the continued success of these and similar efforts, the Dirty Dozen pushed for a revision of the APA accreditation standards and lobbied successfully to place the writer on the revision task force. In addition, they supported Fox's proposal to organize the Association of Psychology Internship Centers to establish a uniform matching date, new standards for accreditation, and greater professional oversight of the internship experience. The reverberations of these and other efforts are still felt within the APA. Professional training needs and issues are on the front burner for the APA, and professional representation from the NCSPP and APIC (now the APPIC) is a given. The Dirty Dozen forever changed how professional psychologists are trained. Recipients of that training are already becoming leaders in their state and national organizations. In 1995, Dorothy Cantor, a Psy.D. graduate of Rutgers University, was elected president of the APA.

Political and Professional Advocacy

Greatly expanded advocacy was the primary motivation that drove the Dirty Dozen's interests and activities. It was at the core of their pressure on the APA to expand its activities in order to better meet the needs of practitioners. Engaging in political and professional advocacy is a basic enterprise of professional societies and organizations, but has little relevance for a scientific society—which is what the APA was when the Dirty Dozen came into being. The intense and prolonged struggle that ensued was, in many ways, a struggle for the heart and soul of the organization: How would it define psychology? What was to be its purpose? Where did it wish to go?

Scientists, who had controlled the APA since its inception, saw little need to change the organization they had created. Practitioners, on the other hand, wanted radical changes, and wanted them at will. Their interests did not easily fit into a scientific society structure, and their goals were unfamiliar, and sometimes objectionable, to academics. With the leadership provided by the Dirty Dozen and the power provided by rapidly growing numbers, practitioners became a force for change in the APA that could not be denied.

Elsewhere in this book, Rogers Wright has detailed many of the changes and concessions won by practitioners, both within the APA and in external political arenas. That discussion will not be repeated here. Instead, this chapter will be limited to a few activities in order to supplement what he has written and thus document the impact of the Dirty Dozen on the APA's advocacy efforts.

It was pressure from practitioners in the Council of Representatives for more action by the APA that led to the creation of an ad hoc Committee on Legislative Affairs (COLA) to determine what needed to be done regarding federal advocacy and make recommendations regarding where and how to proceed. Appointed by President Leona Tyler in 1973, the committee's members included Ted Blau, Nick Cummings, and Ron Fox. Despite some attempts to deflect, change, or blunt the thrust of COLA's many recommendations, the group was successful in identifying significant professional issues and what the association could do to address them. A number of COLA's suggestions and recommendations were implemented, but its most important accomplishment was the legitimization of a more active role for the APA in advocacy and in enacting state and federal legislation. During Cummings' APA presidency (1979), COLA was elevated from an ad hoc committee to a standing committee, with Pat DeLeon as its chair.

Rogers Wright has detailed the creation of the Council for the Advancement of Psychological Professions and Sciences (CAPPS) in 1972, which was funded by contributions and was entirely separate from the APA. CAPPS also formed a political action committee for the support of political campaigns, one of the major consequences of which was the pressure it generated to create a similar organization with the APA. Within just a few years, the APA established the Association for the Advancement of Psychology (AAP), and in 1979, CAPPS and the AAP were merged into a single entity within the APA. Later, the AAP was reconstituted outside of the APA so that it might set up a political action committee as such activities were not permitted under the APA's nonprofit tax status.

Although these developments placed the APA squarely in the advocacy arena, the organization's resources still were inadequate to meet any but the most basic needs at the federal level, to say nothing of those that had to be managed at the state level. Ironically, it was a 1984 resolution of the American Medical Association's (AMA's) House of Delegates to establish a political war chest to resist the incursions of psychologists and other health professionals into medical practice that finally spurred the APA to address the resource and organizational issues that had stymied previous advocacy efforts. The AMA's action was a challenge that could not be ignored if the profession were to survive and flourish.

Obviously, significant new resources were going to be needed in order to respond. But how to acquire such resources was far from a simple matter. Raising dues would certainly be resisted by academic members of the Council, who felt that the existing dues already were far too high. To avert that resistance, health-care practitioners then proposed to assess only licensed health-care providers to fund the new advocacy programs they felt were needed. The funds would be sequestered, would be used to supplement rather than supplant existing APA support for practice, and would be placed under the control of practitioners.

In 1985, the Council of Representatives approved a proposal permitting the association to levy a special assessment to fund such activities as state advocacy efforts, the hiring of experienced lobbyists and advocates, and the development of a strong, national grass-roots network of providers. At its February 1986 meeting a few months later, the Council approved an implementation plan developed by Ron Fox establishing an Office of Professional Practice (OPP) to carry out the new initiatives. In addition, a Committee for the Advancement of Professional Psychology (CAPP) was created to advise the Board of Directors on the expenditure of the special assessment funds and to oversee the operation of the OPP. Rogers Wright was a charter member of the new group.

The creation of a significant new income stream and a major new organizational structure greatly enhanced the visibility of practitioners and practitioner issues. In addition, the changes significantly increased the visibility and influence of state associations, which translated into increased power for practitioners in the Council of Representatives, as more states were able to garner enough support to gain voting seats. Many academic members saw all this as clear and convincing evidence that the APA neither was a scientific society nor was responsive to their needs. It had become a professional association. Whether or not that was true, it was clear that, at the very least, the changes represented a new high-water mark for professional advocacy within the association.

By 1990, the changes in the central office that began with the creation of the OPP had led to the organization of all programs into four directorates: science, practice, public interest, and education. Although financial resources were fairly evenly divided among the directorates, the special assessment made practice first among equals, by a large margin.

Despite all the changes made to accommodate the practice agenda, the APA still was not properly positioned to address many issues as directly and vigorously as needed. As a 501(c)(3) tax-exempt organization, it was forced to operate within strict limits regarding the amount of lobbying that was permitted. In addition, nonprofit organizations are forbidden to make political contributions or to do anything that would advance the interests of one political candidate over another. Because the loss of its tax-exempt status would be catastrophic for the APA, the Board of Directors and the CEO were loath to approve any advocacy or lobbying activities that would place the organization even remotely at risk. Differences between members who favored a more liberal interpretation of IRS rules and those who were more cautious abounded for years. The issue was so important, and yet so esoteric, that even the members of the Dirty Dozen disagreed vigorously about what to do.

On the one hand, by losing its favored tax status, the APA would lose all of its assets. This would be an unfortunate outcome, even for the most dedicated practitioner members. The APA was approaching the legal limit as to how much money could be spent on lobbying, while the needs for such lobbying was rapidly escalating. Major issues of great import to the very survival of psychological practice were playing out at the state level, but the APA was severely limited as to how much direct help it could provide to state associations to deal with these issues. At the very time that health care in the United States was undergoing massive and unprecedented change, the APA could not devote the resources necessary to advance the interests of its practitioners. The association was caught in a major dilemma: protecting its considerable assets versus protecting the income of the largest segment of its membership. Something had to give.

In 2000, the Board of Directors finally proposed that the Council of Representatives retain the APA's tax-exempt status and establish a companion organization under section 501(c)(6) of the tax code, which would then be able to pursue guild interests, participate in the political process, and provide direct assistance to its state associations. The new organization would be funded by the special assessment and would operate under the guidance of the same governance members who oversaw practice activities in the existing organizational structure. In addition to the income from the special assessment, the companion organization (yet to be named) would be able to develop other income streams. In the new structural alignment, the APA would continue to be the only membership organization. The companion organization has no members. Its sole purpose is to provide a tracking and accounting mechanism for professional activities that are not tax exempt.

It is too early to assess the utility of the new arrangement (assuming that it wins the approval of the Council), but, on the surface at least, it appears to be a resolution that allows the APA to address, finally and directly, the issues that the Dirty Dozen have been advocating from the beginning. It is a step that is long overdue from the perspective of practitioners, whose ability to practice has been steadily eroded over the past decade.

Organizational Power Structure: New Faces and New Realities

While the Dirty Dozen as a group was emerging as a new power nexus within the APA, the fact that the percentage of practitioners in the organization was rapidly increasing gave added impetus to their demands. An explosion in opportunities for practitioners, combined with a general constriction in employment prospects for academic and research psychologists, led to changes in the composition of graduate classes and in the types of new members joining the APA. The numerical power of the academic and scientific psychologists, who had been the dominant force in the APA, began to decline. By 1984, over 50% of all Ph.D. degrees were awarded to health-service providers, not counting the numbers of professional school graduates who received Psy.D. degrees. Not only were more practitioners graduating, but they were joining the APA at a much higher rate than they were other groups. Some were predicting that the APA was at risk of losing its "scientific base," and used demographic changes to argue for a restructuring of the organization to make it more responsive to the needs of scientists and academics. Practitioners, for the most part, were reluctant to change the organization now that they were finally gaining ascendancy. In his chapter, Wright deals with the subsequent struggle over a reorganization and how it was played out as a scientists-versus-practitioner issue.

The feelings concerning proposals for reorganization were so strong that the defeat of those proposals inspired several academic/scientific members of the reorganization effort to resign from the APA and to establish a competing national psychological association, the American Psychological Society. Although many scientists and academics did join the new organization, most of them also continued to belong to the APA. This period marked another watershed in the ascendancy of practitioners in the organization.

Prior to the struggle over reorganization, practitioners already had learned how to obtain access to the levers of control. Denied entry by the existing representatives bodies, the Dirty Dozen leaders helped establish new divisions made up primarily of practitioners, which were then entitled to seats on the Council of Representatives. The Divisions of Psychotherapy (29) and State Associations (31) were the earliest, and most influential, examples of such organizations. Division 29 was founded in 1967, primarily by psychologists in independent practice. For a time, it was the largest division in the APA as practitioners flocked to join a division focused on their issues and concerns. Leaders of the division gained visibility among their peers, which helped them attain higher offices in the APA. Ted Blau (the first independent practitioner to be elected an APA President), Nick Cummings, Jack Wiggins, and Max Siegel were members of the Dirty Dozen who became Presidents of the APA after having first served as presidents of Division 29. In addition, the number of "second generation" practitioners mentored by the Dirty Dozen followed the same progression: Ronald Fox, Stanley Graham, Pat DeLeon. Later, other practice divisions were organized, including a Division of Independent Practice (42), initially led by Stanley Graham.

The expansion of new practitioner divisions and the revitalization of many state associations with the assistance of the Practice Directorate meant additional seats on the Council of Representatives, which elected the members of all APA boards and committees. Taking the political process a step further, members of the

Dirty Dozen organized the first caucus group in the Council of Representatives in order to help place practitioners on key governance groups. There are now 10 caucus groups in the Council, but it was the practitioner caucus that showed the way and that continues to set the pace. For example, Council members elect the treasurer and recording secretary of the association, as well as at-large members of the Board of Directors. Presidents are elected by the APA membership. Together, the officers and members-at-large compose the Board of Directors. In 1974, Rogers Wright was the first practitioner to be elected to the board with the help of the caucus: the next year, he was joined by Nick Cummings. In 1976, Ted Blau was elected president of the association (also with the help of the caucus, and other practitioner groups as well). Since that time, members of the caucus have become the dominant constituency group represented on the board.

Closing Note

In just over two decades, the Dirty Dozen had found ways to give voice to the problems and needs of their peers and colleagues in independent practice, an effort that changed American psychology and the American Psychological Association. Their efforts either created, or provided the impetus for, changes that permanently altered the landscape of the association.

- The number of APA divisions with a majority of practitioner members (over 50% pay the special assessment) has grown to more than 20.
- All state associations have been strengthened and now have seats on the Council of Representatives, and all but half a dozen have one or more voting delegates.
- The leadership of state associations is supported and developed through programs sponsored by the Practice Directorate.
- The central office has been restructured into four directorates, the largest of which is the Practice Directorate, with support subsidized by a special assessment on licensed health-service providers.

- Practitioners are well represented on all major boards and committees of the association that deal with practice issues, and typically make up a majority of the Board of Directors.
- Plans are under way to establish a new companion organization to provide an operational umbrella for the pursuit of professional issues that are not permitted to tax-exempt organizations.

These are major accomplishments to lay at the feet of a small bank of determined men (and it was men in the beginning) who sought a professional association that was responsive to their needs and what they had to contribute to society. What they started has not been completed as yet, nor were the results of their efforts always without cost to the organization. Nevertheless, what they accomplished cannot be denied. Practitioners who followed the trail blazed by that small band will be forever in their debt. We are all a bit dryer from being able to walk under the ample umbrella of the Dirty Dozen, and the APA will never be the same.

RONALD E. FOX, PSY.D., PH.D.

CHAPTER 4

A Most Unlikely Prospect

Could a practicing clinical psychologists ever become president of the American Psychological Association (APA)? For three quarters of a century, this seemed to be a very small, if not non-existent, probability.

In 1949, having just received my master's degree from Pennsylvania State University, I looked forward to getting married. I had been engaged for two years, and was somewhat tired of academe. My great and good advisor, at Penn State, Robert Bernreuter, attempted to help me by arranging an interview with Jack Klein & Associates in New York. This industrial testing organization had been using Bernreuter as a consultant for many years and he felt that they needed an in-house research director to help develop more reliable and valid clinical instruments. Since my fiancée lived in New York, this looked like an ideal opportunity to settle down and start a family.

After a day of tedious, and to me, seemingly inane, interviews with various Klein staff members, for my final interview, I had to face the Great Man himself—Jack Klein. A small man, his desk was on a raised dais. I took the chair to which he pointed and he spent some 30 seconds or so staring at me "eye to eye." Suddenly, he leaned forward and asked in an aggressive tone, "What do you wish to accomplish in psychology?" I found his attitude very annoying, and I answered without much thought in what might be considered a hostile manner: "I would like to become president of the American Psychological Association."

During my first year on the board, Abraham Maslow was past president of the APA. He was ill, and often spent the meeting time resting on a couch. To me, he was (and still is) one of the heroes of psychology. We became friendly, and I was astonished when he insisted that I stop calling him "Professor Maslow" and address him as "Abe." We talked quite a bit, and on one occasion, he said, "I was the first clinical psychologist to become president of the APA." I looked at him. "Abe," I said, "You are one of the greatest in the history of psychology, but you are no clinical psychologist." When he asked what I meant, I pointed out that a clinical psychologist is someone who puts the groceries on the table by seeing patients every day in a clinical setting and offering such psychological services as individual psychotherapy, group psychotherapy, assessment, and counseling. He smiled. "Is this what you do?" I answered, "Every day, every week." He then said, "It must be costing you a considerable income to participate in APA activities as often as you do?" "That," I answered, "would be what Abe Maslow would call actualization." We both laughed.

My friendship with Abe Maslow is a cherished memory. For example, at lunchtime during the board meetings, he sometimes would collar me and say, "Since you're a practicing clinical psychologist, let's go for a walk and you can counsel me." Maslow once told me he had had three psychoanalyses—first for his emotional problems, the second as a training analysis, and the third after World War II when he was in the army serving in the military government of Germany, where psychoanalysis had reemerged. The cost of a 50-minute session at that time was the equivalent of 75 cents in U.S. currency. Maslow said, "I couldn't afford not to have another analysis."

In 1971, I was nominated for the office of president of the APA, but was beaten by Ann Anastasi (for whom I voted). The same thing occurred in 1972, 1973, and 1974, when I would be nominated, but would lose, respectively, to Leone Tyler, Albert Bandura, Donald Campbell, and Bill McKeachie.

In 1975, I was again nominated and decided this would be my

last "go." Before the balloting, I was approached by a coalition of clinicians who said that they would support my candidacy if I would agree to a rather long list of expectations that they had put together (as well as make a financial contribution to my own campaign). Being politically naive and somewhat acerbic, I rejected their offer, and they decided to support Nicholas Cummings as an opposing clinical candidate. He earned my eternal support when he told me that he had been approached but had refused out of friendship for me.

I really did not expect to be elected. It was my fifth run, and I had decided that I had things to do other than seeking to become the first practicing clinical psychologist to be elected President of the APA. Then an interesting thing happened. That winter, before the nominations were complete, I was in Boston, and had lunch with a friend, Fred Skinner, dean of Behaviorism at Harvard University. While we were eating in his office at the school's William James Hall, the telephone rang. Actually, there was no sound because Fred had a hearing problem and had rigged up one of his many inventions: a blue light on the wall that flickered when the phone was activated. He picked up the phone:

> "Hello. Oh, how are you [giving the name of a distinguished research psychologist at the University of Illinois]? No, I certainly would not accept a nomination for the presidency of the APA. You say that the clinicians are putting forth a candidate who might have a chance of winning and that the research/academic coalition must have a viable candidate to oppose him? Who is this ogre? Ted Blau? Well that's fine, because he's sitting right here and I'm putting him on the phone."

As it happened, I knew, respected, and was fairly friendly with the man at the other end of the line. I picked up the phone and said, "Hello." After a short pause, he said hesitantly, "This is so embarrassing." I replied, "Don't worry about it. If you can persuade Fred to accept the nomination, I will withdraw and campaign vigorously in his favor. No one in the APA deserves the honor more than Fred Skinner." After a pleasant chat, we hung up.

I implored Fred to accept the nomination, since he had retired and would have the time to serve. He absolutely refused.

That summer, I received a call from the Executive Officer, Kenneth Little. "I have the honor to inform you that you are president-elect of the American Psychological Association." I was shocked, pleased, and a bit nervous. After I hung up I thought about whom to tell first. I immediately placed a call to Robert Bernreuter at Penn State. "This is Ted Blau in Tampa, Florida," I said, to which he replied, "What kind of trouble are you in and what kind of help do you need?" I said, "Do you remember back in 1949 when you tried to arrange a job for me with Jack Klein but he rejected my application?" Bernreuter responded, "Yes, I vaguely remember that he didn't like you for some reason." I filled him in: "He thought I was nuts because when he asked me what my ambition in psychology was, I said, 'to become president of the APA.'" Bernreuter laughed. "Now I remember. You certainly had a big mouth." I laughed. "Dr. Bernreuter, I want you to know that I have just been informed that I have been elected president of the APA." There was a short silence, and then Bernreuter replied, in his usual no-nonsense tone, "Would you please get off the phone now. I want to call Jack Klein."

What I accomplished or didn't accomplish as president of the APA is speculative. We had been meeting with the American Psychiatric Association every year for cocktails and dinner, at our expense. At the first meeting that I attended as president, I asked why we weren't sharing these expenses, or at least alternating them? This led to a rather heated discussion with the Executive Officer, Chuck Kiesler, doing his best to interject some measure of reasoning and sensibility. We never again had a joint dinner with the "little APA" paid for by our APA.

The APA's central office was not terribly pleased when, as president, I insisted on being given, and answering, all mail that was addressed to me. During my year as president, I heard from more than 1,500 members. The central office labeled me the APA's most expensive president ever, since I charged for postage and secretarial time to answer my various letters, although succeeding presidents undoubtedly have exceeded my budget.

My tenure as president-elect, president, and past-president was not particularly remarkable. It was characterized by my insistence that we always do the right thing for the greater good of the most members and my evident lack of political sense concerning a great variety of issues.

My most important experience during my presidency was the opportunity to meet the truly great psychologists who served the APA on the Board of Directors and in the Council of Representatives. I continue to recall these friendships, and sometimes acrimonious interchanges, with pleasure. The leadership of the APA has been, and still is, a representation of the best we have to offer in psychology. I don't always agree with the decision making, but I am aware of the commitment and the good will on the part of most of those who have served our organization.

THEODORE H. BLAU, PH.D.

CHAPTER 5

A History of the Division of Psychotherapy

Editor's Note

The importance of APA Division 29, Psychotherapy, cannot be overemphasized. During the years in which the Dirty Dozen and their supporters were struggling to professionalize the APA, professional psychologists felt displaced within their own national organization. The APA's Division of Clinical Psychology (Division 12) was only occasionally congenial, as it mostly represented the needs of the academic clinicians, rather than those of the rank-and-file independent practitioners. When Division 29 was established in 1967, professional psychologists affectionately referred to it as "a home of our own."

On the occasion of the APA Centennial (1992), Dr. Canter wrote a comprehensive history, which was published by Division 29 as a booklet. We are pleased to reprint her article in its entirety, with the permission of the author and the Executive Board of the Division of Psychotherapy of the American Psychological Association.

Introduction

As the American Psychological Association celebrates its Centennial in 1992, our sense of history becomes increasingly salient, and we find ourselves focusing greater and greater interest on our own roots, our own development as the Division of Psychotherapy. In so doing, we go back more than 30 years, when our story really began. While this is not a very long time by historical standards, it is, unfortunately, a long enough time in which to lose records, reports, and people—the stuff of which such histories are made of. So this recorder has become a detective, trying to piece together from available data, the material which belongs here. Ever optimistic, I have left blanks to fill in names, dates, etc., at times, in the hope that some obsessive-compulsive packrats/old-timers will answer my call and answer my questions! Let me assure you, however, that what I don't have evidence for, I do not include. So this may be taken as somewhat less than complete, perhaps, but hopefully never less than accurate, account of the Division of Psychotherapy of the American Psychological Association.

Beginnings

PIAP: Psychologists Interested in the Advancement of Psychotherapy

A copy of Vol. 1, No. 1, of the *PIAP Bulletin*, dated July 1961, was a real find, and provided the kinds of background information I was looking for: it was during the 1960 APA Convention that a group of APA psychologists sharing interests in psychotherapy banded together to form PIAP, an organization dedicated to the advancement of the teaching and practice of psychotherapy, the training of psychotherapists, and the conduct of research in psychotherapy. This action was based on their shared perception that the APA and its Divisions were not representing adequately their scientific and professional interests.

An active and ambitious group, chaired by Arthur H. Davison, PIAP presented workshops and institutes in major areas of the United States, led by professionals who had made recognized contributions in the field of psychotherapy. They presented programs at APA conventions. And they started plans for publishing a journal, *Psychotherapy: Theory, Research and Practice*, to be edited by Eugene T. Gendlin. Reading the rosters of officers, board members and committee chairs involved in PIAP from 1961 on is much like reading a list of the illustrious psychologists/psychotherapists in the United States! Among its presidents, following Dr. Davison, were Leonard Pearson, Reuben Fine, Hans Strupp, and Gene Gendlin. Other officers and board members included Ronald E. Fox, who served as treasurer, Jules Barron, who was chair of publications and served as editor of the *PIAP Bulletin*, and Vic Raimy, Jack Krasner, Vin Rosenthal, Harold Lindner, Ted Blau, Jim Bugenthal, Al Ellis, Mel Gravitz, Bob Harper, Max Siegel, Lawrence Bookbinder, Henry Guze, Fred Spaner, Erica Chance … the list goes on and on!

Plans to organize a new Division of the APA were discussed— with considerable heat generated, apparently—but the final decision was to defer such action, and see how responsive the APA and its Divisions, particularly Division 12 (Clinical), would be to their needs.

PIAP: A Section of Division 12, APA

In March of 1963, Eugene Gendlin, President of PIAP, received a letter from Victor Raimy, President of Division 12, informing him that on February 23, 1963, the Executive Committee of the Division of Clinical Psychology had unanimously approved PIAP as a section of their Division. This seemed a natural and appropriate affiliation and, according to the PIAP report dated April 1963 and found in the APA's membership files, for the first time psychotherapy as a field was explicitly represented in the APA. PIAP developed its own bylaws, elected its own officers and Executive Board, assessed membership dues, and published a Bulletin for its membership. From the Library of Congress, I was able to get my hands on two more issues of that *Bulletin*, Vol. 3, No. 1, and Vol. 4, No. 2. Such a find!

In the *PIAP Bulletin*, Vol. 3, No. 1, dated June 1963, and edited by Jules Barron, Treasurer Anita Montague reported sending out bills to over 600 members (incidentally, dues were $5, then), and quickly the membership grew to about 1,000. Looking at the list of officers and board, we noted some who went on to lead in Division 29, our past presidents Ted Blau, Bob Harper, Max Siegel, Jules Barron, and Carl Zimet. I also noted with interest mention of the formation of an Administrative Committee to carry on the day-to-day business of the Section, and learned that a Membership Directory, a simple, mimeographed listing, was under way under the direction of Richard Robertson, while Keith Hoover had taken on the responsibility for preparing a comprehensive directory of all institutions or agencies offering programs at the level of postgraduate training in psychotherapy.

Very active programming was one of the major goals of the section, with workshops and symposia planned for presentation during the APA convention and at regional and other meetings throughout the year to provide quality postgraduate training in psychotherapy. Discussion continued regarding the journal on psychotherapy, which had been planned even before PIAP became a Section of Division 12, and efforts had begun to develop policy and structure for the journal in time for presentation to the Executive Board at the APA for final approval. It should be noted that the decision to pursue establishment of a journal was based in part on the results of a research questionnaire dealing with 11 critical issues in psychotherapy and sent to nearly 4,500 psychologists in the APA who listed psychotherapy as an interest in the 1962 Directory. Only 20% of respondents thought that coverage of psychotherapy topics was adequate in APA journals, and 78% thought that there should be a new journal dealing with psychotherapy.

There was a letter dated April 8, 1963, from Leonard Pearson, vice-president of the PIAP, to the Publications Board of APA, indicating that the PIAP had been concerned about the adequacy of publication outlets for theoretical, clinical, and professional articles dealing with psychotherapy practice, teaching, or research. He stated that their decision to establish a journal of psychotherapy had been made before the PIAP became a section of Division

12, and cited an illustrious Editorial Board. (George Bach, John Bell, Paul Bergman, James Bugenthal, Charlotte Buhler, Eric Dreikurs, Reuben Fine, Ernst Hirsch, Sidney Jourard, Arthur Kovacs, Rollo May, Clark Moustakas, William Snyder, Hans Strupp, Julies Seeman, Victor Raimy, Frederick Thorne, among others, were participants.) Even as Len Pearson wrote, manuscripts were being solicited for the first issue, under the editorship of Eugene Gendlin, and in 1964, Vol. 1, No. 1, of that journal, *Psychotherapy: Theory, Research and Practice*, was published.

Vol. 4, No. 2, of the *PIAP Bulletin*, edited by Vin Rosenthal, showed an Executive Board and committee chairs list that included more to-become-presidents of Division 29: Vic Raimy, Fred Spaner (our first president), Jack Krasner, and Vin Rosenthal. It also showed an organization with a membership very much involved not only in the practice of psychotherapy, but also in the teaching, the training, and the researching that are so important to us still.

A letter written by Maury Karpf to President Gene Gendlin in September 1963 concerned the PIAP Executive Board meeting that had been held earlier in the month, and indicated some of the struggles around getting consensus regarding the structure and function of the group. But PIAP continued as an active Section of Division 12. For example, on September 8, 1964, PIAP recommended changes in the accreditation of doctoral programs, including: a minimum of two years of supervised training in psychotherapy, which would be conducted in campus settings serving the community; and appropriate courses in psychotherapy, some of which would be taught by practitioners. And PIAP opposed vigorously any attempt to separate psychotherapy training from the doctoral program in psychology, stating that there should be no "practical or professional program" established separate from, or incapable of leading to, a Ph.D. degree in psychology.

The APA Board of Directors, at its September 1964 meeting, rejected a request from PIAP for the inclusion, in the APA ballot, of slates of candidates for election to PIAP office, on the grounds that "the central office cannot, in general, supervise such an election adequately."

The Section continued its proactive stance, growing by 1966, to a membership of approximately 1,400. But problems for PIAP members within Division 12 continued, including a 50% rejection rate of the programs submitted for the APA Convention and a perceived lack of cooperation regarding PIAP's election ballots, dues billing, and other requests for help. The leaders of PIAP felt that their needs were inadequately met by the governance of Division 12, and discussions about the possibility of achieving divisional status, begun in 1960 but tabled when the affiliation with Division 12 was agreed to, resurfaced.

The leadership of PIAP most involved in the effort to achieve Division status consisted of:

	1965–1966	1966–1967
President	Hans Strupp	Reuben Fine
President-elect	Reuben Fine	Fred Spaner
Past President	Leonard Pearson	Hans Strupp
Secretary	Marjorie Creelman	Nancy Orlansky
Treasurer	Ron Fox	Ron Fox
Rep. to Div. 12	Ted Blau	Ted Blau
Board members	Jules Barron	Jules Barron
	Harold Lindner	Harold Lindner
	Jack Krasner	Jack Krasner
	Fred Spaner	Len Pearson
	(Others unknown)	Vin Rosenthal
		Bob Harper

At the Executive Board meeting on September 1, 1966, Ted Blau led a discussion that culminated in a unanimous vote to draft a petition to be circulated for signature, requesting of the APA Council of Representatives the establishment of a new Division of APA to be known as the Division of Psychotherapy. The petition for divisional status, with the necessary signatures and proposed bylaws attached, was presented to the Board of Directors of the APA at is May 1967 meeting, and was forwarded to the Council of Representatives in August of that year.

As indicated in the petition submitted to the Council (see Appendix A):

"... the purpose of the Division shall be (a) to bring together into one body all members of the American Psychological Association who are interested in psychotherapy and who meet certain standards and qualifications; (b) to stimulate the exchange of scientific information among psychologists interested in psychotherapy; (c) to contribute toward, and aim to enhance the appropriate teaching of psychotherapy to psychologists; (d) to stimulate research into the nature of psychotherapy and to publish, whenever possible, the data so collected; (e) to promote the development of standards for practice that: (1) encourage utilization of the special skills and training of the psychologist-psychotherapist, (2) emphasize the broadest possible background for our practice."

A Home of Our Own:
The Division of Psychotherapy, APA

On September 4, 1967, in Washington, DC, with the approval of the Council of Representatives, PIAP became Division 29, the Division of Psychotherapy of the American Psychological Association. So now our goals were officially recognized as significant for psychology and warranting divisional status to carry them out. And we were on our way and—more or less—on our own! Since PIAP had petitioned for divisional status, and had served as the organizing body of the new Division, it was transformed into the Division of Psychotherapy during the 1967–1968 year, and all PIAP members became charter members of Division 29.

Division 29 has, over its 25 years, been a very special collection of people doing a very special job for psychology and psychotherapy. It was first in so many ways: first Division to hold Midwinter meetings—which changed the face of the APA, becoming a model which many other divisions have emulated over the years. It was the first to offer student travel scholarships. The first to have a central office. The first to have conversation hours and programs in a Divisional Hospitality Suite (a PIAP idea). It was a leader in trying to reshape fellowship requirements for practitioner divisions. And it was, according to Ron Fox, Ted Blau, and many others, a first real home for the practitioner within the APA. One of the things which has made it special over the years has been the sense of family in Division 29. In the early years, it was the one Division within which the young practitioner would find role models. It was also a leader in bringing practitioners into participation in APA governance, on boards and committees, on the Board of Directors, and ultimately into the presidency of APA via such strongly identified Division 29 members as Ted Blau, Max Siegel, Nick Cummings, Stanley Graham, Jack Wiggins, and who knows who else by the time you read this! But now, let's go back to 1967:

1967–1968

The first official Board of the Division of Psychotherapy (for 1967–1968) took their seats following the 1967 Council meeting, and consisted of:

President	Fred E. Spaner
President-elect	Theodore M. Blau
Past President	Reuben Fine
Secretary	Nancy Orlinsky
Treasurer	Ronald E. Fox
Council Rep.	Leonard Pearson (1967–69)
	Jules Barron (1967–68)
	Eugene T. Gendlin (1967–69)
	Fred E. Spaner (1967–68)
Members-at-Large:	Jack D. Krasner (1967–68)
	Erika Chance (1967–70)
	Vin Rosenthal (1967–69)
	Lawrence Bookbinder (1967–69)
	Max Siegel (1967–70)
	Charlotte B. Buhler (1967–68)

Robert A. Harper (1967–70)
Harold Lindner (1967–68)

Having been fortunate enough to find a copy of the *Psychotherapy Bulletin*, Vol. 1, No. 2, dated June 1968, I can tell you that the Division by then had bylaws approved by the membership, and was actively engaged in an impressive variety of projects chaired by an impressive roster of psychotherapists! Gene Gendlin was editor of *Psychotherapy*, and Jack Wiggins was chairing—you guessed it—the Insurance and Related Social Issues Committee, with Gene Shapiro and Ollie Kerner as working members. Al Mahrer was editor of the project entitled *Creative Contributions to Psychotherapy*, and Pincus Gross was editor of the *Psychotherapy Bulletin*, the official organ of the Division, and the successor to the *PIAP Bulletin*. Nat Raskin was heading the Research Committee's efforts, and a one-day conference on "Psychotherapy Research" was planned to precede the 1968 APA Convention in San Francisco. Donald Paull, chair of the Ethics and Ethical Standards Committee, reported that the results of a Division survey on ethical standards were in the process of analysis, and would be published in the next issue. A booklet entitled *Psychotherapy—A Psychological Perspective*, written by Jules Barron, Jack Krasner, and Ben Fabrikant, and designed to educate the public about how and when to use psychotherapy and where to seek it, was nearing publication. Ted Aidman, chair of the Workshop Committee, had, with Gerard Haigh, Leonard Pearson, and Hans Strupp, arranged for two all-day therapy workshops to be held at the 1968 APA Convention. One of the workshops was entitled "How Can We Speed Up the Intensive Psychotherapeutic Process?" and included as participants the following panel members: Eric Berne, Hedda Bolgar, Eugene Gendlin, Harold Greenwald, Frederick Perls, Bernard Reiss, Virginia Satir, and Everett Shostrom, among others! (Impressive, no?) And the other workshop, "The Personal Experiencing of Some Innovations in Psychotherapy," was led by William Schultz. Not bad for a new Division. ... I also noted that Ted Blau and Stanley Graham were among the members of the

Program Committee chaired by Robert F. Schaef. And that among the new members welcomed to the Division were Herb Freudenberger and Irv Raifman.

Division 29 was already soliciting input from graduate students relating to their training, and providing its membership with information regarding the background and legislative effort on the part of the New Jersey Psychological Association (with Gene Shapiro and Morris Goodman spearheading the effort) that led to passage of the first freedom-of-choice law in the United States recognizing psychologists under group major medical policies.

Ron Fox told me the story of how the new Division did not have sufficient funds in their treasury to pay for their needed board meeting. So, at the suggestion of Ted Blau, they held a workshop in Tampa, Florida, from which they raised the funds necessary to meet the financial obligations incurred by their board meeting. It was these workshops which were, in fact, the forerunners of the Midwinter Meetings which helped, later, to put the Division of Psychotherapy "on the map."

1968–1969

Our President, Ted Blau, was elected to the Board of Directors of the APA for a 1969–1971 term. Ted was the first Division 29 officer to serve in this capacity, though Vic Raimy had had two terms on the Board of Directors in 1960–1962 and 1965–1967, before we became a Division.

I couldn't seem to get my hands on much material to tell us about what happened during this year, but a phone call to Ted Blau brought a promise to send along whatever he might find on a back shelf in a dusty carton! Meanwhile, Ted reminisced with me a little about that era, sharing his perception that Division 12 did not represent "real clinical psychology," in the sense that they were a very academically oriented group, and not really interested in practice issues. The "real clinicians" belonged to Division 29, where the young, aggressive, independent practitioners, who felt suppressed and ignored by Division 12, came together to act. It was a time of "showing new psychotherapies," with lots of workshops and demonstrations.

At its last meeting, the Executive Board voted funds for a trial period of four months to test whether the Division could make use of the outgoing president's administrative assistant as a central office resource person. They also discussed the idea of having the 1970 APA Convention program topic for the Division be "Women." Vin Rosenthal, president-elect, discussed with the new program chair, Stephen Mourer, and the outgoing Board the idea that, in addition to holding a board meeting, we have a full-scale Midwinter Convention for Division 29, and they expressed their support of such a plan.

1969–1970

Among the most significant actions taken by the incoming Executive Board was the establishment of what was to become an annual Divisional activity: a Midwinter Convention of the Division of Psychotherapy, to be held in the sunny South.

The Division's Ad Hoc Committee on Psychotherapy Curriculum's draft of recommendations regarding minimal standards for psychotherapy education in psychology doctoral programs, which was published in the August 1969 *Psychotherapy Bulletin*, was very favorably received by the Board. In the discussion that took place, suggestions were made for incorporation, and another draft was to be prepared for discussion at the 1970 Midwinter meeting.

The first Division 29 Midwinter Convention was held in January 1970 in Tampa, Florida. Two hundred members attended, and it was pronounced a great success. It must have been, to have become an annual event, and to have served, as it did, as a model for other Divisions that have gone on over the years to plan similar events for themselves.

Among the efforts of the Division this year were two resolutions passed and implemented by the Executive Board, involving applying to the Office of Communication Management and Development of the APA for funds for the development of films to be used in the teaching of psychotherapy, and for funds and research assistance in planning and carrying out several projects in connection with the Tape Library of the American Academy of Psychotherapists. These projects involved audio and video materials as prime components of information media, and dissemination problems.

Other firsts this year included the establishment of a Distinguished Professional Award in Psychology and Psychotherapy, the first of which was presented at the 1970 APA meeting in Miami to Eugene Gendlin. The exchange of letters between President Vin Rosenthal and recipient Gene Gendlin, as printed in the April 1970 edition of the *Psychotherapy Bulletin*, Vol. 3, No. 1, pp. 20–21, illustrates the warmth, excitement and activities.

Dear Gene:

You are an irascible, cantankerous, exciting, lovable, wise man. You are also the first recipient of the Division 29's Distinguished Professional Psychologist Award.

And I am delighted to be the one to inform you.

I am asking that you give an invited address at the September 1970 meetings of the APA at which time the award will be officially conferred.

I hope this gives you joy. I have a big smile on my face as I write this.

> Affectionately,
> Vin Rosenthal
> President,
> Division of Psychotherapy

Dear Vin:

Thank you, and thank you for the very expressive letter!!! I am happy to accept the award. What does it mean?

> Sincerely,
> Eugene T. Gendlin, Ph.D.

Dear Gene:

It means, in the words of Sid Jourard:

"The Executive Board of APA Division 29, the Division of Psychotherapy, unanimously voted to present Eugene T. Gendlin its first Distinguished Professional Psychologist Award. Gene Gendlin was nominated and chosen for this honor because of his untiring efforts at midwifing, ram-rodding, nurturing, scolding, worrying, politicking, philosophizing and demonstrating, that psychotherapy is a proper concern of the American Psychological Association, and that it warrants divisional status and a journal. Active as he has been, tirelessly, at theory, research, practice, teaching, and organizational aspects of psychotherapy, he earns the respect and esteem of his colleagues who view him as well with affection."

Sincerely,
Vin

The Division, which was cooperating with Division 12 and the Board of Professional Affairs of the APA on the Joint Task Force on Evaluation of Psychotherapy Education in Psychology Training Programs. Its Research Committee had held a research conference at which a new society for psychotherapy research was formed, to deal with problems of psychotherapy practitioners and the meaning and value of research to them.

The Committee on Education and Training proposed that Division 29 sponsor the development of a Center for Advanced Studies in Psychotherapy, to provide advanced practitioners an opportunity to meet once a year for a three or four day colloquium, bringing together a group of nationally known senior psychotherapists to address specific theoretical issues of psychotherapy.

By the end of its 1969–1970 year, the third of its existence, Division 29 had made significant strides. Its membership in January of 1970 was over 1,600, and 21 Fellows had been elected. In addition, 732 membership applications were received and processed in 1970 and subscriptions to the Divisional journal had reached 3,698 by January of 1970, representing a steady growth pattern.

1970–1971

President Vic Raimy, in his first *Psychotherapy Bulletin* column, proposed that efforts be expended to form a coalition with other Divisions and state associations sharing our concerns regarding national health-care policies, ideas, and energies seemed reasonable to Vic.

At the midwinter board meeting, it was agreed unanimously that a campaign be launched to secure support to finance a full-time executive secretary with an office in Washington. Speaking of Midwinter Meetings, I am reminded that Ted Blau told me that the meeting was advertised as "29 in the Sun" and for the first time in 101 years, Tampa, Florida, registered a temperature of 29 degrees! But it was a wonderful meeting, anyway!

In looking through this year's programs in the Division's Hospitality Suite, I noted conversation hours which included the following as some of the speakers: Al Ellis, Peter Nathan, Aaron Canter, Vin Rosenthal, Margaret Rioch, Gordon Derner, Hans Strupp, Al Mahrer, George Albee ... quite a roster!!

As of September 1971, the Division had attracted over 2,000 members, and applications were coming in a steady stream. New members, associate members, and student affiliates were welcomed, and 12 members were granted Fellow status, a new endeavor on the part of the Division (and Hans Strupp, our Fellows Chair), and one fraught with difficulties as fellowship criteria developed by the APA Membership Committee did not seem appropriate to impose on our practicing psychotherapists.

This year, the Distinguished Psychologist Award went to Vic Raimy!

1971–1972

This fifth year for the Division began with Max Siegel's taking over as president. At the incoming board meeting held on September 15, 1971, an Ad Hoc Committee on Nondoctoral Training in Psychotherapy was formed with Arthur L. Kovacs as chair and Ted Blau (East Coast) and Vin Rosenthal (Middle States) as members. They were charged with making site visits throughout the country to examine AA training programs in psychology or mental health. It was established that the site for midwinter meetings would be guided by the principle of annual alternation between the eastern and western parts of the country. At this board meeting, the Publications Committee, chaired by Hedda Bolger, was charged with developing guidelines for publication policies for the Division, and $350 was contributed to the Black Psychologists Organization.

I noted also a $500 donation to the California School of Professional Psychology. It seems that shortly after the founding of CSPP by the California Psychological Association, the Division of Psychotherapy joined as a co-founder and made a significant contribution to the school's endowment. I do not know exactly when this occurred, but it seemed to me that, since this was the first time I found a reference to CSPP in the reference materials available to me, it might be as good a place as any to note this fact.

Division 29 instituted student travel scholarships this year, another APA "first" for the Division, and one of which we are very proud. Much praise was received from other divisions, as well as inquiries about our experience with this program. As the members of this first selection committee (Ron Fox, Max Siegel, and Herb Freudenberger) indicated in their report to the board, "If imitation is the sincerest form of flattery, we may have reason to feel quite flattered at future APA meetings. We can also have the satisfaction of having been instrumental in helping more students become an integral part of their professional organization." This year's winners, who presented at the APA Convention, were:

Marlene Cohen, Fordham University, and Sandy Neuschatz, University of Rhode Island, "Therapeutic Change in a Behaviorally Oriented Experimental Community," a symposium

Roseanne Reed and Sheila Schuster, University of Louisville, "Therapeutic Applications of Autogenic Training with Biofeedback," a symposium

As part of its new public information program, the Division released a booklet by Drs. Jules Barron, Ben Fabrikant, and Jack Krasner, entitled *Psychotherapy: A Psychological Perspective*. It was written as a means of providing students, counselors, teachers, administrators, patients, and the public-at-large with a basic understanding of psychotherapy and the role of the psychologist, and included answers to important questions regarding theory, training, practice, research, and education.

The year's Distinguished Psychologist Award was given to Carl Rogers, theorist and therapist extraordinare.

At its outgoing board meeting in Honolulu in September 1972, a Legislative Committee was initiated by President Max Siegel in collaboration with the president-elect, Jules Barron. The committee, chaired by Morton Schillinger, was charged with functioning as a liaison to CAPPS regarding national legislative activity, to various state legislative committees in regard to local actions, and to APA committees (e.g., Insurance), which were involved in legislative actions such as insurance, national mental health service bills, etc. The journal editor, Gene Gendlin, reported that subscriptions were up to 4,500, and the journal had doubled in size.

It was at that meeting that the Board discussed a request from Dr. Leah Gold Fein, Secretary of the Division, for the establishment of a Committee for Women. Despite the argument that women are often overlooked in organizations, and that women graduate students needed more female role models, the Board chose not to establish such a committee. The discussion reflected a consensus that women were presently active in the Division and should continue to remain active as members, rather than as a special group.

1972–1973

At the incoming board meeting held on September 3, 1972, chaired by the newly seated president, Jules Barron, the Publications Policy Committee was dissolved and the Administrative Committee was charged with examination of the structure and function of the Board and *all* of its committees. The Board went on record as instructing its Council representatives to vote against giving M.A.-level psychologists full membership in the APA.

At the December 1972 meeting of the Council, the Division was represented by Art Kovacs and Gordon Derner, and by Jack Wiggins and Max Siegel sitting in as alternates to Len Pearson and Hans Strupp, who could not attend. Art's report of that meeting gives us a good view of what Division 29 was doing, what positions we were taking, to carry out the perceived mandates of our membership. For one, we worked to defeat a proposal from the Policy and Planning Board of the APA that would have reorganized the APA as a loose confederation. We also opposed changes in Council responsibilities, and were pleased that the Council itself assumed responsibility for studying the further reorganization of the APA. For another we opposed, "at least for the time being" the entry of the M.A. membership issue by referring it to the membership for a referendum. And we fought for a $20,000 donation by the APA to CAPPS, which was finally passed by a vote of over two to one, with accompanying cheers on the floor of the Council.

This was another successful year for the Division. The Midwinter Meeting, held in Freeport under the direction of Vin Rosenthal, was attended by about 400 people. Our annual programs at the APA Convention (Herb Freudenberger, program chair) were greater in number than ever before, and the quality was outstanding. Our pre-convention workshops were led by Drs. Cyril M. Franks and Victor E. Frankl, and excellent Conversation Hours were held in our hospitality suite. The Executive Board discussed the many issues confronting professional and applied psychologists, and gave serious consideration to the matter of effective action. It seemed to the Board that if we combined our energies and resources in the common cause of our mutual concerns and interests, we would markedly increase the probability of success. And so the Division of Psychotherapy, under the leadership of its president, Jules Barron, innovated the formation of an Interdivisional Committee for Professional and Applied Psychology, composed of 10 Divisions and representatives from the APA central office and CAPPS. In April of 1973, the Division issued an invitation to the presidents and presidents-elect of Divisions 12, 13, 16, 17, 22, 29, 30, 31, and 32 to participate in a special interdivisional conference of professional and applied psychology hosted by Division 29 in June 1973 in New York City, the Board having voted the funds for hotel accommodations, the meeting room, and lunch. The agenda was set to involve the identification of problem areas and issues, and to determine ways of taking the kinds of action that would sensitively and productively achieve solutions on behalf of our specialized concerns and our larger association of psychologists. Dr. Barron was elected president of the group, Jack Krasner was elected secretary, and further meetings were scheduled.

And the Division won another seat on the Council, bringing to five the number of people representing us at the August 1973 meeting of the Council. Speaking of the Council, Division 29 participated in the push to hold an emergency meeting of the Council in March of 1973 to consider what should be the APA's response to the phase-out and termination of federal support for training and service programs in psychology and related disciplines. Out of this Council meeting, which seemed to make clear a shift in power within the APA to the professional, applied group, a number of important actions were taken: resolutions passed and disseminated to the mass media in an effort to affect public policy on human welfare matters; a charge to the BPA to gather data regarding mental health services and prepare position papers for possible use in influencing governmental bureaucracies; the appointment of an official staff liaison from the APA to CAPPS for the purpose of improving the public policy effectiveness of both organizations; establishment of a continuing Committee on Legislative Affairs (COLA); the addition of the position of Administrative Officer for Professional Affairs within the central office of the APA charged with the responsibility for articulating psychology with federal programs, etc.

Additional activities during the year? The Office of the Secretary, under Jack Krasner's supervision and with his participation, was very productive, establishing liaisons with some key personnel in the APA, handling materials for the Administrative Committee, attempting to set up a communications system between various Divisional committees, etc., etc., etc.

Fran Rothman, Chair of the Tape Library Committee, developed a Division 29 audiotape distribution library, which made available to psychologists and allied professionals tapes on psychotherapy by outstanding psychologists. Jack Chwast was busily arranging for regional programs sponsored by the Division, which were greeted with great success. Via its Committee on Education and Training, the Division was taking the initiative by working toward the evaluation of postgraduate training facilities in psychotherapy, and was charged with studying the possibility of the Division's setting up accreditation procedures itself for postgraduate training programs in psychotherapy. And the Subdoctoral Training Program Committee's final report was presented on the need and structure of such training. The Research Committee was also actively involved, developing research regarding psychotherapy. The Public Information Committee initiated a series of radio panel programs aimed at education of the public regarding psychologists/psychotherapists. And the Membership Committee processed and recommended to the board approximately 500 new members for the Division, noting that by the end of the year, the membership was about 3,000. Growth continued!

The Distinguished Psychologist Award this year went to Albert Ellis and Hans Strupp! It seems that it was impossible to choose between them ... and that descriptions of their contributions would be "de trop."

The committee that had been established by President Max Siegel to consider issues of Fellow status concluded that the Fellow category no longer fulfilled the function for which it was originally created, and that the current procedures for nominating, selecting, and recommending candidates were unworkable. Other Divisions, in addition to ours, had experienced similar difficulties over the years, and numerous task forces and committees had failed to develop workable solutions. It was recommended that the membership be polled by mail ballot regarding abolition of the Fellow category, and, should Fellow status be retained, that consideration be given to other alternatives.

Publications flourished this year and included:

- *Directory of Post-Doctoral Training Facilities*, 3rd Edition, Arnold Rachman and Priscilla Kauff, Editors
- A new volume of *Creative Contributions to Psychology*, Al Mahrer, Editor
- A volume developed and published through the efforts of the Religion and Therapy Committee, Richard Cox, Chair
- The *Psychotherapy Bulletin*, three issues, Robert Schaef, Editor
- The journal, *Psychotherapy: Theory, Research, and Practice*, Gene Gendlin, Editor (with 5,000 subscriptions)

Members of Division 29 were encouraged to continue their individual efforts to support CAPPS financially as well as spiritually. The Division itself contributed $1,000 to CAPPS and became co-plaintiff in the CAPPS suit against the "Blues." Financial support was given to the CSPP and was authorized for the Virginia Psychological Association in their battle for insurance payment for mental health services provided by a psychologist/psychotherapist.

This year's Student Travel Scholarship winners, who presented at the 1973 APA Convention were:

Judith Katz, University of Pennsylvania, and Jeanne Maracek, Yale University. "Liberated Psychotherapy: Changing Perspectives and Roles Among Women," a symposium

Avraham Frydman, Joseph Klawsnik, Mary Sedney, and Howard Tennan, all from the University of Massachusetts. "The Experiential Qualities of Learning Behavior Therapy," a symposium

Linda Lifur, California State University, "The Possibility of Licensing Adults to Have Children," a symposium

As Jules Barron put it in his last presidential column in the *Psychotherapy Bulletin*, "Since our inception as a division, that was born of PIAP, we have been a significant force in the psychological revolution. While fighting for the legitimacy of professional psychology we have tried to maintain our scientific heritage."

1973–1974

This was the year of Gordon Derner's presidency, and it was another productive year. In keeping with its by-now-established pattern of being in the forefront, Division 29 became incorporated on October 2, 1973, and was working on securing 501(c)(6) tax-exempt status from the Internal Revenue Service. (We got it, though I do not know exactly when.)

Jack Krasner and his Public Information Committee were working toward developing radio programs which included panels sponsored by Division 29. These panels, begun in September of 1973, were to continue for at least a full year of broadcasting, and were heard on Sunday mornings in the New York metropolitan area. One of them was submitted for a special public service radio award!

The 1974 Midwinter Meeting, held in San Diego with Dr. Karl Pottharst as chair, was the best attended meeting to date (650–700 people), and was enriched by the cooperative efforts of the California School of Professional Psychology and the California Psychological Association. It was at this meeting that what came to be known as the Committee for Women was born.

The Distinguished Psychologist Award was given posthumously to Haim Ginott.

The Committee on Student Travel Fellowships, after two years of experience, recommended to the Board that the student awards become an ongoing and permanent annual event, the funds to be given to help students travel to APA conventions to present noteworthy scholarly offerings as part of the Division's program. The Board officially adopted this awards program, with this year's winners to present at the 1974 APA meetings. The winners were:

Karen Corbin, M.A., CSPP, Los Angeles, and David Corbin, M.A., Fuller School of Psychology, Pasadena. "The Psychodrama of Death," an experiential workshop designed to help professionals

Vicky M. Mays, M.A., Chair, University of Massachusetts, Amherst; Supo Laosebekan, Loyola University; and Herman H. Lewis, University of Massachusetts, Amherst, A symposium on "Psychotherapy, Graduate Training, and the Black Student"

Estelle Parness, M.A., CSPP, A paper "The Play of the Dying Child"

The Division was enjoying the success of its journal, but since Dr. Gendlin was retiring as editor, a search committee was formed to find a worthy successor. Dr. Gendlin agreed to serve for two more years, and the search committee was charged with reporting to the Board at the 1975 Midwinter Meeting.

The Division-sponsored active committees kept the membership aware of what was happening in terms of such issues as freedom of choice, and independence for psychologists from the supervision of "medical review." This was the year in which the APA's Council of Representatives voted to establish an organization called the American Association of Psychologists, to function as a legal legislative advocacy body. The Executive Board of Division 29 unanimously endorsed the AAP, while also urging continued support of CAPPS while the AAP "tooled up." The Board also voted to support the APA Council representatives' resolution reaffirming CAPPS's activities in its litigation against the Blues.

A donation of $1,500 was made available for the Committee on Legislative Activity (COLA), the newly established standing committee of the APA charged with monitoring federal legislation and bureaucratic regulations with a view toward making recommendations for involving the APA in legislative programs as appropriate.

Apparently the membership voted to retain Fellow status, because I noted, in my reading, that the Fellows Committee, chaired by Hans Strupp, was developing criteria for Fellows for Board consideration. The Education and Training Committee, chaired by Sam Kutash, was working on standards for postdoctoral training programs, and the Creative Contributions Committee's second volume was taken over by the Social and Basic Science Book Club and volume 3 was in process.

This was the year that the *Psychotherapy Bulletin* had its first woman editor (Constance Nelson). I also noted in the Bulletin a column entitled "News of Members." Any connection? The personal information was nice to read about. President Nixon's stock went up in my eyes when I read, for example, that he had appointed Joe Matarazzo to the new Board of Regents of the new Uniformed Services University of the Health Sciences. Congratulations were extended to the wives of two board members—Mrs. Vin Rosenthal and Mrs. Jules Barron (Nina)—who were currently enrolled in graduate psychology programs, and Vin Rosenthal's editorship of *Voices*, the journal of the American Academy of Psychotherapists, was noted.

Jules Barron was appointed by APA President Bandura from Division 29 to the Committee on the Relationship of Divisions to the APA. The committee among other items was to study and make recommendations regarding the relationship between incorporated divisions of the association and the possible necessity of a fuller report of divisional, financial, and other activities of the association.

At its final meeting, the outgoing Executive Board of Division 29 voted to send a check to the Virginia Psychological Association in support of their case against the Blues. While up to $2,500 had been authorized earlier, $1,000 was as much as the Division's financial condition would allow at this time.

1974–1975

The president, Art Kovacs (Arthur L., officially), was asked by the Board at the above-mentioned meeting to write to the Chair of the APA Membership Committee requesting a meeting of the Division 29 Fellows Committee with the Membership Committee to discuss the issue of Fellow status. Rejection of Division 29 Fellow applications frequently hinged on publication credits, not seen as appropriate criteria for this Division. Drs. Strupp, Krasner, and Barron met with the Membership Committee in September of 1974, and worked out some criteria for election of Fellows in Division 29. At the midwinter board meeting, Art Kovacs was selected as the next journal editor, Student Travel Scholarship Award winners were designated, and the decision was made to shift the Division's workshops from the APA Convention to the Midwinter Meetings, because of what was seen as a coming trend of increasing numbers of competing pre-APA offerings.

Attention was addressed to thorny issues around the Division's incorporation, the way in which the journal had been filing an independent tax return though it belonged to the Division, APA's looking with disfavor upon Divisions which incorporated independently, and similar issues. Legal counsel was to be sought. Items relating to the Council of Representatives agenda were discussed, so that representatives were aware of board positions on various matters to come before them.

The student scholarship winners, who presented at APA in 1975 were Theodore G. Falcon, David M. Young, and Lynn Johnson and David Blair. Unfortunately, the titles of their presentations seem to have been lost. Lost, too, is the citation that went with the posthumous awarding of our Distinguished Psychologist Award to Sid Jourard, this year.

This was the year in which Ernst Beier took over as *Psychotherapy Bulletin* editor, the year in which the Committee for the Treatment of the Aged was established with Carol Dye as chair, and the year in which the Committee for Women became official, its goals were developed, and Joy Kenworthy was designated its chair. The CFW was tentatively charged with examining what is transmitted to women clients in psychotherapy, directions taken in terms of role, function, sexuality, etc. Additionally, it was charged with helping in the integration of women into a full leadership role in the governance of the Division.

Division 29's Committee on Health Insurance (COHI), chaired by Jack Wiggins, was busy cooperating with and assisting the

APA's COHI in its negotiations with insurance companies and government agencies regarding the use of psychotherapy by psychologists, and in negotiating and implementing specific insurance contracts regarding the use of psychotherapy in treating health conditions. This was the year in which clarification was achieved about the status of psychologists regarding disability determinations under the Social Security Administration's rules. There was also ongoing active lobbying for freedom-of-choice legislation, and work with unions aimed at convincing them to include psychologists in their insurance contracts.

By August of 1975, the Division of Psychotherapy was big business, with annual income and expenditures of approximately $50,000. To enhance and facilitate the quality and effectiveness of its work, and to maximize financial economy, it seemed that changes in the way the Division operated might be in order. A central office, that would bring together the functions of the Division would, it was anticipated, eliminate duplication of actions and minimize the possibility of conflicting activities. Additionally, communication with the membership would be facilitated, and official mailings would be eligible for lower postage costs. A central office, as envisioned, would serve as a clearinghouse for information, and would assume routine functions of many committees, freeing committee persons to concentrate on the creative and professional aspects of their duties.

It was at this final board meeting of the year that the Board voted to establish, for a two-year trial period, a central office in the New York/New Jersey area to administer the activities of the Division. At the end of its first year, the operation was to be reviewed. The Board also voted, at the request of the treasurer Stanley Graham, to change the Division's fiscal year to the calendar year, thereby making budget creation, among other things, a more manageable process.

1975–1976

Another busy and productive year for the Division steered by Jack Krasner! Laura Barbanel agreed to chair the newly formed History Committee, and Ted Reiss's International Committee was trying to find ways to relate to our colleagues in different countries and exchange information. The Committee for Women was weighing and discussing the advisability of trying to establish itself as a Section, and the Program Committee, led by Aaron Canter, was effective in providing exciting convention offerings.

Jack Krasner was appointed Administrative Coordinator of the central office, with an honorarium of $1,500 per year for two years.

In 1976, the Division increased its Council representatives from the current five to six, though that number was to be decreased to five the next year, and had been only four the year before. These ups and downs seemed to be typical, and suggested the need to make a point of soliciting apportionment ballot votes from the membership each year.

The 1976 Distinguished Psychologist Award went to Nick Cummings, an innovator and leader in the field whose accomplishments are legion!

The student scholarship awards went to the following individuals, who presented at the 1976 APA meetings:

K. David Schultz, Robert Kreuger, and Joshua Auerback, Conscious Control of Consciousness as Therapeutic Aim and Technique

Marion Walker, Effect of Clinical Supervision on Therapeutic Attitude of Supervise

Michael Feuerstein, Training of Psycho-physiological Therapists

Julia Lewis, Therapy with High-Risk Schizophrenic Families

On the issue of "sexual intimacies between client and therapist," the Division resolved that physical contact aimed at erotic stimulation and/or gratification of the therapist and/or the client is in and of itself an unethical action for the psychotherapist. The Division also reaffirmed its support of then-current ethical standards on advertising and its desire that these be upheld. A $500 contribution was pledged to support and encourage the Ohio

School of Professional Psychology. And a recommendation was made that the incoming president, Carl Zimet, appoint a task force to review and to formulate levels and patterns of training and practice for psychotherapy and formulate some guidelines that could be introduced into the APA structure through our Council representatives.

At the final executive board meeting on September 1, 1976, a $50,000 budget was approved. It was recommended that our Council representatives petition the Council to formally approve continuing the operation of the Division's journal (already in existence for 13 years, and actually predating our attaining Divisional status in APA), and also that they request that the Council establish an Office of Divisional Affairs in the APA. We were delighted with the election of Ted Blau, one of our past presidents, as president-elect of the APA. . . . the first practitioner to be chosen, we believe. Ted would be serving as APA president in 1977. Ted told me that some people considered Abe Maslow the first practitioner president, but that he—Maslow—thought that was ridiculous!

Another of our past presidents, Max Siegel, who was serving as a Council representative for us, was elected to the APA Board of Directors during this year. Max was retained on our Board by the creation of a "Senior Consultant" seat for him, which he filled until 1978.

1976–1977

Carl Zimet assumed the presidency of a dynamic and growing Division. He used his presidential columns in the *Psychotherapy Bulletin* to inform the membership regarding issues of importance: for example, the master's degree psychotherapist, and NIMH plans which would have ended training support for programs in various areas of psychology. NIMH changed its position, and was clearly responsive to Dr. Zimet's column, which made us feel effective and efficient in using our power to shape our profession.

This was the year in which three new committees were formed: Bylaws (Fred Spaner, chair), Professional Affairs (Herb

Freudenberger, chair), and Finance (Jack Krasner, chair). And the
Committee on International Relations, the Religion and Psychotherapy Committee, the Study Committee on Ethical Issues, and
the Task Force on Standards for the Practice of Psychotherapy
were discharged with thanks. The Public Information and Education Committee reported that about 70 radio and TV shows
across the country had featured members of Division 29.

We noted that Ohio psychologists were successful in obtaining
passage of a bill by their legislature establishing a school of professional psychology at Wright State University. Division 29's early
backing of the idea with a financial contribution—and spiritual
support—was seen by the Ohioans as instrumental in soliciting
help from other professional groups. The Division was also continuing its efforts to press for the passage of bills including psychologists in Medicare.

In terms of housekeeping, Jack Krasner was serving as Administrative Coordinator, in charge of the Division's central office, on
an interim basis, until a decision was made regarding one of three
proposals: to have a secretary-treasurer, a new central office, or a
professional administrator. And on recommendation of the journal editor, Art Kovacs, no action was taken by the Board of Directors regarding incorporating the Division's journal.

The Committee for Women, chaired by Hannah Lerman,
decided to drop the idea of Section status, and to concentrate on
its agenda within the current framework. They were devising a
questionnaire to be sent to the membership to gather data regarding men's and women's professional lifestyles. The committee
decided that energies should be directed toward helping women to
prepare presentations for both Midwinter and APA Convention
meetings. A subcommittee with liaison to the Program Committee was established and charged with developing guidelines for
program preparation to be published in the *Psychotherapy Bulletin*
for members and to be made available to new members joining
the Division. While the idea was generated in relation to the perceived need for women to acquaint themselves with the process,
it was felt that this could prove to be of interest to men as well.

At the Midwinter Meeting, the Board moved a statement to communicate to appropriate persons and legislatures urging passage of the Equal Rights Amendment and indicated that "This Board would find it very difficult to support meetings in a state that has not ratified ERA." The Division also sent a letter to the Florida state legislature informing them that we would not return for another Midwinter Meeting as long as the Florida legislature failed to pass the Equal Rights Amendment. In response to concerns brought to their attention by the CFW, the Division, at its annual business meeting, voted to advise the Arizona legislature that while it was too late to cancel our plans to hold the 1978 Midwinter Meeting in Scottsdale, Arizona, in the future we would boycott Arizona unless its negative stance regarding the ERA was changed.

At the 1977 Midwinter Meeting, one of the innovations was the formation of a volunteer panel of supervisors available for individual and small group consultation during the meetings. Another was the presentation of a Master Lecture series dealing with philosophic and professional issues in the work of the psychotherapist.

Student travel scholarship winners this year who presented at the APA in 1977 were:

Paul Lane, Florida State University, The Limits of Confidentiality and the Process of Psychotherapy

Nancy Cooley, Bob Coyle, and Suzanne Imes, Georgia State University, Effective and Ineffective Supervision from Student's Points of View

Jane Rozanasky, University of Minnesota, Beyond Schools of Psychotherapy: The Integrity and Maturity of the Therapist

The 1977 Distinguished Psychologist Award went to Gordon Derner, for his many contributions to the teaching and training of psychotherapists in the country's first professional school of psychology, at Adelphi University.

It was in the spring of 1977 that the policy of publishing statements from candidates running for Divisional office in the *Psycho-therapy Bulletin* was initiated. When the Division's election results were announced this year, it was interesting to see that still another woman had been elected to the board of Directors, making a total of three female members-at-large (Irma Lee Shepherd, Annette Brodsky, and Rachel Hare-Mustin) plus two women officers (albeit secretary and treasurer), Gloria Gottsegen and Ella Lasky. At the final board meeting on August 24, 1977, the completed CFW brochure material written by Matty Canter and Ellen McGrath and entitled "Program Development—Your Guide to Getting It On" was presented, and it was agreed that it be published both in the *Psychotherapy Bulletin*, Vol. 11, No. 1, and as a brochure to be distributed to new members. Also to be published in that issue were the results of the survey conducted by the CFW.

1977–1978

Noted in the news was the fact that another of our past presidents, Nicholas A. Cummings, was elected president-elect of the APA, his presidency term to be in 1979. How proud we were! (And how nice it would have been if we could have had access to a crystal ball and been able to tell this year's Division president, Stanley Graham, that *he* would be president of the APA in 1990!!).

It was interesting to note that our *Bulletin* editor Ernst Beier had invited Norman L. Farberow to submit a paper on "Mental Health Response to Major Disasters," which was published in the Fall 1977 issue. (As I write, in 1992, aware of all that our Division has contributed in relation to Desert Storm and its sequala, this seems particularly significant in terms of our view of Division 29 as being on the cutting edge!)

The 1978 Midwinter Meeting was held in Scottsdale, Arizona, on March 1–4. Its theme, "The Family of Psychotherapies," represented interest in exploring the diversity of current psychotherapeutic approaches while simultaneously identifying the common family ties which provide our shared identity and a basis for appreciating both similarities and differences. A consultation/peer discussion program similar to the format developed for the 1977

Midwinter Meeting was also offered. In protest against Arizona's failure to pass the Equal Rights Amendment, a discussion was held at the meeting by a panel which included local ERA supporters. At its midwinter board meeting, the Board voted to print 1,000 copies of the CFW's brochure, "Program Development— Your Guide to Getting It On," for distribution to new members and to make it available to all in the Division's Hospitality Suite at the APA Convention. Ron Fox was in charge of that Midwinter Meeting, and I did the local arrangements. So I remember particularly well that colleagues coming to the meeting were greeted by what was called, by the natives, "the 100 year flood"—I recall that I kept expressing my regrets (not responsibility, just regrets) to everyone for the sunless, wet weather during the first couple of days. And then, thank goodness, it turned "typical."

This was the year that we formed our first Ethnic Minorities Committee, reactivated our Research Committee, and our president, Stanley Graham, convened a Committee of Young Turks— later called the Members Forum—to encourage communication, innovation, and greater participation among members. This was also the year that the Finance Committee was reorganized, placed under the chairmanship of the treasurer, and charged with the responsibility of preparing an annual budget to present to the Board of Directors for approval. Gloria Gottsegen was appointed Administrative Coordinator of the Division's Central Office, and a Committee on Reorganization was appointed to develop several alternative plans for the structure of the Division. The Bylaws Committee was hard at work, including on its agenda the elimination of sexist language from the bylaws and a consideration of Sections. And our journal issued its first special issue on "Personality of the Psychotherapist."

Ellen McGrath, Program chair, instituted a formal procedure for evaluation of submissions for the APA program, each program being rated by three independent reviewers with expertise in the area under consideration.

Division 29's COHI had a busy year negotiating with labor unions, and their work resulted in the inclusion of psychologists in the United Air Lines contracts for both salaried and hourly workers. Dr. Gene Shapiro of COHI and Dr. Herbert Dorken provided testimony to the Federal Trade Commission regarding psychology's economic loss resulting from the restraint-of-trade practices of the National Association of Blue Shield Plans. The COHI report also addressed the AAP's complaint to the Federal Trade Commission about JCAH guidelines for hospital privileges.

Division 29 appointed a task force to develop an in-house legal office and staff within APA, and the Division's support of the APA's doing so was communicated to the APA Board of Directors.

At the August 1978 board meeting, the treasurer announced that the Division's 1979 budget of $149,000 was the largest of any Division in the APA. A donation to an ERA benefit was approved. And the following statement on reproductive freedom was passed by the Executive Board:

> Childbearing is an event that has the most profound consequences in the life of a woman. Even when a pregnancy is sought after and prepared for, a woman's life is inevitably altered when she bears a child. The sharpest foresight falls short of predicting the scope of the parenting experience that invariably demands more than the best prepared anticipate.
>
> When faced with an unsought and unwanted conception, there is no more reliable an index than the woman's self-assessment of her preparedness to bear a child. No law, practice, or circumstance should be allowed to discount her perception and force a woman to bear a child against her will.
>
> Although elected parenthood does not guarantee beneficial outcomes, forced parenting forecasts the grimmest psycho/social results. Women given no option to an unwanted conception are physically and emotionally jeopardized and their options for progressive self-direction are critically imperiled.
>
> We are particularly distressed by the present governmental climate wherein poor and disadvantaged women are specifically and differentially excluded from the possibilities for

abortion of unwanted pregnancies which are now available only to the more advantaged.

Laws, policies, or practices which force or favor unwanted childbearing detract markedly from goals of improved mental health by contributing to the damaged self-concepts which are the anathema of a healthy society. In the case of the pregnant woman, she suffers loss of control of her body and her self. In the case of the unwanted child, the potential for suffering the effects of child abuse and neglect are enhanced and the potential for delinquency enhanced.

Once again, the Division was taking a courageous stand on a public interest issue!

This year's student travel scholarships for 1978 APA presentation went to:

Chris Baker and Nicholas Caskey, "Dual Perspectives: Client and Therapist Perceptions of Therapy Process"

Julie Parson, "Group Psychotherapy with Mentally Retarded Adults"

Mavis Tsai, "Therapy Groups for Women Sexually Molested as Children"

Pedro Ferreira and Marcia Ferreira, "Barriers and Therapeutic Impasses Encountered When Both Client and Therapist Share a Similar Cultural Base"

Maureen O'Mara, "Acquiring Meeting Skills in Psychotherapy"

And this year, the Distinguished Psychologist Award went to Jack Krasner.

1978–1979

Jack Krasner died on October 6, 1978. His loss was keenly felt, and a memorial program in his honor was held at the Midwinter Meeting in Mexico City in February of 1979. The Jack D. Kras-

ner Memorial Fund was established to honor his memory. The
monies collected for this continuing fund were invested and the
proceeds of the investment were to be awarded as an annual prize.
As formulated initially, this prize was to go to a member of the
Division of Psychotherapy with a doctorate awarded no more
than 10 years prior to receipt of the award, who had made or was
making unusually significant contribution(s) in psychotherapy research, theory, or practice.

An ad hoc committee to study the nominations and elections
procedures of the Division was appointed by President Bob Harper, with Rachel Hare-Mustin as chair, and was directed to prepare recommendations for bylaws changes. Ellen McGrath and the
Program Committee were hard at work systematizing an evaluation procedure, with forms developed by the committee and
provided to program attendees for completion.

The APA had received a one-year contract from the NIMH to
conduct an assessment of research on psychotherapy and women
leading to recommendations for future research, with the project
being a cooperative effort of the Division of the Psychology of
Women and the APA's Women's Programs Office. Division 29's
CFW appointed Joy Kenworthy to represent us at the conference
being held. In recognition of the importance of this conference,
the Division voted a travel supplement for her. The CFW was
also working hard to disseminate and implement the "Principles
Concerning the Counseling and Therapy of Women," developed
by the Division 17 (Counseling) Ad Hoc Committee on Women
with contributions from many Division 29 members, and endorsed by Division 29. The CFW chair, Jaquie Resnick, noted in
one of her reports that Division 29 had been in the forefront of
standing up for equal rights by passing its own resolution to hold
its Midwinter Conference only in those states which had been
ratified by the ERA.

I'd also like to mention that this year the Division made a $250
contribution to the Committee Against Defamation of Scholars.
... and that in response to a questionnaire from the APA regarding reorganization, we responded emphatically against a split and
for an intact APA.

Gloria Gottsegen, going on sabbatical in June of 1979, gave up her post as Administrative Coordinator, and Ben Fabrikant agreed to assume some of those duties. The Committee on Reorganization of the Division, chaired by Annette Brodsky, recommended that the secretary and treasurer positions not be combined, that a central office be maintained, and that a non-psychologist staff it. It was in the minutes of the Executive Board Meeting held on March 3, 1979, that the name of Rhoda Schneider first appeared as an example of the type of office manager being suggested. The location of the central office was to be researched further, in particular regarding the possible advantages of locating near the APA. But a study of central office relocation revealed that moving to Washington would about double our costs, and the board voted to remain in New Jersey for at least another two years.

Jules Barron was appointed as Division 29's representative to a Division 12 Commission charged with drafting criteria for Fellow status appropriate to clinicians. (Some issues never seem to get resolved. . . .)

Thanks to a special assessment, the Division covered its expenses for the year. But we were facing a 1980 deficit budget. This with a membership which stood at 3,803 in July of 1979, including 128 Fellows! The Board voted to raise the Division assessment to $25 in 1980, and to keep the journal as a free subscription to members. This was the first assessment increase in 10 years, and it would keep our budget balanced while allowing the Division to continue its work, providing direction and services appropriate to the Division of Psychotherapy.

This year's Distinguished Psychologist Award went to Max Siegel, in recognition of his many contributions as an academic and a practitioner. And the Student Travel Scholarship awards for presentations at the 1979 APA Convention went to:

Richard C. Baker, University of New Mexico, "The Effect of Length of Session on the Development of Relationships: A Psychotherapy Analogue"

Noa Wieselberg Bell, University of California at Davis School of Medicine, "Comparative Effectiveness of Biofeedback and Brief Psychotherapy in Alleviating Tension Headache"

John C. Patterson and Steven M. Osborn, Texas A&M University, "Psychotherapy Outcome Models for the Independent Practitioner"

1979–1980

Jack Wiggins was president of our Division this year, and led us through a year of growth and purposeful activity. By 1980, the Division's budget was almost $180,000, and we were solvent! Ben Fabrikant was functioning as our Administrative Coordinator, with Rhoda Schneider as his able secretary, and the Division had a payroll! Under the leadership of Jules Barron, we were developing a psychotherapy brochure, and working on the third volume of *Creative Developments* (with Barron as senior editor). Ernst Beier resigned as Bulletin editor, and Ben Fabrikant was selected to replace him. And the journal published a special issue on "Values in Psychotherapy."

It was at the February board meeting that Vin Rosenthal received a special award "for his foresight, vision and dedication in initiating, developing and nurturing the Division's Midwinter Meetings from 1970–1973," and Jules Barron was selected to receive the Division's Distinguished Psychologist Award. Also at that time, the composition of the nominating committee was changed, on the recommendation of Rachel Hare-Mustin, and under the new system, the Nominations and Elections Committee was to be chaired by the president-elect, with two members elected by the Board and two appointed by the president from the membership at large. Concerns about reimbursement policies for women's and children's psychotherapy were routed by the CFW to a Division 29 committee, chaired by Max Siegel, to investigate the issues involved. Our Program Committee, chaired by Ellen McGrath and Alice Rubenstein as associate chair, had done a remarkably fine job, and the Board of Convention Affairs had requested the forms they had developed and the brochure done by

Canter and McGrath, to use as models for other Divisions. The Committee on Group Psychotherapy was preparing to apply for section status and "Burnout" written by Herb Freudenberger came out and appeared in a full-page ad in the *New York Times*, placed by the publisher, Doubleday.

By the August 1980 board meeting, at the close of the 1979–1980 year, the Division decided to combine the journal's business/clerical functions and locate them in the central office of the Division, and the policy was established at this meeting that chairs of standing committees be reimbursed for attendance at midwinter meetings.

At the Council meeting, a revision of the APA Ethical Principles was discussed, and postponed until the adjourned meeting in early 1981. There was also heated discussion on the floor of the Council about the formation of a new Division, the Division of Independent Practice. The Council approved the formation of a Division of Psychology and Law, but defeated the formation of an Independent Practice Division. While a majority of the Council favored its establishment, they did not constitute the two-thirds majority necessary for approval. The defeat was widely interpreted by supporters of a new division, many of whom were members of the Division of Psychotherapy, as a direct vote by academic/research interests against private-practice interests in the APA. Many old wounds were opened during the discussions, and issues of the need for APA reorganization were raised.

Looking at the Bulletins of the Divisions, I was struck by the breadth of concerns addressed: concerns of practitioners regarding substantive psychotherapeutic issues; reimbursement and insurance matters; organizational concerns regarding the profession; master's-level psychotherapists, etc., etc., etc.

1980–1981

Our president, Herb Freudenberger, was writing in the Bulletin about "burnout," and urging us as a division to be sensitive to our colleagues, and to further the development and improve the competence of younger colleagues not only via continuing education opportunities at our midwinter and national meetings, but also via encouraging their participation in Divisional governance.

As of January 1, 1981, all journal business operations were being conducted out of the Division's central office in River Edge, New Jersey. How many of us remember sending correspondence to Helen Merwede, Journal Business Manager, Division of Psychotherapy, at 912 Kinderkamack Rd. in River Edge?

The January 1981 meeting of the Council was memorable. Roberts' Rules of Order were replaced by Keesey's Modern Parliamentary Procedure. And finally a new code of ethics was adopted, after much discussion, revision, and debate. It was at this meeting, too, that Division 42, the Division of Independent Practice, was established. As described by one of our Council representatives, Ron Fox, "Following heated, impassioned, and, occasionally, enlightened argument on behalf of the new division by Council representatives from Division 29, 12, and numerous state associations, the opposition was eroded. . . ." (Oops, I forgot to reference this—but I *did* see it in print.)

At the 1981 midwinter board meeting, resolutions were passed in support of generic licensure for psychologists, with certification authorizing the use of specialty titles to be reserved for psychologists who previously had met statutory requirements for generic licensure and with the adoption of a position opposing nonstatutory credentialing or specialty credentialing as alternatives to generic licensure. The Board also communicated to the APA Board of Directors and the Council its support for the prompt implementation and continuance of an effective mechanism for publicly identifying doctoral training programs in psychology, recommending that such a mechanism be based upon objective criteria for program evaluation and constituted with interorganizational representation from educational, professional, and credentialing bodies; that such a mechanism not be limited to the designation of clinical, counseling, and school psychology programs or programs educating health service provider psychologists.

Discussion also centered around the Division's proceeding with explorations of the commission of a nontechnical paper showing the efficacy of verbal psychotherapy; another detailing the implications of the cost offset in efficacy of psychotherapy in health care, targeting businesspeople, labor leaders, and workers; and one distinguishing psychotherapy from welfare, written from a business point of view. It was hoped that these papers would illuminate psychotherapy's potential contributions to the educational, judiciary, and penal systems, and to the development of a stable society through resolving conflicts within marriages and families. The Board voted $10,000 for the writing of these position papers and $5,000 for a Task Force on Psychotherapy Research, being hopeful of matching funds from the APA's Board of Directors for this efficacy project.

There was also need expressed for a behavioral classification system as a reimbursement alternative to DSM-III, a classification tied to treatment outcome rather than to descriptive symptomatology.

Dr. Art Teicher had spearheaded a drive to form a Group Psychotherapy Section within the Division, and at the midwinter board meeting, its formation was approved in principle. And I noted that the journal's special issue for 1981 was on "Theory and Practice of Group Psychotherapy."

It was also at this board meeting that the question was raised about exploring the inclusion of other Divisions of APA in our midwinter planning. The Board voted that Kay Standley, Chair of the 1982 Midwinter Meeting contact Divisions 12, 39, and 42 as well as the American Group Psychotherapy Association, to explore the idea of a joint Midwinter Meeting.

Candidates for office this early in the decade were all talking about the need for the Division to serve in the APA as a major voice for psychotherapy as a science and profession, to maintain its proactive stance in fostering the acceptance of psychologists as psychotherapists, and to work for social programs to contribute to the public good. Presentations were focusing on the need to influence public policy affecting health service providers, on the promotion of mental health as well as the prevention of mental illness, and, at home, on APA organization and the complex issues facing psychotherapy. These issues were seen as requiring broad understanding and a willingness to make difficult decisions regarding standards for education, training, practice, and research in psychotherapy, and to reflect the emerging needs of various groups and their effect on the family and society. The Division had the foresight to investigate the concept of a model National Professional School program which would integrate training in professional psychology with public policy.

Bylaws changes were voted this year, which provided for student affiliates, developed a mechanism for establishing and maintaining sections, added to and described standing committees, and made changes in the nominations and elections procedures. The following ad hoc committees were designated as standing committees: Fellows, Continuing Education, Finance, Publications Board, Committee for Women, and Ethnic Minorities. The defunct Ethics Committee was deleted.

A search committee, chaired by Carl Zimet, was set up to find a new editor for the journal, and the revised bylaws were adopted, with a large vote of thanks to Annette Brodsky for this work. The Publications Board completed its public information brochure on psychotherapy, written by Jules Barron and Ben Fabrikant and called "Psychotherapy and Psychologist," and the *Creative Contributions* publication effort was terminated.

At the final board meeting held in August of 1981 at the APA Convention, the president highlighted some of the year's activities: an upcoming meeting of the officers of professional divisions to be held during the APA convention; the establishment of a National Commission on Mental Health; work in progress on the possibility of a National Professional School; an active, visible Ethnic Minorities Committee; establishment of a Committee on Contracting and Informed Consent; the Division's joining the Public Interest Coalition; the establishment of a liaison to Division 16; and the opening of the Midwinter Meeting to added sponsors. Karen Zager, History chairperson, raised questions concerning the submission of historic documents to the APA archives, and it was suggested that a legal opinion be solicited from the

APA regarding possible privacy issues where certain correspondence, for example, is concerned.

At the 1981 Convention, Student Travel Scholarships were
once again awarded, the winners presenting their papers at the
APA:

Lynn Rehm, Nadine Kaslow, and Adele Rabin, University
of Houston

Mavis Tsai, University of California

Laura Schnaps and Richard McKeon, University of Arizona

The 1981 Distinguished Psychologist Award went to Carl Zimet,
as deserving a recipient as could be wished for! And the first Jack
D. Krasner Memorial Award was shared by Annette M. Brodsky
and Gerald P. Koocher.

1981–1982

Many exciting things happened during the presidency of Ronald E. Fox! The 1982 Midwinter Meetings of Division 29 marked
a first: a cosponsor! Division 42 had accepted our invitation to
join us in 1982 in Monterey, California, and the meeting was a
very successful partnership ... so successful that the board voted
that from 1983 on, the Midwinter Meeting would be a joint meeting of Divisions 29 and 42, the Divisions of Psychotherapy and of
Independent Practice of the APA.

This was also the year in which we officially established our
first Section: Group Psychotherapy. Chaired by Art Teicher, with
Jules Barron as secretary, Harold Greenwald as treasurer, and
Morris Goodman, Bert Schwartz, Fern Azima, and Saul Tutman
as Board Members, the Section developed its bylaws and established liaisons to the Executive Board, the Division's Publications
Board, and the Division's Program Committee. The Section's mission was seen as fostering, advancing, and developing the practice
and theory of group psychotherapy as an autonomous reparative
modality and milieu within the mental health field. According to
Art's "Inaugural Statement" in the *Psychotherapy Bulletin* (Vol. 16,

No. 2, p. 20), "As our understanding of group psychotherapy becomes more sophisticated and theoretically more substantial, we recognize the need for criteria which will depict differences between modality and technique, between reparative, prophylactic and developmental purpose. There is also a need for clarification of the differences between group organizational (group dynamics) and group psychotherapeutic processes. ... This new modality involves not only new parameters but different processes of interpersonal interaction that both produce as well as reflect a totally different context and milieu for reparative mental health purposes. ... To fulfill this mission without fragmenting or splintering the organizational structure or purpose of Division 29 is the desire of those who are active in forming the Group Psychotherapy Section ... The aims and objectives of the new Section are to enhance both the pragmatic and/or administrative functions that are an integral part of the practice of group psychotherapy such as the establishment of training criteria, confrontation of the clinical-ethical, therapeutic, and legal aspects of the issue of confidentiality; problems of insurance reimbursement relevant to group psychotherapy practice, licensing, and accreditation. ..."

At our midwinter board meeting, central office functioning was reviewed, and everyone was very pleased with the way the office was being run, with the utilization of computerized techniques in the management of the office and with Ben Fabrikant's plans to add appropriate software. His term as Administrative Coordinator was extended through 1987.

The Division's financial condition was very strong, and the Board voted, on recommendation of the Finance Committee, that $20,000 be appropriated from the Division's reserves, to be donated to the special projects funds of the Association for the Advancement of Psychology (AAP). These special project funds were designed for professional interests, the original reason for their creation having been the JCAH challenge on hospital privileges. A $5,000 contribution was allocated to PLAN, a separately incorporated organization managed by the AAP, whose sole purpose was political action. President Ron Fox was planning to meet with other Divisions to try to develop a coordinated strategy of division involvements regarding political action. Another significant action at the board meeting was the authorization of funds to hold a board retreat in May 1982 to articulate the Division's goals and priorities, with their financial implications.

One of the most exciting experiences for Division 29 Executive Board Members—and directly for the membership at large—was that retreat, held on May 14–16 in New York, under the dynamic leadership of President Ron Fox. It was a memorable meeting at which everyone worked hard—and successfully—to develop specific courses of action to at least begin the process of addressing some of the serious issues which were confronting us. It was a retreat which had as its goal action rather than impressive speeches or ineffective position statements. The significant actions and interactions of the retreat really reflected five major areas of concern: quality control and access to the profession; advocacy and social/ethical responsibility; redefinition and implementation of psychological practice; marketing; and utilization of psychological organizations. It ended with 23 actions that were taken by the Board, and included establishment by Division 29 of:

- A Public Relations and Information Committee with an initial charge detailing a number of issues and problems of concern to a broad segment of our membership
- A Task Force on Professional and Public Advocacy
- An Ad Hoc Committee on Professional Education and Training with a specific charge
- A Task Force on Models of Professional Education, Training, and Practice for Psychology, charged with writing a proposal for a "house of our own" and developing/defining essential characteristics of professional education, credentialing, licensure, and definition of specialty areas for further consideration
- An ad hoc committee to study implications of the PUPI (Psychologists' Use of Physical Interventions) report for Division 19 and to formulate suggestions for action
- An Ethical Advisory Committee

In additional actions coming out of the retreat, a variety of proposals were made to the APA Board of Directors, in line with addressing the above-mentioned areas of concern.

At the retreat it was decided to ask the midwinter Program Committee to plan a future retreat meeting on the topic of promoting a broad definition of psychotherapy and psychological practice, and to request the committee to study the feasibility of devoting a program every 6 to 10 years to international or multicultural approaches to psychological problems. The BPA was asked to develop an information package for psychologists interested in becoming involved in reimbursement review mechanisms established by various third parties (insurance companies, HMOs, etc.) And the BPA was to be informed of Division 29's retreat actions which would be of particular concern to them and requested, along with COPP and COLI, to seek relief from medical practice acts regarding the right of psychologists to advise the reduction or elimination of medication in certain instances and to study the effect of state medical practices acts on the unrestricted practice of psychology.

Once again, the Division decided to write the presidents of Divisions 12, 38, 39, and 42, this time summarizing some of the results of the retreat and asking their reactions to the idea of a meeting of division presidents to deal with issues of common concern to the applied divisions. And to help support (with the APA and several other applied Divisions) a project conducted by an external firm to compile data on the costs of providing mental health coverage or for augmenting existing benefits in private insurance plans, they voted to allocate $2,500 immediately, with up to an additional $2,500 committed for the next fiscal year, if needed, and provided that other groups agreed to pay their share. It was quite a retreat!

The Distinguished Psychologist Award for 1981 was presented to Arthur Kovacs, editor par excellence, our golden-tongued—and golden-penned—creative thinker and gift to psychology.

An interesting article appeared in the *Psychotherapy Bulletin*, Vol. 16, No. 4, was Stanley Graham's "A Suggestion for the Development of a National Residency Program in Professional Psychology." In the same issue, the Division's Committee for Women published the results of their survey of the lifestyle and work patterns of psychotherapists in the Division of Psychotherapy. Not surprisingly, men and women responding to the questionnaire had similar degrees, specialty areas, and number of years in the profession, but in terms of rewards and recognition (salary, ABPP, and Fellow status), women were far behind men, who reported working more paid hours, whereas women worked more unpaid professional hours and spent more hours in home/child care.

Donald K. Freedheim was selected by the board as the next editor of *Psychotherapy: Theory, Research and Practice*, to take over from Art Kovacs in the fall of 1983. This year, the Division published four issues of its Bulletin and four issues of its journal plus a special issue entitled "Psychotherapy in Later Life." And approximately 20,000 public service brochures on psychotherapy, printed by the Division, were distributed to state psychological associations, other organizations, and psychotherapists, for a minimal fee. Fran Pepitone-Rockwell was reviewing all articles going into the journal for sexist language and removing such language. The consciousness of the Division was really kept raised!!

The Ethnic Minorities Committee was very active, and established a newsletter and network among members interested in minority issues related to psychotherapy theory, practice, and research.

And Student Travel Scholarships were forthcoming for the following talented students:

Carl Stoltenberg, Brian McHeill, Richard Pierce, and Lane Ogden, "Examining the Developmental Levels and Needs of Therapists-in-Training"

Robert G. Sutton, "Negative Clinical Bias Toward Lower Socioeconomic Groups: Some New Findings"

Stephen J. Naifeh, "The Live-in Therapist: Some Problems and Possibilities"

The Division was involved in developing informed-consent

procedures for psychotherapy, a controversial topic which the Division had a strong commitment to examining.

The Division was extremely concerned also about the processes under which the APA Membership Committee made decisions regarding new Fellow status in 1982, and submitted two resolutions to the APA Council. The first asked that the Policy and Planning Board of the APA draft a bylaw amendment which would define the membership of the Membership Committee of the APA to consist of two members each from the research/academic, public/social, and professional/practice sectors of the association. The second resolution requested that the Membership Committee of the APA submit the guidelines for its decisions to the Council of Representatives for ratification as official policy of the association to be officially included in the rules of the Council.

We were also pleased with the election of Ron Fox, our fearless leader, under whose stewardship Division 29 had accomplished so much, to the Board of Directors of the APA.

1982–1983

Jack Chwast, our president, saw us through another busy year. In the aftermath, of its generous contributions to worthy causes, this year was one of financial austerity for the Division, but as a result of close budgeting and cost containment in all programs, and an increase of 540 in membership, we were able to hold our own and expected to break even.

Committees continued to be very active. Division liaison relationships were established with Division 17 (Counseling Psychology) and Division 42 (Independent Practice). The Public Information Committee developed a media directory questionnaire as part of compiling of a directory of members willing to share their professional expertise via TV appearances, radio, public media (letters to the editor, newspaper columns, etc.), or legislative consulting. The Ethnic Minority Affairs Committee announced with delight the election of former chair Maxine Rawlins to the APA Board of Ethnic Minority Affairs. The EMAC was active in addressing the concerns of ethnic minority psychotherapists and their clients, successfully increased ethnic minority presentations at conventions, and enhanced Divisional liaisons with other APA ethnic minority bodies. The EMAC was instrumental in helping the Massachusetts Psychological Association to form its own Committee on Ethnic Minority Concerns. Since the Division had supported the appointment of Maxine Rawlins as its BEMA liaison, we were particularly pleased to learn that, largely on her impetus, BEMA had decided to establish an interdivisional caucus to provide a mechanism for increased liaison among interdivisional ethnic minority groups. The EMAC was also active in giving input to state legislators regarding the training and licensure of psychologists.

The Committee on Independent Practice, chaired by Stanley Graham, noted that 85% of the Division's membership was interested in issues of practice, and was focusing on areas of peer review, master's-level issues, and the organization of health providing services. The Committee on Professional Education and Training, chaired by Ben Fabrikant, was working to put together a list of postdoctoral programs in psychology, particularly psychotherapy, throughout the United States and Canada, and was also exploring postdoctoral clinical respecialization programs.

If you recall, at the May 1982 board retreat, a task force was appointed to develop a model of professional education, training, and practice for psychology. Art Kovacs, Ron Fox, and Stanley Graham put their heads together and, throwing caution to the winds, came up with a provocative, intriguing, sometimes revolutionary set of ideas designed not as a "final word," but rather as a catalyst for creative input from all of us. Some of the principles they set forth for discussion involved schools of psychology affiliated with accredited universities for graduate education and training in professional psychology; the Psy.D. as the appropriate degree; education and training to be at the doctoral level, at least four postbachelor years, and generic, following the practitioner/ scientist model; professional schools to organize curricula to provide master's-level people the opportunity to earn the doctorate, and provide a track for part-time study; specialization to be offered initially to advanced students and specialty training to be undertaken only in well-defined postdoctoral sequences; that the APA should proceed to develop a mechanism for the identification of specialties in professional psychology, and that the current specialties should be updated, with the most likely areas in need of review being psychotherapy, health/neuro/rehabilitation psychology, public health psychology, advocacy and public policy psychology, environmental psychology and psychopharmacology. If such ideas were to be implemented, it was recommended that licensure of psychologists be generic.

Our Group Psychotherapy Section was going strong, providing excellent programs at the APA, including an afternoon of conversation hours in the Division's Hospitality Suite. They reported receiving a telegram from the president of the American Group Psychotherapy Association congratulating them on finding a home within the APA. In their first official election, they gave a vote of confidence to their pro tem officers and committee who had worked on achieving section status and elected Arthur Teicher as chair, and Jules Barron as vice chair and chair-elect.

A bylaws change was proposed by the Board of Directors of the APA, relative to disputed elections, and was sent to the membership for their vote and approved by them.

For more than a decade, Division 29 had been holding midwinter meetings. The 1983 Midwinter Meeting, held at the Greenbrier in West Virginia, was the first one that was jointly sponsored. Combining forces with Division 42, the Division of Independent Practice, was a very successful, enriching experience, and it was decided to make this joint sponsorship permanent. Guidelines for the establishment and constitution of a Midwinter Convention Committee, with procedures for decision making delineated, were adopted by the Board. And Division 29 applied to, and was approved by, the American Psychologist Association as a sponsor of continuing education programs.

This year, the 1983 Student Travel Scholarship award winners made their presentations at the midwinter meeting held at the Greenbrier in West Virginia. They were:

Jack Wright, Richard Gilbert, and Harry Parad, Stanford University

Barbara J. Graham, University of Washington

David A. Miller, Iowa State University

Deborah I. Couk and Randall S. Cheloha, University of North Dakota

Many significant things happened in the arena of Division publications. Don Freedheim took over as editor of the journal, and we looked forward to continuing the tradition of excellence of one of the Division's most important contributions to its members and to psychotherapy! The psychotherapy brochure printed by the Division was revised to take into account the times when confidentially may have to be broken because of state or federal law. Upon recommendation of the Publications Board, the Division voted to change the name of its journal, *Psychotherapy: Theory, Research and Practice* to *Psychotherapy*, with the words "Theory, Research, Practice, and Training" on the lower legend of the page. This change came coincidentally with (and without knowledge of) the change in the name of the APA journal *Professional Psychology*, which added the words *Research and Practice* to its title. Interestingly, Don Freedheim had founded *Professional Psychology* in 1970. Ben Fabrikant edited his last issue of the *Psychotherapy Bulletin* (Vol. 17, No. 4), before handing the editor-elect, Laura Barbanel, the reins. And a Special Recognition Award was given to Fran Pepitone-Rockwell for her work in keeping the journal free of sexist-language.

The year's Distinguished Psychologist Award went to Herbert J. Freudenberger, psychotherapist, psychoanalyst, author, workshop leader, and active participant in APA and Divisional governance. The Jack D. Krasner Memorial Award was shared by Jaquelyn Resnick and Gary VandenBos.

1983–1984

I noted in a Committee for Women Report (*Psychotherapy Bulletin* Vol. 17, No. 4, p. 9) an acknowledgment that this Division "is presently adequately represented in officers and candidates for office by persons of both sexes ..." I believe this to be a measure of the ability of the Division's leadership (not surprisingly another "Old Boys' Club" in many respects at one time), not only to be open to having their collective social consciousness raised, but also to be willing to incorporate and act on what they had learned!

As the first woman president of the Division of Psychotherapy, I was handed the gavel at the annual business meeting of the Division, held at the APA in August 1983. (I must confess, it was really a special experience!) There were then three women on the Administrative Committee (Secretary Suzanne Sobel and Treasurer Shirley Sanders, in addition to me, Matty Canter). With past President Jack Chwast and President-elect Ernst Beier, we were the group that, along with the Board Members-at-large, had the 1983–1984 service year extended for an extra four months to December 31, 1984, in order for the Division to change to a calendar-year-based schedule, to fit with our budget year, APA office terms, etc. The president started something new that year: sending monthly updates to the Board Members and committee chairs to keep them apprised of what was going on for the Division between regularly scheduled meetings, as, for example, correspondence, requests for action, etc.

We were saddened by the death, on September 12, 1983, of Gordon Derner, a past president of the Division, and organizer of the first school of professional psychology in the country at Adelphi University, where he served as dean and professor of psychology at the Institute of Advanced Psychological Studies. He was a distinguished colleague who made a significant contributions to professional psychology, and was a wise, warm, and gentle man.

The 1984 Midwinter Convention of Divisions 29 and 42 was held in San Diego, with Division 39 overlapping. At the CFW meeting there, it was noted that Hannah Lerman was in the process of annotating the extensive bibliography she had developed on "Sexual Exploitation in Psychotherapy" and support of the Division was reaffirmed by its additional funding for this project.

It was voted at the 1984 Midwinter Meeting that the title of our major professional award be changed to: "Distinguished Psychologist Award for Contributions to Psychology and Psychotherapy." It was felt that this would better reflect the Division's mission, and the amended title was unanimously adopted by the Board. Robert A. Harper—Bob Harper to almost all of us—was unanimously selected to receive the Distinguished Psychologist Award for 1984, which was presented to him at the business meeting of the Division held during the APA meeting in Toronto, in August. Ronald F. Levant, a family therapist was named recipient of the Jack D. Krasner Memorial Award. The Student Travel Scholarship award winners, who presented their papers during the APA Convention in Toronto, were:

Sharon Harrison and Suzanne E. Weld, University of Ottawa

Sarah Anderson-Powell, Illinois School of Professional Psychology

M. Katherine Hudgins, Virginia Commonwealth University

Moli-Dawn Terrell, Michael Neale, Rick Ochberg, Lisa Silverstein, Jefferson Singer, and Richard Sussman, Yale University

Keeping in mind our multiple interests involving psychotherapy, we needed to direct our strongest efforts not only toward our survival in the marketplace and our inclusion in legislation concerned with the provision of health services, but also toward programs involving training and research in the area of psychotherapy. We took a very active role in encouraging and supporting the APA's focus on these issues, and in providing input in those instances where we believed we could and should have an impact. At our February executive board meeting, we appointed and funded Suzanne Sobel as our Observer to the BPA Subcommittee on Professional Services Review (SOPSR) and recommended her appointment to the SOPSR. We gave $1,000 in financial support to the Group for the Advancement of Psychotherapy and Psychoanalysis in Psychotherapy as it geared up to take action against the American Psychoanalytic Association, not only to fight the exclusion of psychologists from psychoanalytic training, etc., but also because the basic issue appeared to be psychiatry's escalating attempts to re-medicalize psychotherapy in general.

As president I wrote many letters for the Division expressing our concerns and viewpoints. We were in contact with the president of the APA regarding a proposed CHAMPUS joint venture agreement with the American Psychiatric Association for peer review, and our concerns, and those of other practitioner-oriented divisions, were apparently heard by the APA governance and modifications were negotiated which would be more protective of our peer status with psychiatry in CHAMPUS matters. We requested Mike Pallak, APA's Executive Officer, to secure a legal opinion regarding an issue of breach of confidentiality of the doctor/patient relationship in psychotherapy when an insurance claim is filed. We recommended that the BPA reestablish a Committee on Health Insurance to address the issues involved and implementations appropriate for fostering the recognition of psychological services by the insurance industry. We sent Evelyn Hill as our Observer to attend a BPA meeting, and a joint meeting of the BPA and the APA Insurance Trust. And we were particularly gratified to note that the APA extended a special invitation to all APA Divisions interested in professional issues, to send representatives.

The Group Psychotherapy Section established a Peer Review Committee under the leadership of Malcolm Marks and Larry Kutash, to define and designate the problems of peer review in group psychotherapy and develop principles related to peer review for group psychotherapy.

The Division was approved as a continuing education sponsor by the APA, thereby increasing its potential for becoming instrumental in providing high-quality continuing education experiences regarding psychotherapy for our membership. Once again, at the suggestion of the Division's Continuing Education chair, Aaron Canter, the Board voted to recommend to the APA that the APA CE Committee immediately develop procedures to grant APA CE credit for attendance at national, regional, state, and midwinter meetings; to substantially reduce fee requirements, reports, and research requirements for APA Divisions and state associations; and, if necessary, to have the Council intervene in order to make the APA CE Committee more responsive to divisional, state association, and membership needs.

Responses received to the principles concerning education, credentialing, and licensure, developed by Fox, Graham, and Kovacs, included one from the Council of Schools of Professional Psychology, and one indicating that the BPA would be considering the principles. (Responses seemed to have, perhaps, lost sight of the thrust of the principles—catalytic, not conclusive—and the matter was referred to the Committee on Graduate Education and Training.)

As president I wrote a series of letters to the APA requesting a change in procedures to enable new members of Divisions to be placed on the divisions' rolls more frequently. As I observed at the time, when a system does not meet the needs of the membership, it is time to change the system, not adjust to the unmet needs! And the system was indeed changed, making the addition of new members to divisions easier and more timely.

At its retreat, the Board discussed organizational problems of the APA, and what developed was a sense that there was not an urgency for a total reorganization, but rather that a change in some of the procedures might be useful. The board passed a resolution that the originator of a Council item be kept up to date on the item, whether or not that individual was still on the Council, this resolution to be referred to the Committee on Structure and Function of the Council, or introduced to the Council by our Council representatives, should the CSFC not act. In addition, the president of the Division was instructed to write to the chair of the Policy and Planning Board of the APA, requesting reactivation of the APA Committee on Organization, reconstituted with new members. The Division's own Committee on Organization was instituted, to be chaired by Jack Wiggins, and charged with making recommendations to the Division on the organization of the APA and with designing some creative legislation.

I was also asked to write to the AAP regarding the Reagan Administration's proposal to place a cap on the amount of dollars which could be used to purchase health insurance as a tax-deductible item and to write to the APA regarding the general mood in Congress to provide insurance converge for the unemployed.

The Division stayed within budget this year, but had to vote a $5 increase in the assessment for 1985. The increase was clearly felt to be more desirable than cutting the Division's activities on behalf of the membership! We were very proud of our journal, which was publishing four issues a year, plus special issues—this year's being on "Psychotherapy with Children and Youth." We now had about 5,000 members in our Division and seemed to be growing slowly but steadily, despite new Divisions which were drawing from the same pool as we. But probably as the result of a related phenomenon, we were advised that the Division had lost a seat in the 1985 apportionment ballot and would therefore have only three seats on the 1985 Council. We noted a letter from Dick Mikesell, speaking for the newly formed Division 43, the Division of Family Psychology, thanking us for our strong support during their efforts to attain Divisional status. Did our seat go to them?

1985

Taking the helm on January 1, 1985, were President Ernst Beier, President-elect Suzanne Sobel, past President Matty Canter, Secretary Ellen McGrath, and Treasurer Shirley Sanders.

At the February board meeting in Miami Beach, the illness of Ben Fabrikant, our Administrative Coordinator, was noted with much distress. An Ad Hoc Committee to Establish Guidelines for Central Office Functioning was created, with the mission of reviewing central office functions and making recommendations not only as to how the office could function more effectively, given its increasing duties and complexities, but also concerning how that office should function if the Administrative Coordinator is unable to perform his or her duties, for whatever reason. The committee was asked to report back at the August board meeting.

At this meeting, Stanley R. Graham, practitioner, trainer, educator, organizer, etc., etc., etc., was selected to receive the Distinguished Psychologist Award, and Raymond A. DiGiuseppe, an outstanding young research/practice/training psychologist active with the Rational Emotional Therapy Institute, was named to receive the Jack D. Krasner Memorial Award. The board also voted to give Ben Fabrikant a special Distinguished Service Award. At the April Administrative Committee meeting, the following was created for it:

> "To Dr. Benjamin Fabrikant, a man of stature in psychotherapy who by years of dedication and effectiveness as administrative coordinator has contributed significantly to the growth and maturation of the Division of Psychotherapy, American Psychological Association, 1985."

On May 12, 1985, Ben Fabrikant, our central office coordinator, former Bulletin editor and Midwinter Meeting chair, esteemed colleague and good friend, died. Ben was an essential ingredient of our growth and development as a division. He was to be much missed. With Ben's illness and death, the central office underwent some times of crisis, as new people stepped in on a part-time basis to try to keep us afloat, with mixed success. In the spring of 1985, President Ernst Beier asked Rhoda Schneider, an 11-year employee of the central office, to take over our functions on a part-time basis until the August board meeting, and she graciously (and charitably) agreed to do so. The crisis was weathered, and the Committee on Central Office was commissioned to investigate management firms with a view toward going to that form of central office functioning. Bids were received from Rhoda Schneider, as well as from Washington, DC, and Phoenix, AZ, management firms. At the August board meeting, after lengthy debate and soul-searching, it was decided to pursue the search by securing more data from the interested parties, and to give the Search Committee the authority to make the final decision. After much discussion not only of relative costs, but also the goals of the Division, it was decided to contract with the Administrators, the Phoenix firm, because of their broad capacities, their desirable financial proposition, and the presence of a Divisional past president to provide local supervision. A three-year contract with a three-month nonpenalty cancellation clause was signed, which provided for the general functions of the central office, as well as work related to the journal, the Bulletin, and some Midwinter

Meeting tasks. Matty Canter was appointed Administrative Liaison and was directed to attend both Executive Board and Administrative Committee meetings. A date of October 12 was scheduled for moving the central office equipment and materials from New Jersey to Phoenix and Matty agreed to sort out the materials packed and shipped by Rhoda Schneider when they arrived in Phoenix, and to help the new central office administrator, Pauline Wampler, and our "account executive," Marie Timberlake, to organize the office and the files. It was agreed that the Division would request a "compilation and review" of our finances once the new central office was reestablished. Marvin Stein, CPA, was designated as the new accountant for the Division.

During the time of crisis in the central office, Rhoda Schneider really managed to keep us from having to close up shop and we owed her a tremendous debt. Even though we had not chosen to contract with her to take over management of the central office (a decision based on the felt need for a resource with broader capability), she cooperated fully and graciously in seeing us through our crisis and in the difficult job of packing up the central office and moving it from New Jersey to Arizona. Rhoda was honored and given a gift by the Division at the 1986 Midwinter Meeting, to which she and her husband were invited.

The Program Committee, chaired by Harold Bernard, reported a very successful year, with submissions so numerous that a 60% rejection rate was the result. Don Freedheim, in his journal report, indicated that he was instituting a Book Review Section, with Mary Jansen as its editor. The journal's special issue in 1985 was on "Psychotherapy with Ethnic Minorities." And the struggle to have the APA award continuing education credit for meeting attendance continued.

The following 1985 Student Travel Scholarship awardees were invited to present their research at the 1985 APA Convention in Los Angeles:

Lynne E. Angus, York University, Ontario, Canada

DeVera L. Foreman, University of Pennsylvania

Jacob I. Melamud, Northwestern University Medical School

Jeffrey L. Pickar, University of Michigan

At the retreat meeting of the board in August 1985, the strengths and weaknesses of the Division and plans for future directions were considered. It was felt that the Division had lost its momentum and "cutting edge" position as a leader in psycho-therapy issues and practice, becoming too diffuse as a specialty area. With the proliferation of other divisions with similar—though not necessarily identical—interests, and with the difficulty in developing clear directions and expertise in our advocacy/professional survival activities, it was agreed that our scholarship activities, particularly the journal *Psychotherapy*, were a great and unique strength of the Division. It was recommended that we invite Divisions with similar interests to meet with us at our 1986 Midwinter Meeting, to discuss coordinating activities more effectively, that we develop proactive strategies in the advocacy area, and that we unite with other professionals involved in health-care activities to define our common interests. It was recommended that the Division's central office become more involved in informing Division members and leaders of significant national issues related to psychotherapy.

The Publications Board, chaired by Jules Barron, reported that the brochure "Psychologists and Psychotherapy" was finished, and would be available shortly. Dr. Alice Rubenstein, the Membership chair, announced that the committee was able to have people automatically accepted for membership in the Division when they are accepted for membership in the APA, thus allowing our members to receive the journal faster and to participate in Divisional activities sooner. At this meeting, it was agreed to change the length of term of the Program Chair and Associate Program Chair to two years, instead of three, with the president appointing the Associate Chair every two years. Ellen McGrath, chair of the Public Relations and Information Committee, reported the development of a Division 29 media project, and presented a proposal to the Board regarding development of a videotape based on a lecture series at the New York Academy of Sciences on women's identity and eating disorders. The Board supported development of the videotape, as an experiment.

The Division's board suggested that malpractice insurance coverage for board members and officers be investigated, and that a Political Action Committee should be reorganized and become very active for the Division. Also, an elaborate bylaws change was suggested by the board to be sent to the membership for its vote.

Division 29 applied for acceptance as a Continuing Education sponsor, and was planning to reapply in 1986. For the 1986 Midwinter Meeting, on an experimental basis a new procedure was to be developed to proved Continuing Education credit for meeting attendance, with a $25 fee to cover expenses.

Plans were made to discuss, at the 1985 Midwinter Divisional Joint Board Retreat, proposals to promote programs where all the Divisions and state associations have the ability to grant Continuing Education credit, as does APA, without our groups having to pay $200 every few years and do an enormous amount of paperwork, as we currently must do in order to grant Continuing Education credit.

Stanley Graham presented to the board his interest in developing an advanced training program for psychologists, analogous to a medical residency.

The Division agreed to see the secretary, Ellen McGrath, and either Suzanne Sobel or Pat DeLeon, to the Division Leadership Conference scheduled for May of 1986. The conference was planned to help identify the mission of each division and provide leadership training. One of our delegates was asked to propose to the conference planners that he or she make a presentation at the conference sharing the extensive experience Division 29 had accumulated regarding organization of a division and the pros and cons of having a central office.

Gloria Gottsegen, outgoing Fellow chair, reported that 25 "old fellows" were elected to Fellow status in the division in 1985, and that a symposium honoring Fellows was being planned for the 1986 Midwinter Convention, a "first" such program for the Division.

1986

President Suzanne R. Sobel, President-elect Pat DeLeon, past President Ernst G. Beier, Secretary Ellen McGrath, and Treasurer Stanley R. Graham composed the Administrative Committee of the Division for 1986.

Harold Bernard, Program Chair, indicated that the division's program "theme" for the 1986 APA Convention was "Therapeutic Effectiveness: What Have We Learned?" In line with this theme, one of the Division's invited addresses was to be given by prominent Division member Hans Strupp.

President Sobel proposed, at the midwinter board meeting, that a Marketing Committee be constituted, perhaps as a joint venture with Division 42 to prevent duplication of efforts. The Board voted to establish a Task Force on Marketing and Promotion of Psychological Services (MAPPS) with Herb Freudenberger as chair, and directed that it work not only with Division 42, but also with other appropriate groups to establish a mechanism to ensure the integrity of psychotherapy practice.

The Division's Continuing Education Committee was asked to establish a liaison relationship with the APA's Continuing Education Committee, in an effort to provide better communication and understanding between us.

Our president attended the first Division's Leadership Conference sponsored by the APA in May of 1986, and noted her sense of pride in Division 29 for being way ahead of other divisions in servicing our members, for being in good shape financially, for being in line with federal IRS regulations, and for operating as an independent entity. We seemed to have everything that most Divisions did not have, that is, our own tax ID number, a central office, a midwinter convention, a newsletter, and a journal that we own. We had active committees reporting to the Board and working for our members, and we also did not seem to have problems with continuity, as so many other divisions did.

The Fellows Committee chaired by Gerry Koocher had as its priority this year the increase in recognition of Division 29 members who were already Fellows of other Divisions. The committee wrote to targeted individuals who were Fellows of other Divisions and who appeared to be good candidates for fellowship in Division 29, inviting them to apply under an expedited process. As a result of their efforts, 50 "old Fellows" were elected Fellows of Division 29.

The Ethical Advisory Committee, chaired by Joe Kobos, was asked to develop some guidelines for the transfer of patient records in the event of the death of a therapist. The Board of Division 29 unanimously endorsed these guidelines, which were published in the *Psychotherapy Bulletin* (Vol. 21, No. 1, pp. 5–7) and forwarded to the APA Committees on Professional Standards and Ethics.

An Ad Hoc Committee on Student Development was appointed to address the special needs and interests of graduate students. Liaisons were appointed to the task force on Scope of Accreditation, the APA Continuing Education Sponsor Approval Committee, and Division 20. Two members, Gerald Koocher and Patricia Hannigan, were appointed Divisional representatives to the APA Committee on Professional Standards regarding revision of the Standards for Providers of Psychological Services. At the request of Ernst Beier, the Research Committee was reinstated and charged with the responsibility of carrying out research projects on psychotherapy for the benefit of the membership. And the name of the Malpractice Committee was changed to Committee on Professional Liability.

A task force was appointed to study the structure of standing committees with respect to the bylaws and make recommendations at the August 1986 Executive Board Meeting.

At the annual business meeting of the Division, held in Washington, DC, in August, President Sobel reported on the many and varied activities of the Division, including a meeting she attended of APA and CIO-AFL leaders, designed to educate unions concerning the benefits to their members of psychological services, and responses to requests for input from the APA regarding the training of psychotherapists, and the model licensing statute being developed.

A joint meeting of the Boards of Division 29 and Division 42 was held at the Midwinter Meeting in order to work through some of the complex problems generated by joint sponsorship of Midwinter Meetings. At that meeting, it was agreed that Division 42 should share in the Midwinter Meeting costs that to date had been shouldered by Division 29. A proposal from the Administrators to provide services required was approved. Division 43 (Family Psychology) presented a request for inclusion as Midwinter Meeting sponsors. The Boards of Divisions 29 and 42 voted to extend an invitation, in principle, to Division 43 a partner for the 1987 Midwinter Meeting and for years beyond. Since Division 43 indicated that they were financially unable to assume a one-third share of the costs, it was voted that shares for profit and loss be assigned on a 5:5:2 basis, with annual adjustments.

An APA proposal to establish an Office of Divisional Affairs and a continuing Committee of Divisional Affairs was approved by the Board.

In February, Laura Barbanel resigned as Bulletin editor, and the Administrative Committee, working closely with Pauline Wampler of The Administrators, was acting as editor. A call for editor of *The Psychotherapy Bulletin* was issued. It was noted that the revised bylaws would be included as an insert in the next issue.

At the August 1986 board meeting, a task force was formed to provide information to the APA on issues of nonphysician healthcare provider statements which deal with professional practice. A Planning Committee was established, consisting of the president-elect, president, past president, and such others as need be appointed, its mission being to serve as a sounding board for the president-elect in developing his/her agenda for the next year. On the recommendation of the Committee for Women, the Board approved the sending of a letter by the president to the president of the American Psychiatric Association in support of a resolution against diagnostic abuses. Membership chair Evelyn Hill reported a membership of 4,639, plus 235 new members to be approved by the Board.

The Division's 1986 Distinguished Psychologist Award for

Contributions to Psychotherapy and Psychology was given to Ronald E. Fox, a former Division president, dean of the School of Professional Psychology at Wright State University, active in APA governance, and a very special pillar of professional psychology. Dr. G. Rita Dudley was the recipient of the 1986 Jack D. Krasner Memorial Award, honored for the many innovative programs she had developed at Boston City Hospital for multicultural clients. No applications were received for the 1986 Student Travel Scholarship awards. An Ad Hoc Committee on Student Development was formed to work on student recruitment, and to reexamine the student awards. Ellin Bloch was appointed chair, and Ernst Beier agreed to serve on the committee.

The Division worked well with the Administrators this year to improve the effectiveness of our services to members, streamline for our journal, and organize our procedures and policies. An updated and more comprehensive policy and procedures manual was being developed. The June meeting of the Administrative Committee was held in Phoenix. The President and the Treasurer met with the Division's accountant, who indicated that we were in line with IRS reporting forms, and that due to the transition, an extension had been applied for filing Form 990. Mr. Stein indicated that our former accountant, Larry Stoloff, had done an appropriate job in filing the necessary reports and all records were in order.

As a measure of the Division's wish to be involved in issues affecting its membership, liaisons were appointed to the Task Force on Scope of Accreditation (Matthew McDonald), APA Continuing Education Sponsor Approval Committee (Rachel Hare-Mustin), Division 20 (Aphrodite Clamar), and COPS, the Committee on Professional Standards, which was revising the Standards for Providers of Psychological Services (Gerry Koocher and Patricia Hannigan).

A task force was created to study standing committee structure with respect to the bylaws and was asked to report back to the Board in August of 1986.

The Graduate Education and Training Committee mission

statement was adopted by the Board. In addition to formulating and recommending policies concerning graduate education and training to the Board, particularly as related to the professional practice of psychotherapy by psychologists, the committee, chaired by Tommy Stigall, was authorized to develop position statements concerning graduate education and training on its behalf, following submission and approval by the Board. The committee was charge with broadly monitoring activities and trends in graduate education and training and to serve in an advisory capacity to the officers and board of the Division. The committee chair was authorized to serve in an observer/liaison capacity with respect to other organizations and units of the APA governance concerned with graduate education and training.

The Committee on Professional Liability, chaired by John Currie, and then by Elizabeth Stewart, a J.D./Ph.D. was just beginning its work, which was seen as serving as a resource for members on malpractice issues, informing members about malpractice, surveying the membership to identify areas of concern, and publishing relevant informational articles in *The Psychotherapy Bulletin*.

Clarification of legal issues around the development of the Public Relations Committee video was requested before any money be spent on this project.

The president was authorized to sign a contract with RPJ, which, for a modest annual fee of $42.32, would tape-record *Psychotherapy* for visually handicapped psychologists and distribute the material at cost to each visually handicapped member of the division. And speaking of *Psychotherapy*, the special issue for 1986 was on "Gender Issues in Psychotherapy."

The Division at the end of 1986 was clearly doing well. As our outgoing president indicated, it was a strong force within the APA, instrumental in getting the APA to work on marketing of psychological services. Our voice had been heard about the structure of the APA, and we served as a resource for other Divisions on organizational structural management, a valuable service to them. Our journal continued to be one of the most prestigious publications in the field of psychotherapy, publishing important and high-quality, timely manuscripts, with many graduate programs in psychology relying on the journal as a teaching tool. We needed to develop our advocacy role ... and that was likely to become a reality, particularly in view of the next president!

1987

With Pat DeLeon as president, Don Freedheim as president-elect, and Suzanne Sobel, Stanley Graham, and Ellen McGrath continuing as officers of the Division, we had another productive year. As Pat DeLeon pointed out in his presidential column in the *Psychotherapy Bulletin*, Vol. 21, No. 3, written right after the Midwinter Meeting, a great deal was accomplished at the midwinter board meeting. Support was given in principle to the efforts of the Section on Group Therapy to credential diplomates, and the functioning of the three-Division Midwinter Meeting was solidified. We began the process of searching for a new associate editor for special supplements, as well as business manager for the journal, with the clear recognition that *Psychotherapy* was, in fact, economically viable. The Board voted at its midwinter board meeting to pay the journal editors the same honorarium as the APA pays: $5,000 per annum for the editor, and $2,500 per annum for associate editors.

Possible bylaws changes were reviewed which would be sent on to the membership later in the year. A Task Force on the Elderly was established and funded, with Laura Barbanel as chair, as were several projects recommended by the women on the board. A Task Force on Adolescents chaired by Alice Rubenstein was set up, as was a mechanism whereby the Board would become more intimately involved with the functioning of our various committees. To facilitate the workings of the Division, Pat DeLeon instituted regular conference calls for the Administrative Committee, and a new monitoring system in which Administrative Committee members served as liaisons between the Administrative Committee and the Division's committees and task forces was established.

Wade Silverman was unanimously recommended by the Publications Board for the position of *Psychotherapy Bulletin* editor, and the board approved his appointment. Contributing editors were named with responsibility for providing regular articles in the following areas: Washington Scene, Stanley Graham; Medical Psychology, David Adams; News and Notes, Matty Canter; and Media, Marketing and Psychotherapy, Ellen McGrath. Donald K. Freedheim was strongly recommended by the Publications Board for continuation as editor of the journal, and the board appointed him for a second five-year term, a tribute to the esteem in which his work and the journal's high quality were held. In his annual report to the board and membership, Don reported that over 800 pages and nearly 100 articles had been printed in four issues this year, plus a special supplement on "Psychotherapy with Victims." Statistically, this was a banner year, with the highest number of articles and greatest number of pages published to date. And in addition, we had book reviews in each issue. At this point, the backlog of manuscripts held earlier had been taken care of and Don's goal was to speed up the publication process so that the winter issues would come out in the latter part of the calendar year.

After many drafts and detailed discussions, the bylaws were extensively revised, updated, and streamlined by Art Kovacs, approved by the Board of Directors, and sent to the membership for final approval (which was forthcoming). The Division participated actively in the Division Leadership Conference sponsored by the APA, sending both our president-elect, Don Freedheim, and our secretary, Ellen McGrath. Don was elected chair of the group designated to plan the 1988 Conference.

The Board gave Section 1 approval to proceed with developing diplomat status for its members, and hard as it is to let go of our children, the Board turned over to the freestanding Midwinter Meeting Committee the responsibility for site selection!

Treasurer Stanley Graham pointed out that the hiring of the Administrators was a financially efficient move for the Division, and that in 1986, for the first time, the journal showed a profit. At the August 1987 board meeting, a $5 reduction in Divisional dues was voted, and it was the first time in anyone's memory that an APA Division had reduced its dues! It was a triumph for Treasurer Stanley R. Graham and another first for Division 29!

At the APA Convention, we were able to sponsor a number of Divisional representatives to the various caucuses. Division 29 had taken the lead in bringing graduate students into the fold, with the establishment of a Student Development Committee under Ellin Bloch. Our Committees on Student Development and Ethnic Minorities (Lisa Porche-Burke) recruited more than 275 new student members, with 49 of these being minorities! Special commendations were expressed to Ellin Bloch and Lisa Porche-Burke. And to think that the year before we had only six student members! The Division clearly was thinking ahead by placing much importance on recruitment of potential colleagues!

The Board voted a $5,000 "forgivable loan" to help defray the expenses of the American Psychoanalytic Association suite, repayable only if the case is won and the plaintiff receives attorney's fees and court costs.

This was the year in which, at the suggestion of the APA Insurance Trust, we provided liability insurance coverage for the officers and Board of the Division. It was also the year in which we purchased a camera so that our *Bulletin* editor could take candid snaps at Divisional functions and we funded a new computer for our journal editor.

The 1987 Midwinter Meeting in New Orleans was the first to include Division 43 as a sponsor, and a joint retreat meeting of the Boards of the three sponsoring divisions, Divisions 29, 42, and 43, was an opportunity to discuss issues of critical importance to practitioner survival, such as access to hospital privileges, prescription privileges and training opportunities, and problematic forensic issues. Bryant Welch, Director of the newly designated APA Office of Professional Practice, addressed OPP's focus on practitioner issues.

Mathilda B. Canter was selected unanimously to receive the 1987 Distinguished Psychologist Award for Contributions to Psychology and Psychotherapy, in recognition particularly of her contributions on state and national levels to the regulation of psychology and the practice of the profession, as well as her role in facilitating the Division's central office move and the establishment of the new office. No Krasner Award was given, and a committee chaired by Gerry Koocher and including other prior recipients of the award was formed to look into the criteria for the Krasner Award, with the objective of creating an award that would have more recognition and impact.

The chair of our Ethnic Minorities Committee, Lisa Porche-Burke, was designated to serve as the Division's liaison to the new Division 45 (Society for the Study of Ethnic Minority Issues), which planned to cosponsor a social hour at the APA for ethnic minority psychologists.

Our Marketing Committee, spurred by Jack Wiggins, Ellen McGrath, and Herb Freudenberger, was very active, directing its energies, among other places, into collaboration with Divisions 42 and 43 on a project for which Division 42 had received a grant, for the establishment of a corporate consultation service. They planned to gather data from corporations on availability of psychological services. The Ethnic Minority Affairs Committee, in addition to working on student recruitment, was collaborating with Division 45 to produce a special collection of papers pertaining to ethnic minority issues in psychotherapy, education, and training, with Division 29 committing to $1,000 on this project. The Committee for Women, among other activities, was involved in distribution and updating of the Lerman Annotated Bibliography, as well as in the drafting of a "patients' rights" statement, and was working with the APA's Director of Women's Programs and Divisions 35 (Psychology of Women) and 42 (Independent Practice) in the development of resource materials. The Graduate Education and Training Committee under Tommy Stigall's chairmanship, was very active in coordinating with counterpart committees of other practitioner Divisions on matters of mutual concern, evaluating materials sent to Division 29 by APA groups for consideration, and planning and participation in programs. It also prepared some proposals regarding accreditation and exemption for school psychologists, and was asked by the Board to develop an intensive workshop and panel discussion for the 1988 Midwinter Meeting to examine the implications of the proposals.

Central office and the administrative liaison completed a *Policies and Procedures Manual*, which was compiled and sent to each member of the Executive Board.

In August, the Board passed a resolution introduced by Gloria Gottsegen that the National Committee on the Status of Women (CSOW) recommend to the local COSWs that they investigate conditions in jails and prisons in their areas, with special attention given to health care for pregnant women and for mentally and physically ill women.

Quite a year!

1988

With Donald Freedheim assuming the presidency, with Aaron Canter as president-elect, and Patricia (Trish) Hannigan as the newly elected secretary, plus Pat DeLeon and Stanley Graham composing the Administrative Committee, we were, as usual, in good hands.

During 1988, all four issues of Vol. 25 of the Division's journal were published, with a special issue on "Psychotherapy and the New Health Care Systems" printed. Operations of the journal went smoothly, not in small measure owing to the able assistance of Anne Mello at the Administrators, the Division's central office, who organized the many administrative tasks necessary for producing the journal, and who served as liaison to the printer, located in Utica, New York. Anne came on board in June of this year, replacing Marie Timberlake.

We noted with sadness the death of Max Siegel, one of the founders of our Division and a past president not only of Division 29, but also of Division 12, New York State Psychological Association, and of the APA. An educator as well as a practitioner, he could be accurately designated a father of professional psychology.

The Student Development Committee, with Board approval,

created an Annual Graduate Student Paper Competition to be implemented in 1988, winners to be given a monetary prize plus the opportunity to present their papers at a session during the annual APA Convention. The 1988 winners were:

First Place: Stephen M. Saunders, Northwestern University, "Correlation Between Therapeutic Bond and Treatment Effectiveness"

Second Place: Michael A. Ichiyama, University of Cincinnati, "Social Self Theory and Cognitive-Interpersonal Therapy: The Interface"

This was an exciting and gratifying year for the Student Development Committee! In April, Chair Ellin Bloch and Student Coordinators Scott Mesh and David Pilon met with the staff of the APA Office of Educational Affairs to investigate the range of possible activities that the APA might consider to increase student membership. Using as a model Division 29's success in recruitment, exciting possibilities were explored. Scott and David were invited by the APA OEA to address the Division Leadership Conference.

In February of 1988, at the request of the CFW, the Board passed a resolution voicing its opposition to federal regulations which restrict or prohibit the "provision of counseling concerning the use of abortion as a method of family planning or the provision of referral for abortion as a means of family planning."

A Division of Psychotherapy Media Hotline questionnaire was sent to the membership, and over 300 responses were received, rather than the 50–75 anticipated! Thanks to the ideas and energies of Ellen McGrath, Herb Freudenberger, and Don Freedheim, work was ongoing to develop a referral list from which the central office could provide media representatives with the names of appropriate resource people to contact for professional information.

The Task Force on Children and Adolescents planned programs for Midwinter and APA Meetings, as well as further work on legal and ethical issues in psychotherapy with children and adolescents. This year the task force focused on a possible brochure on psychotherapy with children and adolescents to be used by clinicians for parents.

Our Section on Group Psychotherapy reported rapid growth, and an enthusiastic membership. Their first directory already needed updating, and they had begun a newsletter, which was published and well received. Work continued toward the establishment of the ABPP diplomat specialty in group psychotherapy, and the Section's ultimate goal appeared to be the formation of a separate Division of Group Psychotherapy within the APA.

At the Midwinter Meeting in Scottsdale in February of 1988, a Coalition of Practice Divisions was formed, with Don Freedheim, Evelyn Hill, and Jack Wiggins as the nucleus. It was planned that presidents, presidents-elect, and past presidents of each Division would meet on a regular basis, and Divisions 29, 42, 43, 39, 12, and 17 were working toward further cooperation.

The membership recruitment drive, instituted by Membership chair Ron Levant and modeled after the Massachusetts Psychological Association's recruitment plan, appeared to be quite successful, though maximum benefit could not be assessed until some years later. The Membership Committee recruited 253 new members and 42 new associate members, bringing the total membership to 4,961 current dues-paying members.

In August of 1988, the American Psychological Association of Graduate Students (APAGS) was formed, the Division 29, through Student Development chair Ellin Bloch and our two Student Affiliates, Scott Mesh and David Pilon, being in the forefront in the formation of this organization. Division 29 helped by its giving initial financial support and encouraging Dr. Bloch to participate in APAGS' formation. The Division's Student Development Committee reported a student membership of 406, including 100 ethnic minority students. The committee also initiated a Student Legislative Internship in cooperation with the Hawaii Psychological Association.

At the 1988 Midwinter Meeting, held in Scottsdale, Mathilda B. (Matty) Canter, a past president of the Division, and Aaron H. Canter, president-elect of the Division, were honored at a reception for all attendees, arranged by the Scottsdale Camelback Hospital, a local psychiatric hospital, and the Maricopa and Scottsdale Psychological Societies, for their contributions on local, state, and national levels to psychology and to practice.

The Distinguished Psychologist Award for Contributions to Psychology and Psychotherapy was awarded to Ernst Beier, distinguished teacher, author, and ski expert! And the Jack D. Krasner Memorial Award went to Alice Rubenstein for her effectiveness not only in this Division's governance, but also for her growing recognition as a therapist, and a role model. How nice it was to see people pouring into the room to hear Ernst give his presidential address to an SRO crowd!

1989

Aaron Canter as president, Norm Abeles as president-elect, and Alice Rubenstein as treasurer: a good team, with Trish Hannigan and Don Freedheim to complete the officers' roster! As our secretary, Trish Hannigan wrote in our Annual Report, "The year 1989 was an active one for the Division of Psychotherapy. Overall, the Division continues to pursue its purposes of fostering collegial relations among members of the APA who are interested in psychotherapy, stimulating the exchange of scientific and technical information about psychotherapy, encouraging the evaluation and development of the practice of psychotherapy as a psychologist art and science, and educating the public regarding the services of psychologists who are psychotherapists, as well as promoting the general objectives of the APA."

During this year, under Tommy Stigall's chairmanship, our Committee on Education and Training, which had been working with similar committees in other practice divisions, became part of a Joint Commission on Professional Education in Psychology, established with Tommy Stigall as its chair, and including, in addition to Divisions 29, 42, 43, 39, 12, and 17, the American Association of State Psychology Boards, the Association of Psychology Internship Centers, and the National Council of Schools and Professional Psychology. Joint efforts such as this one would, it was hoped by the leadership of Division 29, avoid duplication, enhance communication and clout, and be facilitated via the Coalition of Practice Divisions now in existence.

The significance of the Joint Commission on Professional Education in Psychology was underscored by its receiving a grant from the Practice Directorate to further its work. And Tommy Stigall was named a member of the Interim Advisory Committee for an Education Directorate for the APA. A Special Commendation was voted for Tommy Stigall and presented to him by Division 29 at the social hour during the APA Convention, to acknowledge the magnitude and effectiveness of his efforts on behalf of the Division and the profession.

Others honored at that time were Jack Wiggins, Len Haas, and Matty Canter. Jack G. Wiggins, recipient of the Distinguished Psychologist Award for Contributions to Psychology and Psychotherapy, is a past president of Divisions 29 and 42, a practitioner whose contributions to psychology, psychotherapy, and psychotherapists over the years are immeasurable, a man of integrity and dedication. Leonard J. Haas, recipient of the Jack Krasner Memorial Award, was at the time a full-time member of the Department of Psychology at the APA Ethics Committee, a toiler in the field for Division 29 and the Midwinter Committee, and a role model for up-and-coming psychologists! Matty Canter was given a Special Award for her service as Administrative Liaison.

Despite growth in membership, the Division was faced with the choice of cutting back its activities or raising the divisional assessment after a short-lived reduction. It was strongly felt by the Board that this was no time to cut back on the Division's involvement in matters of importance to psychotherapy, and that even with the increase, members would be receiving excellent value for their dues. By mid-1989, our hard-working Membership chair, Ron Levant, was able to report the recruitment of 783 new members over the last 12 month period, an impressive total, given the proliferation of divisions tapping the pool from which Division 29 members were likely to come. And this year we won back a Council seat!

The two winners of the Student Paper Competition this year were:

First Place: Pam Hazelrigg, University of Missouri, "The Current Status of Closed Head Injury Family Therapy"

Second Place: Mark Koltko, New York University, "How Religious Culture Affects Psychotherapy: The Example of Mormonism"

The first place winner received $350: the second place winner $150. Both presented their papers at the APA Convention in New Orleans.

The Committee for Women had a busy year, participating in educational, professional, clinical, and public policy matters within the Division and in concert with representatives of other Divisions. They were continuing to pursue a distribution arrangement for the Lerman annotated bibliography. "Sexual Intimacies between Psychotherapists and Patients," which, since its original publication in 1984, had generated broad general interest and been a consistent source of revenue each year.

Under Ellen McGrath's leadership, the Committee on Professional Practice was finishing the coding of applicants for the Media Hotline, and focusing on developing marketing tools for psychotherapists, with a plan to pilot the project in New York, Los Angeles, and Phoenix. A very successful workshop at the Midwinter Meeting was led by Herb Freudenberger, and Ellen's absence was noted (but excused, as her second son was about to be born, and Division 29 has always been family-oriented and all that sort of thing)!

The Professional Liability Committee, ably chaired by Leon VandeCreek, published articles regularly in the *Psychotherapy Bulletin* all year, and saw to it that programming was provided our members and the profession in general at Midwinter and APA Conventions.

At the instigation of Norman Abeles, a Task Force on American Indian Mental Health was formed, with Diane Willis as chair, to work toward a National Conference on American Indian Mental Health. With initial funding from Division 29, the task force will seek monies from the APA and other relevant Divisions.

The Division's Task Force on Men's Roles and Psychotherapy, chaired by Ron Levant and Herb Freudenberger, was gaining attention, with a feature article in *The APA Monitor* reporting on Ron's development of a course which utilized life-span developmental psychology to help men in becoming better fathers. The task force was offering information to psychologists to assist men in becoming less bound up in traditional roles and to become freer, more nurturing, and more oriented toward expressing their feelings.

The CFW undertook a survey of the Division's membership about the depression patterns of their individual practices. A questionnaire on "Depression in Clinical Practice" was included in the *Psychotherapy Bulletin*, Vol. 24, No. 1. In the main, responses yielded trends similar to those found by the APA Task Force on Women and Depression, chaired by Ellen McGrath. Depression in women was seen as truly widespread and deep in our society, respondents showing divided opinions about medication and the role of psychologists in recommending medication as an adjunct to treatment, in treating patients who are on medication, and in prescribing medication themselves. The CFW also published a model letter to politicians on the freedom of choice for abortion issue, as well as tips on effective letter writing now that the issue has become a states' rights matter.

In 1989, our Group Psychotherapy Section became actively involved with the Group Psychotherapy Section (Section 7) of Division 12, planning a national conference and expanding its newsletter to include the latter group. These Sections, plus Sections from Divisions 19 and 39, formed in an Interdivisional Council on Group Psychotherapy, with Art Teicher as president, Morris Goodman as treasurer, and Mike Andronico as secretary.

Don Freedheim began preparation, for the Division, of a volume on the *History of Psychotherapy*, in conjunction with the centennial celebration of the APA, and a search commenced for the next editor of the journal, who would assume full editorial responsibility by 1994.

A demographic profile of Division 29 compiled by ODEER, the APA Office of Demographics, Employment, and Educational Research revealed that of the total 1989 membership, more than two thirds were male, though 43% of the associate members were female. Mean age of members was 50.5 with 89% having an earned doctorate and a little over 70% describing their major field as falling in the health service provider area. Sixty-three percent were employed full time, only six members stated that they were unemployed and seeking employment, and about 4% were retirees or students (but a significant 21% did not specify employment status). Eighty-nine percent of the members were licensed and/or certified, approximately 28% stated that they were involved in research, 43% in education, and 93% described their activities in the area of health and mental health services. All APA Divisions appeared to have some Division 29 members, and, in fact, 30% of our membership belonged to four or more divisions and 74% belonged to state psychological associations. About 11% of the membership had the ABPP diploma.

1990

Norm Abeles was a fine president, from whose administrative skills and personal know-how we all could learn! The Division continued in its purposes of fostering collegial relations among members of the APA interested in psychotherapy theory, research, training, and practice. Through its many committees and task forces, as well as its publications, the Division actively attended to a variety of issues facing psychologist psychotherapists.

The Student Development Committee implemented a 120-hour legislative internship in Rhode Island with the state psychological association and conducted a student paper competition. Winners of the Third Annual President's Award for Psychotherapy Research (Student Award) for 1990 were:

First Place ($350): Cindy Ford, York University, "Effects of Intimate Self-disclosure in Marital Therapy"

Second Place ($150): Stephen C. Messer, University of Mis-

sissippi, "Development Psychopathology and Psychotherapy: An Integrative Approach"

Winners of the Ethnic Minorities Paper Competition for 1989–
1990 were:

First Place ($350): Marisol Muñez, Florida State University,
"Toward the Psychological Empowerment of Ethnic Mi-
nority Clients: A Competence Paradigm for Psychotherapy
Practice"

Second Place ($150): Gayle Y. Iwamasa, M.S., Purdue Uni-
versity, "Cultural Psychotherapy Model

Student award winners in both competitions presented their
papers at the 1990 APA Convention in Boston, and had abstracts
printed in *The Psychotherapy Bulletin*.

At the end of the adjourned meeting of the Council on February 3, 1990, the APA presidential gavel was passed on to Stanley
R. Graham, a past Division president and twice its treasurer. Another local boy made good! Another Division 29 former president
made it to the top of the APA with the election of Jack Wiggins
as president-elect. Jack will be wielding the gavel when the APA
celebrates its centennial in Washington, D.C., in 1992. How nice!

At the midwinter board meeting, Tommy Stigall was designated as recipient of the 1990 Distinguished Psychologist Award for
Contributions to Psychology and Psychotherapy, based on his
tremendous contributions to the Division and the profession as
chair of the Joint Council on Professional Education in Psychology, his contributions to the regulation of psychology on state and
national levels, and his impressive history of service. Victor R.
Nahmias was name to receive the Jack D. Krasner Award, in recognition of his service to the Division and the Midwinter Conference, as well as his achievements in modeling and fostering good
clinical practice within a managed-care framework. Scott Mesh
and David Pilon, who were among the first student affiliates recruited by Division 29, and who, with the Division's support
helped to establish APAGS, were honored by the Division for

their accomplishments, at the Social Hour/Awards Presentation at the APA. Bryant Welch, head of the Practice Directorate, was given a certificate of appreciation by the Division 29 Board for his outstanding work in the Practice Directorate.

The Board voted for the first time to offer small "grants" to help defray child care expenses for elected or appointed members of the Board who must attend executive board meetings before the convention begins. While only $50 to $150 in amount, and to be given only when expenses are documented for attendance before the actual convention, they were considered an important symbol of supporting work and family and hopefully would convey the message that the Division was encouraging the younger or less experienced members, who are more likely to the parents of younger children or adolescents, to become involved in the leadership of the Division. Another first for the Division? We also were encouraging the APA to establish a day-care center at the new APA Building.

At this meeting the Board voted to send a bylaws amendment to the membership to permit the Division's Membership Committee to officially approved membership without an action of the Board, on a monthly basis, and immediately offer these new members the benefits of the Division prior to formal acknowledgment by the APA. The Board also reaffirmed its position in support of mandatory continuing education.

The Task Force on Men's Roles and Psychotherapy, with Ron Levant and Herb Freudenberger co-chairing, continued to pursue its agenda, presenting programs, and linking up with emerging networks of men who treat troubled men. This year, an initiative emerged to form a Division on the Psychology of Men.

The CFW continued with its educational and political thrust, and the Chair, Carol Goodheart, served as liaison to the Interdivisional Task Force on Gender, with Division 35, Division 12, etc. The Committee on Professional Practice conducted marketing training workshops at the Midwinter Convention, and continued the development of the Media Hotline. The Task Force on Men's Roles developed and edited a special section of the journal *Psychotherapy*.

The Task Force on Children and Adolescents was busy collating responses arriving from the letter sent out to all state associations regarding confidentiality and ethical issues in psychotherapy with children and adolescents. Chair Alice Rubenstein, with her committee, consisting of Gerald Koocher, Penny Norton, Gloria Gottsegen, and Karen Zager, was drafting a brochure for practitioners on psychotherapy with children and adolescents, designed to be given to parents. They completed the first draft of this brochure and prepared materials in conjunction with the Trauma Response Group on support groups for children and parents deployed in the Middle East.

The Task Force on American Indian Mental Health, appointed by President Norm Abeles, with Diane Willis as chair, got off to a busy start with a March meeting to establish goals and priorities toward meeting the mental health needs of American Indians and determining the need and possible funding sources for a National Conference on American Indian Mental Health.

The Section on Group Psychotherapy formed a newsletter called *The Group Psychotherapist* with Larry Kutash as editor. Begun by Division 29, it became this year a joint organ of Division 12's Section VII, as well. Among her other activities, our secretary, Trish Hannigan, was busy this year publishing in the *Psychotherapy Bulletin* questionnaires to get feedback from the membership on such issues as attitudes toward continuing education, referral networks, etc.

As part of its response to the crisis in the Persian Gulf, the Division of Psychotherapy sponsored a project undertaken by Ellin Block and Jon Perez of the LifePLUS Foundation, aimed to deliver psychological support and educational materials, at no charge, to meet the needs of families nationwide. Dependent upon volunteer services of psychologists in their own communities who would act as facilitators and resources, this community project generated considerable interest from the U.S. Congress and the Department of Defense.

In August of 1990, Ellen McGrath was asked to run a support group for the wives of servicemen at Fort Bragg, NC, for the

"Home Show" on ABC. She did so, collecting some research data, as well, analysis of which the Division underwrote. Results were summarized in *The Psychotherapy Bulletin* and *USA Today*. Ellen, our president-elect, asked the Administrative Committee of the Division of Psychotherapy to establish a Task Force on Trauma Response and Research co-chaired by Ellin Bloch and Jon Perez, with Harry Wexler and Wade Silverman coordinating the research facet of the work, collecting and evaluating data from the volunteer psychologists and their support groups regarding the impact of these interventions. The task force was established in October of 1990, and was planning to create a national network of volunteer psychologists who wished to provide outreach to those affected by the Middle East crisis and to assess the process and outcomes of interventions. Through efforts of the committee the Division published, in conjunction with Project Me of Tucson, Arizona, materials that were disseminated through the Family Life Units of the Department of Defense. A pilot study conducted by Ellen McGrath and Harry Wexler, funded by Division 29, looked at data collected from military wives on attitudes and stress reactions.

Work continued on the preparation of the *History of Psychotherapy* volume, and the journal's special issue for 1990 was "Psychotherapy and Religion."

The Division conducted a self-study on the role and functions of its numerous committees and task forces, and continued to promote the effective interface of Division activities with other Divisions of the American Psychological Association. The Committee on Committee Structure (Ron Levant, chair; Don Freedheim; Trish Hannigan) did its work and reported that the Division appeared to them to have three functional categories of committees:

- Organizational/Administrative Committees (all Standing Committees)
- Member Service Committees
- Issue Committees

The Committee on Committee Structure recommended that

all Member Service and Issue Committees review their current missions in the light of both parallel committees existing in other divisions and the work being done by paid staff in the APA directorates, and consider whether it would be appropriate to continue as a divisional committee, to form an interdivisional committee or task force, or to function as a liaison, either divisional or interdivisional, to one of the directorates. It was also suggested that the existing liaison structure should be updated to reflect the reorganization of the APA's central office, and that consideration should be given to the sharing of liaisons with other practice divisions.

In terms of membership growth, this was a good year for the Division. Assisted by a change in APA procedures to facilitate members' joining divisions, we got 2,466 interest slips, more than double the number received last year! And we recruited 565 members. The Division was also pleased to welcome seven new Fellows: Drs. Claire Brody, Jan Carlson, Marvin Goldfried, Diane Hill, Lynn Rehm, Stanley Sue, and Leon VandeCreek.

The Task Force on Psychotherapy with the Aging, chaired by Laura Barbanel, prepared a questionnaire which was published in *The Psychotherapy Bulletin* and in the publications of Divisions 42 and 43. The low response rate limited its value but the results did suggest that education and training in this area are extremely important.

The Division began to offer for sale this year a 12-cassette Tape Series Library on Psychotherapy with Families which consisted of a representative sampling of current thinking on the advancing edge of family therapy, featuring philosophical/foundations, theory, research, and practice, and representing the emerging maturity of the 40-year-old subfield of psychotherapy.

Division 29's representatives to the Joint Commission on Professional Education in Psychology (JCPEP) were Art Weins and Tommy Stigall, the chair of JCPEP. The JCPEP report was completed and approved for publication and distribution at the August 1990 meeting of the Joint Council.

Division 29 cosponsored and endorsed, along with Divisions 42 and 43, an all-day conference of SPAB (Society of Psychologists on Addictive Behavior) held in Boston in August of 1990.

With the help of the Division's Central Office, the Program Committee created a "Program Binder" to specify the complex process of doing programs at the APA, and including procedures, sample correspondence, rating forms, deadline dates, etc. It is planned that this binder be updated yearly.

Our president-elect, Ellen McGrath, was chair of the APA Task Force on Women and Depression, which published its findings this year. The book, *Women and Depression: Risk Factors and Treatment Issues* was very well received, as have been presentations that Ellen has made on the subject. We in the Division were proud to claim her as one of us.

The 1990 election results were as follows: Reuben Silver, president-elect; Patricia Hannigan, secretary; Carol Goodheart, Council representative; and Ernst Beier, Sandra Haber, and Ronald Levant, Members-at-Large. As usual, more good people!

1991

Ellen McGrath started out her presidential year with a "bang" as Operation Desert Shield became Operation Desert Storm, and she mobilized the Division impressively, facilitating some significant contributions to the government and the public, in the name of Division 29.

The Task Force on Trauma Response and Research was divided into three sections, as the Division's outreach efforts expanded. In the Community Intervention Section, Ellin Bloch and Jon Perez were successfully mobilizing support groups at the community level for families separated by the Middle East conflict, serving as consultants for local groups and doing a wonderful job as spokespeople in the media about the plight and needs of these families. In the Education Section, co-chairs Alice Rubenstein and Dennis Embry developed a book for the principals and counselors at schools with a substantial number of kids who were coping with military separation. The book was sent by the Department of Defense to all the military base schools in the United States and Europe in January of 1991, along with a research questionnaire, and was available to other schools and to Division members. The Division paid approximately $5,000 toward the cost of this undertaking ... money well spent! Dr. Ellin Bloch was first author of a position paper which was submitted to the Congress, the Department of Veteran Affairs, and the Department of Defense outlining recommendations for services and research. The third section of the Trauma Task Force was on General Applications in Trauma and the group planned to work on such areas as how psychotherapists need to respond to natural (earthquake) and human-made (plane crash) disasters. The Division worked with the Practice Directorate to coordinate and develop activities in this area. The Trauma Task Force's commitment to research was reflected in the appointment of Harry Wexler and Wade Silverman to co-chair this endeavor.

It should also be noted that a brochure written in conjunction with the Practice Directorate was part of a packet cosponsored by Division 29 which was presented to every member of Congress for distribution to their districts.

The Committee for Women was sunsetted, on the recommendation of its chair, Carol Goodheart, and reconstituted as the Gender Issues Committee.

The Publications Board had much to occupy it this year! Again we had a special issue of the journal, this one on "Psychotherapy with Victims." *The History of Psychotherapy* volume, edited by Don Freedheim, with an illustrious list of associate editors, was well on its way to publication in time for the APA Centennial. The APA is doing the publishing, and it will be a volume of fine quality, of which we can be proud, for it is part of Division 29's contribution to the APA Centennial! The Task Force on Adolescents and Children completed its brochure on Psychotherapy with Children and Adolescents, which was printed and enthusiastically received. A marketing plan was being developed to increase its sales. Some articles on topics of interest to students were written by the Publications Board members and circulated to university newspapers for publication. And Wade Silverman was designated to take over editorship of the journal from Don Freedheim in 1994.

At its February 1991 meeting, the Council of Representatives overwhelmingly approved the establishment of Division 49, the Division on Group Psychology and Group Psychotherapy. This was a real victory for our Section 1, which had skillfully shepherded the measure through the Council. Section 1, Group Psychotherapy, voted overwhelmingly to disband and designate the newly formed Division 49 as its successor organization. The Section president, Gordon Boals, indicated the intention of the Section members to continue as active participants in Division 29.

At the Midwinter Meeting, the Board, agreeing with the Student Development Committee's suggestion, voted to change the name of the Student Paper Awards to the Donald K. Freedheim Student Development Award, in acknowledgment of Don's encouragement, guidance, and instrumental support for the creation of APAGS. The 1991 winners of the Fourth Annual Donald K. Freedheim Student Development Award were:

First Place: Steven Herman, Rutgers University, "Therapist Client Similarity as a Predictor of Psychotherapy Outcome"

Second Place: Maureen Corbett, University of Maryland, "A Brief History of Research on the Process of Individual Psychotherapy"

Both papers were presented at the APA Convention in August 1991, with Ellin Bloch as discussant.

At the request of the Ethnic Minority Affairs Committee, its name was changed to the Multicultural Affairs Committee, because the term "ethnic minority" was seen as denoting a negative image of ethnic individuals, not in line with changing demographics. Further, the committee felt the new title would be much more reflective of the mission and goals of the committee. The Multicultural Affairs Committee announced that the winner of the 1991 National Students of Color Paper Competition was Christopher J. Barker, a student at Seton Hall University. His paper, "Working with the People: Ethical Issues in Counseling and Suicide Assessment with a Native American Population," was given by him at the APA Convention in San Francisco.

Following up on the APA Task Force on Women and Depression, Division 29 conducted a pilot survey of gender differences in depression.

Donald K. Freedheim was designated recipient of the 1991 Distinguished Psychologist Award for Contributions to Psychology and Psychotherapy. Just from reading this history, one must have a sense already of why! A professor at Case Western Reserve, Don has given yeoman service to the Division and the field via his editorship of the journal for two five-year terms, his presidency of the Division, service on the Council of Representatives, his work on developing student membership, etc., etc., etc. The Jack D. Krasner Award for 1991 went to Lisa Porche-Burke, a faculty member at the California School of Professional Psychology and coordinator of Ethnic Minority Studies (rising to Acting Provost at CSPP-LA, *after* she was designated as the reward recipient, just proving how right we were in seeing her as "going places")! Her service included being the Division liaison to the APA's Board of Ethnic Minority Affairs and chair of what has become the Multi-cultural Affairs Committee. The awards were presented at the Division 29 Social Hour at the APA Convention in San Francisco.

Efforts were begun by Secretary Trish Hannigan to collect information about members for a database which would be used to maximize the exchange of scientific, educational, and professional information among members.

At the Council meeting in August 1991, Ellen McGrath and Ellin Bloch received Presidential Citations from Charlie Spielberger, APA president, in recognition of their superb work in response to the Gulf crisis.

The Division formed a new committee, the Employee Benefits Committee, chaired by Trish Hannigan, with Victor Nahmias as a member and James P. Farley, an employee benefits administrator, as an ex officio consultant. The committee's goals were stated as follows: to promote the professionalism of psychologists in relation to employee benefit plans; to educate employers about the appropriate role of mental health in their own and their employees' lives and about the impact of employee mental health or benefits utilization; to promote quality utilization review; to serve as an adjunct to APA-level efforts in advocacy for mental health coverage; and to serve as an information clearinghouse for Division members on the current topics in health benefits management.

Norm Abeles and Carl Eisdorfer made recommendations to

Division 29 on the kind of education and training experiences needed by trainees in order to be competent to work clinically with older adults. They asked that Division 29 encourage action on their specific recommendations by providing publicity in our printed materials, by urging the inclusion of aging in lists of diversities as in accreditation criteria, by setting up communications channels with the Practice Directorate, and by reinforcing colleagues who take steps to incorporate more aging content in the programs that they lead. The idea of a Section on Aging in the Division was raised for consideration.

At an interdivisional Gender Issues Committee meeting at the 1991 Midwinter Meeting, it was decided to try to arrange for a day at the 1992 Midwinter Meeting for women, a day during which leadership development content would be combined with nurturing, play, and re-energizing activities, offering women an opportunity to make new friends, to relax and unwind, and to discuss the barriers and solutions for women in leadership. Evelyn Hill and Matty Canter agreed to co-chair the event, and a committee was constituted, which met at the APA Convention in San Francisco to work out some of the details.

Looking through the Bulletins, one can see how active and effective this Division has been and continues to be! Articles on such topics as substance abuse, prescription privileges, marketing opportunities, malpractice insurance, the Psy.D. degree, the use of hospital referral services, trends in psychotherapy, education and training recommendations on the kind of education and training experiences needed in order to be competent to work clinically with older adults—these are just some of the topics addressed in just one of the 1991 issues!

Election results suggested that the Division would continue to be in good hands in 1992, with Reuben Silver as president, with the election of Gerald Koocher as president-elect, with Ellen McGrath as past president, Trish Hannigan-Farley (Congratulations, Trish and Jim!) as secretary, incumbent Alice Rubenstein as treasurer, and Jules Barron, Lisa Porche-Burke, and Carl Zimet as members-at-large. And so it would be.

But on December 18, 1991, Jules Barron died, suddenly to

some of us, and sadly for all of us. Jules was a founder of the PIAP, a founder of our Division, our past president, a friend to so many, a warm and wonderful human being who helped to shape us and who helped to make the Division a force in our profession and a pleasure in our lives. Although he had been active in many facets of the APA's governance, Jules always considered Division 29 his home. And we considered him ours. He will be sorely missed. In accordance with the bylaws, Morris Goodman was designated to be seated as a member-at-large in his stead.

1992

As I write, I am looking ahead to what should be an exciting Midwinter Convention at Amelia Island Plantation, near Jacksonville, Florida, in mid-February. The Winter 1991–1992 edition of *The Psychotherapy Bulletin*, Vol. 26, No. 4, arrived while I was writing, and a glance through it suggests that we shall have another very productive year. Articles reflect such diverse issues of significant concern as the feminization of psychology; substance abuse; media, marketing, and psychology; national health insurance; professional liability; the employee health care benefit system; concerns of graduate students, etc., etc., etc.

This year the journal special centennial issue will be, what else? "The Future of Psychotherapy." And the 1993 special issue "in the works" is on "Psychotherapy and the Addictions." Our *History of Psychotherapy*, edited by Don Freedheim, is in press, with a foreword by Rollo May. We expect it to be a very special year!

Another former president of Division 29, Jack G. Wiggins, takes over the presidency of the APA on March 1, at the conclusion of the adjourned meeting of the Council, as our former president and twice treasurer Stanley R. Graham ends his term on the APA Board of Directors as APA past president, and our former past president and current APA recording secretary Ron Fox ends his term and is replaced by our former past president, Pat DeLeon, who becomes APA recording secretary! Ron is running for president-elect of the APA. . . . who knows! We may have still another past president going to the top of the ladder! And as for the APA Board of Directors, of the six members-at-large who will be seated on March 1, three (Dorothy Cantor, Robert Resnick, and myself) are Division 29 Fellows and one, Bruce Bennett, is a Division Member. How about that! Certainly the Division of Psychotherapy has served as a training ground for many of us, has nurtured its members and sent us on to fight the good fight.

Concluding Remarks

We do not wish this history to be a finalized version of our first 25 years. We really want it to be a living document, open to additions and your enrichment. So if, on reading this, you find that it has stimulated some memories, comments, or additions, please communicate them so that we can add to what we hope will be an ongoing, living document, as the Division itself is a growing, developing organization!

MATHILDA B. CANTER, PH.D.

CHAPTER 6

One Psychologist's Journey to Professional Activism and Advocacy

A s with many other important developments in life, my work as an activist and advocate for my beloved profession of psychology began in early childhood. My parents inculcated in their three sons (two of whom became clinical psychologists) a strong sense of responsibility and duty to family, country, and society in general. We also learned that if we wanted to accomplish something, then we should work toward that goal both by ourselves and with like-minded others. In time, that led to my enlistment at the age of 17 in the U.S. Navy during the final months of World War II.

It was while serving as a medical corpsman at the Bethesda Naval Hospital that I discovered psychology, and I am indebted to that experience for my ultimate decision to become a member of that profession. Together with many of my peers in the service, I learned to escape the routine (termed "goofing off" by the cognoscenti) by finding other things to do. In my case, that was accomplished mainly by retreating to the professional library, which was a quiet and secluded venue where one could get a few moments of respite, and even sleep, in a small space between a sofa and the wall. The stacks were a treasure trove of wonderful distraction, though, and books by and about mental health in particular attracted my attention. As a result, after my discharge from active duty, I entered George Washington University and declared a psychology major. I clearly remember my father's asking, when I told him about that decision, what kind of crazy profession that was, because in those early days there truly was no profession of psychology: it was a scientific and academic discipline. But my father eventually got his answer, since not only I, but also my brother, entered that field. Upon receipt of my B.A. degree, I married, and Harriet's understanding and support of my professional activities have always been there.

There was another important career development during my undergraduate senior summer. I began working as an aide (as an attendant, as it was then called) at the world-renowned psychoanalytically oriented Chestnut Lodge Sanitarium in Rockville, Maryland, a suburb of Washington, DC. Shortly before I came to the Lodge, Harry Stack Sullivan, who had been director of psychotherapy, had died, and Frieda Fromm-Reichmann (who was fondly called Frieda From-Rockville behind her back) had replaced him in that position. At the Lodge, I was privileged to attend staff conferences and other presentations where eminent staff members and visiting professionals discussed theoretical and clinical issues that I found fascinating; I also did much reading at the extensive library. The Lodge clinical psychologist, Margaret Rioch, was an impressive, thoroughly competent, and autonomous professional; furthermore, she was, most of all, a psychotherapist, a role for a psychologists that was rarely mentioned in my undergraduate classes. Working there established the theoretical interpersonal orientation in understanding human behavior that has ever since been an important part of my professional grounding. On one occasion, a senior staff psychiatrist, whom I greatly respected, urged me to enter medical school and become a psychiatrist. When I asked him how knowing that there were 206 bones in the body and how to deliver a baby would help me to understand how *people* function. He paused for a moment, and then said that I was right and that I should become a psychologist instead. And I told him that I was planning to do exactly that. And I did.

After that summer, I returned to George Washington University where, one year later, I received my master's degree in clinical psychology, while working part-time at the Lodge. I fulfilled my two-semester master's degree fieldwork requirement on the acute psychiatric admissions service of a large municipal hospital. The clinical psychologist there was a respected professional who enjoyed her work and reinforced my growing sense of professional identity, whereas the senior psychiatrist allegedly kept a loaded gun (and a bottle of bourbon) in his desk. He also stayed in his office most of the time because he was afraid that a patient might attack him. What a difference in role models!

My sense then, and now, was that being a professional psychologist required a doctorate, and so I applied for admission to doctoral programs at several East Coast universities. Fortunately for me, I elected Adelphi University in Garden City, New York, because of its emphasis on training psychologists to be *professionals* rather than scientists/researchers/academics, as did all the other schools. Adelphi was the nation's first APA-approved professional program in clinical psychology, and I was a member of its second class of eight students (see the chapter by Nicholas Cummings on the development of the professional school movement for further information about Adelphi). The new director of clinical training at Adelphi, whom I initially met on my first day, was Gordon F. Derner. He was the consummate professional role model. A graduate of Columbia University's clinical psychology program who had after completing the training program at the William Alanson White Institute, he became for me not only an important educator in the Sullivan model, but a dear friend and esteemed colleague. Gordon Derner was also the first professor I knew who invited his students to address him by his first name. Through him, I learned that teachers could also be people; and I have ever since enjoyed teaching students the elements of *professional* psychology. He emphasized our responsibility to give back to the field, while providing skilled high-quality psychological services to those who sought our assistance. He always reminded us, by his personal example, that we had the responsibility and the opportunity to build psychology as an independent profession, even though, at that time, it was ancillary to a medical-model organized psychiatry that sought to exert stifling control. One day, Gordon organized a motorcade of students and faculty, and we drove into New York City, where psychologists had convened a mass meeting to advocate for the licensing of psychologists in New York State. I had never seen so many psychologists in one place before, and I was impressed by their energy and effort.

After a first-class internship in 1953–1954 at Springfield State Hospital near Baltimore, in my native state of Maryland, graduation from Adelphi in 1955 was followed by several years of work as a staff psychologist at various facilities. Wherever I was, I joined the local and national societies, believing that as a professional, one should always support one's institutions. As a young intern, it was my privilege to be present at the founding meeting of the Maryland Psychological Association (MPA), and I had become a student member of the American Psychological Association (APA) while at Adelphi. The APA was my organizational home, and always will be, and I valued my membership. If there were programs that I wanted to change or initiate, I worked to effect them. For many years, I have been taking on various APA governance and committee assignments, demonstrating my strong support for that important organization that has changed significantly since I first became part of it.

By the late 1950s, my family and I had returned to Washington, DC, where I worked for the Department of Public Health before entering private practice. We lived in nearby Maryland, and I became a member of the MPA, as well as of the District of Columbia Psychological Association (DCPA). The former was more professionally oriented at the time, so I became more involved in MPA affairs. Soon I was asked to serve on committees (e.g., three years as program chair), and in 1961–1963, I was elected state treasurer. In about 1958, the Federal Employees Health Benefits Program (FEHBP), the largest health-insurance plan in the country, became the first major program to include reimbursement for mental health services. However, the services of physicians were covered, which meant that any medical doctor could offer psychotherapy. Psychologists were not then generally recognized by the insurance industry as providers of mental health services, let alone as autonomous professionals. In those instances where we were permitted to be part of the so-called mental health team, our role was usually limited to the administration of tests. That was particularly offensive to me, as I had taken a sequence in psychotherapy at the Washington School of Psychiatry.

Eventually, through the hard work of several Washington psychologists, and with more than a little assistance from friendly members of the Congress, we were able to get the rules changed a bit. At that time, the U.S. Civil Service Commission contracted, and still does, with a number of insurance carriers to provide health care under the FEHBP, and thus was amenable to "advice" from the Hill. The new rules stated that psychologists could do psychotherapy, but only under medical supervision. That requirement was a travesty; I knew psychologists whose psychotherapy was "supervised" by dermatologists and proctologists. It was then that I learned the value of utilizing legislative means, in this case, federal, but later at the state level, to help achieve our profession's goals. The exclusion of psychologists as autonomous providers was disturbing to other colleagues, as well as to me, and when we realized that the APA was not interested in pursuing efforts on behalf of our professional concerns, several of us founded the Washington Society of Clinical Psychologists, the first professional organization in the area. Harold Lindner was the first president, and I served as secretary-treasurer, later replacing Lindner at the helm. Several dozen local professional psychologists joined us, and we undertook to prod the APA and DCPA into action. Our small, but assertive, group wrote letters to local newspapers, buttonholed politicians, made contacts in the insurance field, and, in general, became *the* activist society in Washington. In the meantime, while serving on the MPA executive committee, I persuaded that group to establish its first Committee on Health Insurance. Having been the spur, I was appointed chair and served in that capacity from 1963 through 1966. It was not until a decade later that the DCPA named an insurance committee, which I chaired from 1973 to 1979.

Meanwhile, the APA was persuaded mainly by West Coast activists, including Rogers Wright, but also by colleagues from other parts of the country, to establish the Ad Hoc Committee on Insurance and Related Social Developments (AHCIRSD). The acronym for this temporary committee quickly became translated into "Accursed," which reflected the attitude of a significant segment of the then-powerful APA governance. I was invited to become a member of this group. Our initial meeting began with breakfast, continued through a lunch of sandwiches, and then went on into the very late evening. At around 2:00 A.M., I fell asleep on the floor wondering what I had gotten myself into. But whatever the demands on my time, I had to acknowledge that it was a privilege to be associated with such effective, hard-working professionals. The APA was dragged, at times kicking and screaming, into recognizing that many of its members wanted, and needed, strong action on several fronts, but principally on the health insurance issue. After much travail, AHCIRSD was superseded by the APA's Committee on Health Insurance (COHI). Nick Cummings (who served as COHI's first chair) and I went directly from the "ad hoc" AHCIRSD to the new standing committee.

As an example of how one person can influence important developments, I had a patient who was an employee of a federal agency and his local FEHBP plan would not reimburse him for my services. Only physicians could provide psychotherapy then, and there was no provision for any participation by psychologists. Through him, I arranged to meet with the agency committee that provided oversight of the health plan. I explained to this small group how we are trained, what a professional psychologists does, and how cost-effective psychological services are and how they could result in a more effective workforce. This agency became the first in the federal government to recognize licensed psychologists as independent providers whose services could be utilized without medical referral and/or supervision. This success served to further reinforce my activist efforts on the insurance issue.

Within this time frame, and mainly because of our impatience with the slow pace of official APA efforts, a small group of us organized ourselves as the Council for the Advancement of the Psychological Professions and Sciences (CAPPS), which later became known (not always with affection) as the Dirty Dozen. It was intended to be an activist body that could operate outside of the APA and thus initiate efforts that the APA could not, or did not want to, undertake. I was there at the beginning because of my contacts in Washington with the federal establishment. I recall on occasion when I invited about 15 Washington colleagues to a meeting in my office. I told them that CAPPS was planning to file suit against the national Blue Cross organization alleging restraint of trade and related legal issues. In less than half an hour, our group had pledged $12,000 to support such actions. And in those days, that sum was real money! It demonstrated that CAPPS was serious and that we would have the support of our colleagues if they perceived us as prepared to engage in actions on their behalf. The Dirty Dozen membership included, but definitely was not limited to, Jack Wiggins, Nick Cummings, Rogers Wright, and Ernie Lawrence. We toiled long, hard, and effectively on behalf of our emerging profession. I shall always treasure working with this dedicated group during those tumultuous years when psychology was growing into the profession it has become.

Although I am now in the latter years of my professional career, I continue to follow professional developments closely. I do whatever I can to participate in, and assist the growth of, psychology. I am active in the APA and state affairs, as well as in other organizations, and if I cannot be there personally, my check speaks for me. I urge those who read this account, especially the younger psychologists new to the field: *Get Involved!* As a profession, we are facing critical times, and only if *you* do your share, and more, can we continue to grow as a discipline that provides the valuable benefits of professional psychology to society.

MELVIN GRAVITZ, PH.D.

CHAPTER 7

A History of the Reimbursement
of Psychological Services:

The Education of One
Psychologist in the Real World

When asked to write a chapter about the history of insurance reimbursement for psychological services, at first I declined. Then I was reminded that most of the relevant activities took place in the 1970s, and so any psychologist in practice for less than 30 years might be unfamiliar with how that history developed. Thus, since most psychologists currently in practice have entered the field since 1980, I felt an obligation to inform, and remind, our colleagues of the struggle we underwent to achieve professional recognition as a health discipline. My memories were revived by the honors accorded the Dirty Dozen at the 1999 APA Convention in Boston, an event that allowed nine of the group to get together again and swap "war stories" of our mission to create a profession of psychology. My documentation is in the *Archives of Psychology* at Akron University. My professional vita is my only reference for this project. The first section focuses on insurance reimbursement and the resulting "spin-offs." The second section deals with the repercussions within the APA from the success of insurance reimbursement. The third section addresses the future of psychology and things left to do.

Professional Psychology Following World War II

The growth of the profession of psychology must be seen in context and not judged by retrospective revisionism. Although there may be many things that we wish had been done differently, it is remarkable that we did it at all. We were in a hostile environment, even in our own discipline. It was to be expected that other professions, such as psychiatry or medicine, would fight bitterly against the rise of professionalism in psychology. What was even more surprising was that this same attitude existed within the APA. Academicians considered practitioners' needs and interests mundane or unworthy; and, above all, the "scientists" and "academicians" were resistant to practitioners' attempts to challenge their control of the APA.

After receiving a Ph.D. degree from Purdue University in 1952, I went to a demonstration clinic in Cleveland to try to prove that outpatient services could reduce admissions to the state-operated Cleveland Receiving Hospital. I found that psychologists with their Ph.D. degrees were not welcomed by the psychiatric community. Psychiatry owned the facilities and psychiatrists were thoroughly indoctrinated with psychoanalytic thinking. Addressing community mental health needs through short-term psychotherapeutic interventions was alien to the community wisdom. Social work was a willing ally in this scenario. As I learned in corresponding with my psychological colleagues, Cleveland was not a unique situation, but represented the country's mental health climate at that time.

Psychologists banded together out of self-protection. Universities did not nurture practitioners, except for allowing them to teach courses that the regular faculty did not want to teach. Psychology departments were research driven and practitioners were looked on as failures of the training system. The state and local psychological associations that did exist were often weak. There were exceptions, of course. In Connecticut, in 1948, Karl Heiser while president of the Connecticut State Psychological Association, prevailed upon the state legislature to enact the first law giving statutory recognition to psychology. Thus began the protracted national struggle for state licensing of psychologists.

It would be many, many years before psychologists attained licensing in all states. Communication and transportation were archaic by present standards, hampering the development of a national concerted effort. Computers were unknown; and although telephones were available, long distance calls were very expensive. When I first called the APA in the 1950s, secretaries had to hand the phone to each other to complete the call. Carbon paper was used to make copies for files; and mass communications were effected by hectograph or mimeographs; that is, a "stencil" was cut, which, in turn, was applied to an ink-filled rotating drum that then imprinted the message on paper. Professional psychology began its development in this era. Journals principally presented research reports, leaving the dissemination of professional news to "word of mouth."

Given the residue of more than 50,000 "neuropsychiatric casualties" from World War II and the increasing acceptance of "mental health" and "psychotherapy," there was an apparent need for mental health services, a need that initiated a major movement of mental health personnel (psychologists, psychiatrists, and social workers) from the "mental health clinic" into private practice.

Working for, or with, a psychiatrist or other physician became one of the main entrees into private practice for psychologists. Fees were in the $10 to $15 range and "testing fees" were commonly $75 to $100. These were costly services and were paid "out-of-pocket" at a time when the average worker earned about $100 a week. Insurance for outpatient psychiatric services was unheard of until 1959, when psychiatric services were first included in federal employee contracts and in the Kaiser Health Plan on the West Coast.

Health insurance in the United States, although an invention of hospitals during the Great Depression of the 1930s did not "catch on" immediately, but did result in the formation of a "Blue Cross franchise network." The idea of prepaying physician's fees through a Blue Shield plan came later.

Psychology's Entrance Into the Health-Insurance Market

Despite misgivings by many in the health-insurance industry, coverage for "nervous and mental disorders" became a benefit for federal employees in 1959. This breakthrough in prepaid health insurance began to spread in the "boom time" labor market energized by the Korean war.

It quickly became apparent to psychologists that if psychiatrists were going to be reimbursed for mental health services whereas they were not, professional psychology would not long survive. Psychologists in California and New York were the first to sound the alarm, and soon were joined by those in Washington, DC. The lack of APA support for these early actions engendered considerable disaffection and bitterness among professional psychologists, and the battle lines still remain. This lack of APA action also directly resulted in the formation of the Ad Hoc Committee on Insurance and Related Social Developments (AHCIRSD), popularly called "Accursed," a history of which is told elsewhere in this book.

I first became aware of the APA's insurance committee in my work with the Cleveland Psychological Association (CPA). I had initiated the CPA Information and Referral Service in 1957 to facilitate practice opportunities for psychologists. Through the referral service, I would often hear from callers that their claims were not being paid (or would not be paid) if their mental health care were provided by a psychologist. The seeming insolubility of the problem led to many discussions with my colleagues and with my family. My father was an executive in life and health insurance and an uncle was an insurance actuary and the principal owner of a life insurance company.

A concurrent issue, and one in which I was also heavily invested (along with numerous other psychologists), was that of psychologists and psychotherapy. In February 1963, Psychologists Interested in the Advancement of Psychotherapy (PIAP) met in Chicago with Len Pearson as the presiding president. I attended as president of the CPA. We discussed whether PIAP should affiliate with the APA as a section of its Division 12 (Clinical Psychology). The failure of the APA to list psychotherapy as a training requirement was a matter of grave concern, as it still is. The dozen or so members in attendance encouraged me to follow up on this "insurance development," and I began reporting in the PIAP newsletter the bits and pieces of information about insurance that I was able to gather.

Eventually, the "freestanding" PIAP became a section of Division 12, but this relationship did not last long. It soon became apparent that the Division 12 governance (which epitomized the scientist/practitioner model) emphasized science and was ambivalent about accepting practitioners. Consequently, the Psychotherapy Section of Division 12 petitioned for, and was granted, Division status by the APA Council, becoming Division 29 (Psychotherapy).

Psychologists across the country were very excited by the prospect that the APA, by establishing a Division of Psychotherapy, was finally recognizing that psychotherapy was an important part of the practice of psychology. We thought that once the APA "legitimized" the practicing of psychotherapy by psychologists, everyone else would follow suit. Of course, this was not to be, but it did result in a critical mass of psychologists focused on problems germane to practice. A Divisional insurance committee was established under the leadership of Oliver J. B. Kerner of Chicago. Soon thereafter, after hearing Nick Cummings report his medical cost-offset research at an APA Convention, Kerner handed me the minutes of the Division 29 Insurance Committee and said, "You understand these things. You do it." I did not realize it then, but this was to be the occasion for my meeting the stalwarts who ultimately came to be known as the "Dirty Dozen," and the beginning of a career in the furtherance of professional psychology that would be a prominent feature of the rest of my life.

Milt Theaman, chair, and Rogers Wright, Nick Cummings, and Mel Gravitz, members of the APA's AHCIRSD, began to correspond with me and to talk with me by phone. Later, I was invited to attend an AHCIRSD meeting and to meet Bill Schofield, George Coppel, and William Smith, who rounded out the committee. It was a highly charged meeting, and I was impressed by their commitment, energy, and determination. However, it was also confusing because there was a decided lack of unanimity; and I could not figure out whether it was the insurance companies or the APA (or both) that was the target of their efforts. The insurance industry, with its denial of reimbursement for psychology, was clearly a major concern, and AHCIRSD was also hammering the APA for its failure to become involved in the reimbursement and mental health service delivery issues (Medicare was being conceived by the Congress—a possible precursor to universal health care), in licensure for psychologists, or in providing current information on matters related to psychology.

I subsequently learned that after having been forbidden to meet by the chair of the Board of Professional Affairs (its parent board), AHCIRSD nevertheless met concurrently with an APA Council of Representatives meeting and proposed: (1) the establishment of a standing APA Committee on Health Insurance (COHI); formal recognition of the *Washington Report* (mimeographed monthly covering professional matters) as an official APA publication (thus was born the APA's *Monitor*), and the discharge of AHCIRSD as having completed its mission. The Council concurred with AHCIRSD's proposals, and COHI came into being. I was named a member of the new "Insurance Committee."

The Committee on Health Insurance

The APA Committee on Health Insurance (COHI) was established in 1967 under the leadership of Nick Cummings and with a different cast of characters, and, following AHCIRSD's recommendation, with a committee "charge" clearly and solely focused on the inclusion of psychologists in health insurance.

The dropping of the phrase "related social developments"

(forced on the Dirty Dozen militants responsible for the formation of the original AHCIRSD by an APA establishment unwilling to accept the legitimacy of psychology's concerns with health insurance) from COHI's title and mission statement was widely viewed as more than a semantic exercise because it symbolized a small, but significant, APA commitment to the interests of professional psychology.

AHCIRSD's efforts in attempting to negotiate an acceptable solution to the "reimbursement problem" with insurance carriers, limited as it was by the breadth of its charge and its meager resources, gained much (and badly needed) experience, but only a few contracts that formally recognized the reimbursement of psychology. In fact, less than ½ of 1% of group insurance contracts contained provisions for reimbursing patients for the cost of psychological services.

Meanwhile, the California State Psychological Association (under the leadership of Dirty Dozeners Nick Cummings, Ernie Lawrence, and Rogers Wright) and the New Jersey Psychological Association (driven by Dirty Dozeners Marv Metsky, Gene Shapiro, and Bob Weitz) initiated and saw passed legislation that included psychological services.

Cummings, as COHI's first chair, focused the committee's efforts on such legislation. I suggested the term "freedom-of-choice" for the legislative thrust, a term that emphasized a patient's right to choose among providers of mental health service and COHI accepted it enthusiastically. Other COHI members were Bill Schofield, Cooper Clements, and Russ Bent. John McMillan was APA staff liaison. COHI lacked the participation of the other original members of AHCIRSD, who (in recognition of the controversy occasioned by their militance) had declined nomination to COHI, but Cummings and Schofield served us well as the institutional memory of the movement. In approximately the middle of his three-year term, Cummings resigned to head psychology's first professional school. Having overseen the passage of California's and New Jersey's freedom-of-choice laws, and having launched COHI on its legislative programs, he asked if I would be willing to succeed him as chair. I accepted, thereby assuming the responsibility of continuing the drive for state-by-state freedom-of-choice legislation.

In addition, my first year as chair involved defining other tasks for the committee. Team building was essential since we did not know each other very well and had only scant knowledge of the insurance industry. We also tried to familiarize ourselves with federal programs, such as Medicare, Medicaid, and the Federal Employees Health Benefit Associations (FEHBA). In this process, we heard about the Civilian Health and Medical Plan for the Uniformed Services (CHAMPUS).

As the Veteran's Administration (VA) was the largest employer of psychologists at that time, we contacted Cecil Peck, the VA's chief psychologist, to enlist his help. We also joined with the Dirty Dozen Divisions 29 and 31 in contacting the APA Insurance Trust to discuss why the APA Health Insurance Plan reimbursed psychiatrists but not psychologists: a source of embarrassment for psychology, and one that represented a substantial stumbling block to us. Without much success, we contacted the U.S. Department of Health, Education and Welfare (Education had not yet become a separate department) to try to get psychologists' services covered by Medicaid, only to find that Medicaid was a federal–state plan and was not controlled by the same rules as Medicare.

There were two pieces of federal legislation that worked in our favor. The Hill Burton Act (1958) funded the building of hospitals to make health care more generally available. This act was designed to provide high-quality health care to all citizens and included psychiatric services in general hospitals. The other was the Community Mental Health Act (1963), which created a series of national community mental health centers (CMHCs) to provide outpatient services. This legislation did include psychologists, and authorized them to administer direct services. It was a major breakthrough in the recognition of psychology, but it did not immediately translate into recognition by insurance carriers. A major irony was that, despite the fact that CMHCs could bill and be paid by insurance companies for the services of psychologists, the insurance companies refused to pay for direct billing by psychologists practicing independently.

We also found that there were federal and state barriers to the implementation of insurance benefits. For example, COHI learned that the Joint Commission on the Accreditation of Hospitals (JCAH), now the Joint Commission for the Accreditation of Health Organizations (JCAHO), had been given "deemed status" by Medicare to regulate hospitals because federal agencies were not equipped to perform this function. Accordingly, the JCAH was regarded as a "quasi" federal agency. However, it was controlled by medicine, and medicine controlled the hospitals. Thus, the JCAH wrote the regulations that denied psychologists staff privileges in hospitals, thereby relegating them to minor roles as members of an "ancillary profession."

Yet another issue confronting COHI was that health insurance was regulated by the states, not by the federal government. Thus, since psychologists in most states were not recognized by statute, and anyone in those states could claim to be a psychologist, the state insurance commissions were reluctant to mandate that benefits be paid to psychologists, and the insurance companies were not about to "broaden their risks by recognizing psychologists as reimbursable providers" (the Cummings-Follette studies on cost-offsetting notwithstanding).

Fortunately, California and New Jersey had passed mandatory licensure and direct recognition laws (freedom-of-choice laws), thus giving COHI hope and assurance that we were on the right path. The New Jersey law alone (through Prudential Insurance contracts) resulted in covering more lives than negotiations with insurers had accomplished in all the previous years.

The original New Jersey and California laws were flawed, however, and had to be amended because the mandatory recognition of psychologists applied only to the state where the service was delivered, not to the state where the contract was issued. Nevertheless, these new laws gave psychology invaluable legislative and regulatory experience. For example, the experience reaffirmed AHCIRSD's earlier insistence on the importance of state licensure for psychology and of the relationship between state-mandated credentialing and insurance-industry recognition of psychologists as reimbursable providers of mental health services. We also learned from the New Jersey experiences that passage of the licensing bill in 1966 had established the political contacts necessary to pass the freedom-of-choice legislation the following year. Ohio and other states followed this patter of "striking while the iron is hot" by passing freedom-of-choice bills shortly after adopting licensure.

Soon after establishing COHI, the APA formed a standing Committee on Legislative Initiatives (COLI), initially chaired by Ron Fox, which was charged with helping states that wanted to secure licensing. COHI and COLI decided to hold a joint meeting at the APA Convention in San Francisco in order to address (1) reaching an understanding of how COHI and COLI would work together and (2) APA staff tensions. From the COHI standpoint, it was essential that states seek licensure containing a defined scope of practice, including provisions for both the diagnosis and treatment of nervous and mental conditions. COLI was agreeable, and a division of labor was reached in which COLI would focus on states without a statutory definition of psychology and COHI on Freedom-of-Choice legislation in states with laws already in place.

State-mandated regulation of psychological services provided yet another area of conflict between the APA's practitioners and academics. Academics, many of whom earned 20% or more of their incomes through private consulting, did not want to be regulated. They claimed it was an infringement of their academic freedom, thereby stretching the concept of "academic freedom" to an absurd limit. Many of the academics who opposed licensing said they would accept "certification" as the preferable form of statutory recognition. Unfortunately, certification did not define the scope of practice of psychology (but merely protected the title "psychologist).

Many states (either to avoid a confrontation with the academics, or in accordance with psychology's beloved principle of "let's talk") compromised and passed certification-type legislation. As psychology more recently has learned (to its dismay) such certification as "mandated regulation" applies only to the use of the term "psychologist" and does little or nothing to regulate the practice itself. Consequently, more than 25 states have had to reexamine the issue of mandatory control.

The ill-advised "compromises" also were otherwise problematic from the outset in that the teaching of psychology was exempted from licensing. It was a high political price we paid, as this compromise has created problems for psychology ever since. Specifically, it has resulted in proliferation of psychology treatment/ training programs outside universities by professors with little or no experience in the practice of psychology.

COHI and the state associations faced other problems as well; for example, many psychologists felt it unseemly for psychology to go back to the legislature to ask for insurance reimbursement so soon after licensing legislation was passed because it would make us appear greedy. In fact, such academicians as George Albee opposed insurance reimbursement of psychological health services altogether, and arranged debates about the mercantile aspects of health care.

Albee predicted (in journal articles and public debates) the "short, unhappy life of clinical psychology" because he strongly opposed psychologists, using what he called the "medical model." He argued that psychology should own its own training facilities and not be housed in medical institutions controlled by physicians. The idea of being independent of medicine and the abuses of medical control had great appeal, but like so many great ideas emanating from college professors with only limited "real world" experience and knowledge, it was just a wonderful dream, and overlooked the political and financial realities; both then *and today*. Insurance pays for health care, not psychosocial development. Albee enjoyed debating and was facile in his arguments, but he lost the debates "going in" because of economic and social forces beyond any group's control.

That the statutory definition of psychology was the only way to survive as a profession was a lesson to be learned. Economic survival requires constant vigilance in the changing marketplace, a sector in which most psychologists have little interest. The APA still does not have the capacity to analyze economic trends or to forecast practice and training patterns in order to adapt to the market.

COHI attempted to capitalize on the new freedom-of-choice laws and made a concerted effort to have psychology defined in the federal and state laws in order to assure the right to practice. Because of the overriding presence of Medicare and the restrictions of the JCAH in hospital practice, we selected our outpatient care as more amenable to our efforts. This also coincided with common practice patterns of psychologists. We found Medicare unassailable. It was too new, and already cost estimates were providing unreliable. Everyone to whom we spoke felt that Medicare "had to be given a chance to work" before tinkering with it by adding new providers from a profession that was not licensed in all states and who might adversely affect "program costs." We turned our attention to the federal employees' contracts, FEHBA.

Aetna and the Federal Employees Health Insurance Program

The federal government offered a very comprehensive health plan for federal employees with several options for health insurance coverage; that is, different carriers offered different benefit programs. The federal employees' health program afforded a highly competitive and lucrative market, and carriers wanted to make their benefits as attractive as possible. Our first break came when psychologists working for the federal government noted that Aetna had not clearly specified in its brochures who would be reimbursed under the program's mental health benefit section. Thus, in Aetna's description of benefits, it appeared that psychologists' services would be covered, whereas in reality they were not being paid. COHI arranged a meeting with Aetna, one we expected to be contentious. However, the Aetna representatives proved to be reasonable, acknowledging the error and agreeing to rectify it by including psychologists in their FEHBA contracts.

After Aetna's revision of the FEHBA contract (to include psychologists) had been in effect for a full calendar year, we met with the company's representatives to determine whether there was any increased cost to FEHBA as a result of the inclusion of psychologists. Although the cost of mental health claims had increased slightly, overall health-care costs were down by about 4% (a result to be expected because of the medical cost-offset phenomenon earlier described by Cummings and Follette). We asked the representatives for a letter to that effect. After some equivocation, Aetna informed COHI that its record keeping did not permit formalizing such a conclusion, but that it would attempt to "do a study" to see whether the reduced costs reflected the "offset phenomenon" as opposed to Aetna's greater efficiency in "claims management."

In a later meeting with Aetna, we again, successfully, tried to obtain the Aetna medical cost-offset data, but we did get a commitment that Aetna would follow the insurance codes of the various states. However, it would not recommend coverage in states where psychologists were not licensed, because it could not identify legitimate psychologists in those states. I asked, "If the APA were to supply a list of qualified psychologists in those states, would Aetna honor their claims?" The Aetna representative indicated that if they had such a list, as well as a listing of the named psychologists' credentials, Aetna would consider recognizing those psychologists for reimbursement. I said I thought that we (the APA) could provide the required lists within six months.

In fact, a basis for formulating such a list already existed. AHCIRSD and Divisions 29 and 31, in earlier struggles with the licensure problem (i.e., the lack of mandated regulation of psychology in all the states), had persuaded the APA to adopt a "Definition of Psychologist for Insurance Purposes" that would allow for the identification of legitimately trained psychologists. Although the "definition" was useful, it failed to solve the problem, because most insurance companies were unwilling to spend the time and money and to assume the liability of evaluating the credentials of those submitting claims.

Knowing this, I thought that some group psychology could apply the "definition" and so derive a list of eligible, legitimate psychological practitioners; hence my proposition to Aetna. Thus was born the idea that ultimately became the *National Register of Health Service Providers in Psychology*.

By this time, the Dirty Dozen had founded the Council for the Advancement of Psychological Practices and Sciences (CAPPS), and that organization was deeply involved in the "reimbursement" issue. Given my six-month timeline, my knowledge of the glacial speed of the APA's response to any new idea, and the rapid response capability of CAPPS's Executive Committee, I proposed that CAPPS develop this Register. CAPPS considered the idea at length, and although very supportive of the concept, declined to develop it. The decision was based on its concern about a conflict of interests because CAPPS already was functioning as an advocacy organization for psychology, engaging in lobbying, as well as participating in a class-action suit against the U.S. Civil Service Commission (because of the exclusion of psychologists from FEHBA).

CAPPS recommended and supported my taking the proposal to the APA's Division 29 and/or 31. I found support, but both organizations (and, indeed , all of the APA) declined to participate because of yet another "conflict of interest" (i.e., the APA's activities as an accrediting body). Almost three years later, and with the unflagging support of Gene Shapiro and the American Board of Professional Psychology, we launched the National Register as a private agency.

Blue Shield and the Federal Employees Health Program

Extended negotiations with Blue Cross/Blue Shield (BC/BS) and the Civil Service Commission (which managed federal employee health insurance contracts) by CAPPS and COHI were unsuccessful, and the recognition of psychologists in the Aetna portion of the FEBHA had no effect on the "Blues." Repeated contacts with the Blues met with polite refusals to offer the "psychologists reimbursement." The common saying was, "The Blues will nice-nice you to death." The failure of these negotiations was a constant source of irritation, occasioned in no small part by the APA's unwillingness to become involved with "issues" in the "private sector" and by its 501(c)(3) tax status, which deterred the organization and its subordinate bodies from taking some of the desired (and militant) actions necessary to address the recalcitrance of the insurance carriers. We even had problems with the Blues regarding our freedom-of-choice legislation, because some of the early freedom-of-choice state laws continued language that applied to commercial health insurers, but not to nonprofit organizations, such as Blue Cross/Blue Shield. Clearly, a different approach was necessary.

CAPPS and the "Blues"

The Council for the Advancement of Psychological Professions and Sciences, or CAPPS, was founded on June 25, 1971, as an independent 501(c)(6) business and professional organization, unrestricted by the 501(c)(3) regulations limiting the APA. Under a charge from Division 31 (State Psychological Associations), CAPPS was conceived by Rogers Wright, with Nick Cummings and Ernie Lawrence becoming its organizing members. As CAPPS wanted to be representative of psychology across the country, and because of my experience in insurance, I was asked to join CAPPS EX-COMM, which soon also included Max Siegal of New York, Ted Blau of Florida, Helen Sunukian of Illinois, and James McCall of Texas. Special consultants to CAPPS were Robert Weitz of New Jersey, Logan Wright of Oklahoma, and Don Schultz of California. The CAPPS EX-COMM elected Rogers Wright as chair and directed him to seek incorporation in Washington. Now we had an action arm ready and able to fight for psychology.

With legal guidance from counsel Joseph Nellis (formerly counsel to Senator Estes Kefauver's anticrime committee), EX-COMM conceived and implemented a class-action suit against the Blues and the Civil Service Commission, charging restraint of trade because of their recognition of psychiatrists, but not of psychologists, in the FEHBA program. A campaign to support the suit with voluntary contributions was organized, and within less than a month, we had collected over $50,000. This energized the practitioner community. The APA was silent, but pleased that it didn't have to be involved. CAPPS had captured the hearts of practitioners and grew as a result.

The filing of the class-action suit against the Blues and the Civil Service Commission was followed by the Commission's decision to direct the FEHBA contracts be amended to include psychologists as independent and reimbursable providers of mental health services. This action, although welcome, was a mixed blessing because whereas it solved the initial problem (the nonrecognition of psychologists as independently reimbursable providers under FEHBA), it "mooted" CAPPS's class-action suit and thereby denied psychology a court precedent against the Blues (in what seemed to many to be a clear instance of restraint of train in favor of physicians). In light of this development and CAPPS's limited resources, EX-COMM decided to practice a concurrent strategy of pursuing "hearings" before the Congress. Strange as it may seem (in the current political context of the economics of national health plans), the early 1970s saw the Congress deeply involved in considering a national health plan as a follow-up to the passage of Medicare and Medicaid.

It was an extremely problematic time for psychology, despite CAPPS's success with FEHBA, because the APA's failure to act had foreclosed our participation in Medicare, which was presumed to be the model for the anticipated and rapid passage of a follow-up National Health Plan. Through personal contacts with the chairs of the House Ways and Means Committees and the Senate Post Office Committee, CAPPS was invited to present testimony before both committees on the appropriate role of psychologists in mental health programs. Mel Gravitz, Gene Shapiro, and I were designated by CAPPS to testify about our grievances with Blue Cross/Blue Shield and the importance of psychology's participation in national health planning before the Post Office

Committee, which was chaired by Senator Quentin Burdick of North Dakota. Gravitz, because of his familiarity with FEHBA, explained how requiring medical referrals adversely affected federal employees by limiting their freedom of choice and reducing competition. Gene Shapiro spoke of how psychologists were defined as physicians for the purpose of insurance contracts in many states, characterizing it as "featherbedding"—a term I originated and CAPPS made public during the filing of its suit against the Blues. My testimony addressed the unnecessary "extra" fees paid to physicians for referral.

CHAMPUS

At the instigation of Senator Daniel Inouye's office, CHAMPUS (the Civilian Health and Medical Plan for the Uniformed Services) was identified as a target for COHI attention. The senator and his aide, Dr. Pat DeLeon (a psychologist), were concerned about both the quantity and quality of mental-health care available to the members of the Armed Services owing to the small number of psychiatrists in the military. The inclusion of psychologists as fully independent providers would help alleviate that problem. COHI knew little about the mental-health provisions in CHAMPUS; and it was not a high priority for us until Colonel Charles Thomas, a career army officer and ranking psychologist in the Pentagon, called my office. He explained that CHAMPUS, one of the largest health plans operated by the government, also provided services for the dependents of military personnel and for retirees from the military and their dependents. He had seen how we obtained coverage for psychologists' services in the Aetna federal employees plan and thought this might be possible in CHAMPUS as well. We identified the documentation he needed, and John McMillan furnished it.

Eventually, John McMillan called my office to say that Colonel Thomas had arranged for an appointment with General Rousseleau, who was in charge of health services for the Joint Chiefs of Staff, and McMillan, Gene Shapiro, and I met with the general and his aide. After hearing our presentation the general asked if we wanted recognition for psychologists in CHAMPUS for the entire world, or just for the United States. Having never previously considered the question, we looked at one another, and I finally said that as a representative of the APA we were requesting the provision only for the United States (since we could not speak for the standards or credentials of psychologists in others countries). The general seem satisfied with my answer, thanked us for our presentation, and dismissed us without giving any indication of his thoughts on the matter.

Several weeks later, Colonel Thomas called McMillan to inform him that General Rousseleau had sent a letter "requesting" that psychologists be reimbursed under CHAMPUS, and as we were to learn, when a general "requests," it is actually an order. We were included in CHAMPUS! It should be noted in passing that a large part of the CHAMPUS recognition of psychologists was attributable to the continuing interest of Senator Inouye and his aide, Dr. DeLeon. Also, notable is that, at the time, Senator Inouye was chair of the Senate Armed Forces Committee.

The CHAMPUS recognition was extremely important because CHAMPUS covered more lives than the Aetna contracts did, and, furthermore, it covered inpatient psychological services in hospitals as well as outpatient care, making this our first breakthrough in hospital recognition. CHAMPUS data were a matter of public record, and thus, for the first time, we were able to obtain claims data for a large number of insureds who had utilized the independent services of psychologists. These data were extremely valuable when negotiating with insurers in the private sector and with the Health Insurance Association of America. Meanwhile, Herb Dorken was elected to COHI and was able to use CHAMPUS data for several studies that were useful in making the case for the inclusion of psychologists and independent providers in health plans. A final note on the importance of the CHAMPUS recognition of psychologists: when CHAMPUS VA legislation was adopted that gave beneficiaries of deceased veterans the same benefits as retired military personnel, psychologists' services were included among its provisions. The number of such beneficiaries was not large, but the action underscored the fact that psychologists are an integral part of the health team.

The Vocational Rehabilitation Act of 1973

On one of our many trips to the Capitol with regard to national health insurance, Gene Shapiro and I learned that testimony on the "Perkins Bill" (a major revamp of Vocation Rehabilitation) was ongoing and we decided to see how it was proceeding. Although the hearings were over, we found a staff person handling the testimony for the bill who was kind enough to ask about our concerns. This staffer agreed to extend the period for testimony for two additional weeks to allow the APA/COHI time to submit a written statement. The testimony was prepared and submitted by John McMillan. We had two major objections; (1) We wanted the requirement that a person must have a physical impairment in order to receive mental health care deleted. (2) We wanted psychological services to be provided at parity with psychiatric services.

With the help of Durand "Dewey" Jacobs of the VA, COHI formed a coalition of rehabilitation psychologists in support of this legislation. The legislation passed the House with ease. The Senate hearings were chaired by Senator Alan Cranston, who had become a friend of the Dirty Dozen psychologists. Although CAPPS had arranged for psychologists to testify, the senator just asked a few questions about our written testimony and the hearing was over in 20 minutes. The final bill was passed by the Congress, and it included the language we requested. We were both shocked and disappointed when then-President Richard Nixon vetoed the bill. Subsequently, the bill was returned to the Congress, again was passed (with our recommendations intact), and was again vetoed. On a third try, Congress once again passed the bill, and this time it was finally signed into law (1975) with our "language" still included. It was a welcome surprise to the APA governance that through the efforts of CAPPS and COHI, mental health was now on a parity with physical health in Vocational Rehabilitation, and, furthermore, that psychology was on a parity with psychiatry.

Hospital Practice

Beginning in the mid-1970s psychological advocacy experienced a difficult time. The APA had changed executive officers, and it was a transitional period for the federal government, as well. The interest in national health insurance legislation had subsided with the election of Nixon and it was a new ball game in Washington. The expansion of social legislation had come to a virtual halt. And the APA, severely threatened by the many successes of CAPPS, had established a competing advocacy organization, the Association for the Advancement of Psychology (AAP). Recognizing the idiocy of having two organizations advocating for psychology, CAPPS and the AAP decided to amalgamate.

At the dinner arranged for CAPPS and the AAP to "join together," I presented a citation of a 1975 decision (*Goldfarb v. Virginia State Bar*) for discussion. This citation described a federal court decision to the effect that professions were subject to antitrust laws in the same way as other trade associations. In light of the decision, I wondered whether it would be possible to bring an antitrust action against hospital staffs that excluded psychologists from membership. The concept was added to the AAP agenda.

In the process of reviewing an antitrust suit regarding hospital practice, we learned that the Commission for the Accreditation of Rehabilitation Facilities (CARF), a peer organization of the JCAH, was very supportive of psychologists. CARF accreditation required psychologists to be on the staffs of rehabilitation hospitals and of facilities attached to the hospitals. There was great disparity between how psychologists were treated according to CARF standards and by JCAH regulations that placed them in restricted and subordinate positions. We believed, and were supported by legal counsel, that in comparing the two sets of regulations, the JCAH regulations constituted restraint of trade.

After unfruitful deliberations with the JCAH, it was determined that the best way to proceed would be to file a complaint with the Federal Trade Commission (FTC) charging antitrust violations under the McCarren Ferguson Act, the Sherman Antitrust Act, and the Clayton Act. This initiative was used as a fundraiser for the AAP, and found significant support among practitioners.

It was a time when general hospitals were starting to develop psychiatric units to meet the increased demand for mental-health care (made available by the coverage of nervous and mental conditions in third-party insurance contracts). The FTC took up the complaint, which named the BC/BS and the JCAH as coconspirators. I was appointed chair of an AAP Special Projects Task Force to follow up on the complaint. However, before completion of the investigation, the political fortunes of the FTC changed. The American Medical Association (AMA), through legislation, came within a whisker of removing professions from FTC jurisdiction, and our complaint was lost in the FTC files without resolution.

Nevertheless, the ebbing of the FTC investigation did not close down the Hospital Task Force. From a newspaper article, I learned that a lawyer in the Cleveland office of the Ohio Attorney General had been granted $50,000 to investigate antitrust issues in health care, and I met with him. After much negotiating, the Ohio Attorney General (a future gubernatorial candidate) expressed interest in pursuing the case. However, by a quirk in the Ohio law, hospitals were not defined as medical institutions, and so, in 1979, the Attorney General filed an antitrust complaint against the JCAH.

The case dragged on for nearly three years, and we had all but given up; when we were told that the JCAH wanted to depose us. Based on the questions asked and our testimony in response, our lawyers felt we had done a good job. A few weeks later, the Attorney General's office informed us that a settlement had been reached whereby the JCAH would abide by state laws in its regulations and policies relating to staff membership and hospital privileges.

The JCAH settlement turned out to be more of a victory than it seemed. With this principle established, Dorken, acting on behalf of the California State Psychological Association, lost no time in introducing a hospital practice bill to the California legislature, and getting it passed and signed. The Ohio Medical Association also wasted no time in getting Ohio law changed to protect the status quo and to punish psychologists. The new punitive law denied psychologists the right to admit, discharge, or transfer patients in hospitals. Then, to add to our consternation, the California Attorney General refused to implement the new psychology hospital practice act. The resulting *CAPP v. Rank* suit , which resulted in psychology's ultimately gaining full privileges in private hospitals is well documented. Ironically, California's state mental hospitals did not have to comply with the decision, and this required yet more legislation. A further irony was that psychologists gained full hospital privileges just as hospitals were cutting back on "psychiatric" beds due to the effects of HMOs.

Medicare, Medicaid, and Social Security Disability Income Programs

In 1976, the APA Board of Professional Affairs (BPA) asked me to chair its Task Force on Medicare to investigate how psychologists might be included in Medicare. Drs. John D. Robinson and Tommy T. Stigall joined me in tackling this major block to the insurance reimbursement of psychological services. Lack of recognition by Medicare was used by the JCAH as a rationale for not permitting psychologists to be on hospital staffs. This, in turn, created a major barrier to the hospital practice of psychology. Our objective was to be included in the definitions of physicians in Section 1861R of Title XVIII (Medicare) of the Social Security Act. The fact that psychologists were listed in group health insurance contracts under the definition of "physicians" was to no avail. In fact, psychologists are not listed as physicians under 1861R today, a quarter of a century later, which impedes the full recognition of psychology in federal regulations and limits the access of psychology students to training funds.

The task force also searched for enabling provision for psychological services in Social Security Titles XVI (disability), XIX (Medicaid), and XX (block grants). Medicaid was found to be a federal–state program in which the individual states define the providers. The disability and block grants programs were also federal state programs somewhat like Medicaid, and as state-controlled programs, their recognition of psychologists was not a practice issue that the APA could address directly. However, the

APA could, and did, assist the various states in considering these issues.

Title XVI and eligibility for Social Security Income programs, an area in which psychology was involved at the state level, were regulated by the Social Security Administration (SSA). Psychologists were hired by states on a contract basis to carry out psychological evaluations to determine the eligibility of the physically and mentally impaired for Social Security benefits. This was a natural follow-up to the work COHI had been doing under the Vocational Rehabilitation Act. As the regulations were written, psychological test findings could be used by the Medical Examiner under contract to the SSA, but the psychologist providing the data could not testify directly about a person's evaluation.

The APA Office of Professional Affairs succeeded in getting psychological testing accepted as medical evidence by the SSA. However, a change in the language of the law was required to permit psychologists to be medical examiners for SSA disability beneficiaries. Our work with the state and regional Social Security offices brought us into contact with Dr. Steven Morin, a psychologist knowledgeable about the SSA, and he identified the section of the regulations requiring modification. Through his continuing efforts, the section was amended, but it took seven years to get the seven words of enabling language incorporated into the statute.

This new recognition has not been fully appreciated by psychology. Based on work on SSA disability determinations, it has become apparent that one of the major tasks of psychology in health care is to prevent or ameliorate the disabling emotional effects of physical illness and injury, and not necessarily "to cure disease." This is a market upon which psychology must focus if it is to survive as a health-care profession in the 21st century.

Peer Review of Insurance Reimbursement

The increased recognition of psychology in insurance reimbursement gave rise to a demand by insurers for demonstrations that the "treatment was medically necessary." Psychology responded to the challenge by developing a peer-review program. But because of its cost, the length of time required for the review, and the variations in state laws regulating health insurance contracts, it was never really utilized. Nevertheless, the plan did provide psychology with valuable experience in the process of peer and/or utilization review. Later CHAMPUS, which had recognized psychologists for some time, instituted a program-wide peer-review process and requested that the APA contract with CHAMPUS to perform peer reviews. These programs were troubled from the outset, in part because CHAMPUS was more devoted to "cost control" than to a true peer review, and also in part to the APA's design of its CHAMPUS program. And again, the APA's CHAMPUS Committee was dominated by academics and staff members, who had little knowledge of and/or experience in designing and operating large service-providing and service-review programs based on a fee-for-service model. Consequently, the APA CHAMPUS program was an overly idealistic, unrealistic effort that encouraged reviewers to function as "professors" rather than as colleagues, had many reviewers who were themselves inexperienced and lacking in knowledge, and allowed negative evaluations based on nothing more than theoretical bias. At best, the program can be described as unfortunate and very problematic.

When the program became operative, a significant number of APA members saw fit to institute a legal action against their own organization that called for the program's complete redesign. However, this consequence did occasion a new milestone in the APA's history: the establishment of a "committee" composed exclusively of members primarily identified with practice. This group, which included Dirty Dozeners Nick Cummings, Gene Shapiro, C.J. Rosecrans, Jr., and Rogers Wright, revolutionized peer-review programs by requiring that reviewers truly be peers of the reviewed, and by developing a data-based peer and utilization review system. Initially, this system worked well, and was expanded to offer service to the health insurers in the private sector.

However, it was short-lived because CHAMPUS was pioneering the health insurance industry's move to "managed care," a scheme whereby "peer review" would become "utilization review" performed by employees of the insurer. The vicissitudes of attempting to operate a meaningful and objective review program under managed care became so great as to lead the APA to terminate its participation in the CHAMPUS program, and ultimately to shut down its Professional Service Program completely.

Nursing-Home Regulation and Legislation

During this period, the billing practices of nursing homes also came under the scrutiny of federal investigators. States had discovered that elderly patients in mental hospitals who did *not* require active treatment could be cared for in skilled nursing facilities (SNFs). Furthermore, by "dumping" these state mental patients into private nursing homes, the costs of care could be transferred to federal funds.

Although the practice never became a major public issue because it was a controversy between the state and the federal government, it was an issue for psychology, and both the AAP and the APA Practice Directorate confronted it. Since many elderly patients are on psychotropic medication and are often overmedicated, prescriptive authority would materially enhance the diagnostic/evaluative and treatment services that psychology provides. Psychologists could suggest alternative care if they could titrate psychotropic medications so as to coordinate treatment with the alternative-care plans. This remains an area for future initiatives.

ERISA

If state freedom-of-choice laws were one of the high points in the story of the reimbursement of psychology, ERISA was the low. The 1975 enactment of the Employee Retirement Income Security Act (ERISA) and its subsequent judicial interpretation dealt a severe blow to all health-care professions, including psychology. This law, as judicially interpreted, basically destroyed state control of the health-insurance industry's employer-sponsored health plans without providing remedies for the beneficiaries for whom the employers had originally purchased the insurance protection.

ERISA's deregulation of health insurance, an unintended consequence of a Retirement Security Act, was particularly hard on mental health services because: (1) diagnostic codes were so vague and overlapping that almost anyone could be diagnosed as having a mental disorder; (2) the diagnostic nomenclature was not predictive of the type of treatment required; (3) it was very difficult to specify the product of psychotherapy; and (4) there were no objective measures of outcome. All insurers really knew about mental health services was that once patients got into the mental health system, they were apt to be there for a long time and could cost a lot of money. And the attitudes that these problems engendered plague the mental health professions to this day.

What is clear is that the court's interpretation of ERISA put employees and the insurance companies in charge of health insurance; and there still are no state or federal governmental checks and balances, so health-care benefits are now left to the tender mercies of the marketplace. Thus, "managed care" was born as an offspring of industrial commerce. Whether health care will, or even should, remain the legacy of commerce is a social dilemma left unresolved a quarter of a century later. And an unfortunate concomitant is that the experience with *all* national health-care plans to date indicates that the government cannot manage health care satisfactorily. The bureaucratic bungling of Medicare, Medicaid, and Worker's Compensation suggests that controlling health care and its costs is beyond the government's capabilities at this time. The same data and experience argue convincingly that the concept of universal health-care system is a dream and an illusion. Until we can agree on a single standard of the value of life, we cannot place a common value on health or its costs. Although I cannot foresee the outcome of this argument, I am willing to stick around for the debate.

The full effects of ERISA were not felt immediately, but it soon became apparent to psychologists deeply involved in the reimbursement issue that outpatient, office-based practices would be much more severely limited than before. It was speculated that hospitals would be setting up panels of providers to contract their

services with self-insuring businesses. Therefore, additional emphasis was placed on facilitating psychologists' participation in hospital-based practice. In order to survive in practice, it was felt that
the psychologist's best bet would be to become a member of a
hospital staff. Since psychology as a profession largely catered to
outpatients, and JCAH regulations limited hospital membership,
special attention was given to JCAH regulation of hospital-based
practice. It was also thought that larger group practices would
survive better than solo practitioners. We attempted to translate
these developments into ideas and suggestions to psychologists in
the field, but were hampered by the lack of communication with
our members. We suggested the combination of practices and the
negotiation of service contracts with employers. Whether the reason was that our warnings were unheard or were just ignored,
little happened within psychology to deal with ERISA and its
managed-care component. It was as though we were in a state of
denial until the federal HMO law was renewed. By then it was
too late.

Other Developments Affecting the
Reimbursement of Psychological Services

One effect of the HMO Renewal Act of 1982 was that many
HMOs were created, along with Preferred Provider Panels (PPOs).
Federal guidelines proved to be too difficult to follow, and not all
HMOs were federally qualified. But the race was on, with insurance companies leading the pack. Prior to the 1982 HMO Act,
states required health plans to set aside reserves of millions of
dollars, just like insurance companies (a requirement that thwarted psychology's efforts to set up a psychological service plan
called Blue Psi). However, a California psychological service cooperative called the California Health Insurance Plan was formed
and operated for several years; and a number of mental health
treatment plans were established by psychologists and psychiatrists. The most successful of these was American Biodyne, or
simply "Biodyne." Within five years, this clinically driven company, with Nick Cummings as its CEO, covered 14.5 million lives

and employed 8,000 psychologists as service providers. Disappointed that Biodyne was essentially ignored by psychology, and having reached age 70, Cummings sold the company, and Biodyne's treatment policies rapidly changed. Biodyne subsequently was sold several more times, and now is part of Magellan, the largest behavioral managed-care company in the world with 60 million covered lives.

The Criminal Justice Code

Another sidebar to the mainstream developments in insurance reimbursement was the revision of the federal criminal code. Psychology, although previously included, had a somewhat marginal and unclear status in the justice system, and the improvement of that status was not covered in COHI's charge. However, the AAP was alerted to the possibility that criminal code legislation (held up in congressional committee for years) might, at last, be moving. As chair of the AAP, I asked Bruce Bennett, who was then in charge of the AAP's special projects, to undertake the task of negotiating the enhancement of psychology's position in this legislation to reach parity with psychiatry. Despite Washington's conventional wisdom that the bill would come to naught, the legislation passed and was signed into law. This gave psychology increased stature in criminal justice; and as a profession was now also recognized by the Congress. The legislation has been instrumental in the development of forensic psychology as well.

Insurance Reimbursement as Viewed from the Other End of the Kaleidoscope Effects of Insurance Reimbursement on the APA

According the laws of Newtonian physics, for every action, there is an equal and an opposite reaction. Up to this point, this chapter has focused on the external effects of obtaining insurance reimbursement for psychological services. Such reimbursement also had significant effects on the APA, and on other psychological organizations as well.

Effects on Representation and Election

As mentioned earlier, the APA historically was primarily an academically oriented scientific organization with little room or patience for concerns relating to the practice of psychology. Insurance reimbursement was one of several issues that created a radical change in the membership of the APA. In 1950, only about 10% of the 10,000 APA members identified their primary work practice. Currently, nearly 80% of the 89,000 APA members are licensed to practice. Of those, approximately 70% earn a substantial portion of their incomes by providing health services. This shift would not have happened without the many changes in the APA, one of which was insurance reimbursement, which place a monetary value on a licensed scope of practice. Another major factor was that state psychological associations became organized and began to fight for representation of the APA Council. The resulting competition between divisional interests (traditionally academic) and those of state psychological organizations (predominately professional) created a dynamic contest for representation that still continues, *and the APA has grown in numbers and stature as a result.* This tension ultimately became focused on a proposal to reorganize the APA that, when roundly defeated in 1989, resulted in the formation, by a relatively small group of academic/scientific psychologists, of the American Psychological Society (APS) as an independent organization. Most of the members of the newly formed APS retained their memberships in the APA.

In the 1950s, the APA's Office of Professional Affairs was staffed by a single psychologist and a secretary. Most of the resources of the association were devoted to academic interests and the scientific meetings, including the annual APA Convention, which were held on college campuses. There was outright antipathy toward the development of state psychological associations, and the licensing of psychologists was a controversial matter that was opposed by the academicians. Even among practitioners, there was heated debate as to whether to seek licensing or certification laws. Those discussions concerning state associations representation on the APA's Council resulted in the establishment of the Albee

Commission in the late 1960s to develop "an equitable way" to resolve issues surrounding the APA Council representation.

The Albee Commission's solution was an apportionment ballot of 10 votes for each member to distribute among the Divisions and states in accordance with how his or her interests should be represented on the Council. The Council representatives would be elected using the Hare system, whereby candidates would be ranked by preference so that a centrist candidate would be elected. This system was adopted even though it appeared to practitioners that if was stacked in favor of those with high name recognition, such as academicians who were the leading presenters and authors represented in APA publications. The Board of Directors, which included the APA secretary, treasurer, and members-at-large, would be elected by the Council representatives. Only the president of the APA would be elected by a referendum of APA members.

It took three or four elections for practitioners to learn how the system could work in their favor. It gradually became apparent that having representatives from state psychological associations on the ballot was the key to the election of practitioners to the Board of Directors. Bullet balloting, voting only for one candidate, did not work. In the redistribution of second, third, and fourth choices, a commanding lead on the first count could be overcome by candidates with fewer votes in the arcane Hare system, whereas on five-person ballot, it was essential to load the slate with candidates with interests similar to one's own. This made the nomination process as important as the election itself.

As state organizations grew in strength thanks to licensing and insurance reimbursement, they elected more and more representatives to the APA Council. Rogers Wright was the first practitioner to be elected to the APA Board of Directors, followed by Nick Cummings, and then by S. Don Schultz. In this election process, Ted Blau was able to become the first practitioner president, to be followed by other members of the Dirty Dozen, Nick Cummings, Max Siegel, Ray Fowler, and myself.

Volunteer Versus a Staff Model of the APA

A second major effect of insurance reimbursement on the APA after the development of state associations into a political force related to the question of a volunteer implementation versus a professional staff implementation model. In its early "academic/scientist" history, the APA had a very small "paid" staff, and most of the work was accomplished by volunteer members of the APA's boards and committees. Given that these members were academics with an institutional staff and backing, "volunteer" effort could generally "get the job done," especially as there was not much work involved. However, the advent of such issues as state and federal advocacy, licensure, insurance reimbursement, and communications soon made clear the urgent necessity to hire a paid staff with skills, knowledge, experience, expertise, and full-time availability.

Although in reality these issues affect *all* of psychology, the APA's academic/scientist wing still persists in viewing them as "practice concerns" and so is unwilling to support them through increases in dues and voluntary contributions. Thus, any request for additional staff or economic or developmental support becomes a battle over an "unnecessary dues increase." Over time, the necessity for expertise applied on a consistent basis toward achieving a resolution to the many recurrent crises confronted by psychology, coupled with the increasing political power of representatives of professional practice within the APA's Council preordained the outcome of enough of these budgetary skirmishes that a professional staff could begin to be developed.

It was not until the establishment of the Practice Directorate funded by a differential dues structure paid for exclusively by practitioners, however, that the staff implementation could become fully functional. This has been a very successful strategy for the last 15 years. It has enlarge the scope of the practice of psychology by strengthening state psychological associations. And has enhanced the position of psychology in the legislative, regulatory, and judiciary arenas at both the state and federal levels.

Networking, Collaboration, and Independence

Psychology's 40-year struggle for recognition as an independent profession has left is marks on the discipline. The internal resistance within the APA and the adversarial struggles with medicine for independent practice engendered resentment on the part of practitioners. Although legislative and regulatory victories were achieved, public and professional acceptance of the new independent profession was slower in coming. It has created a certain amount of awkwardness in collaborations between psychology and other health-care professions.

Collaboration has been defined by Dennis King as an unnatural act engaged in by nonconsenting adults. The health-care field is on of the interactive areas that is facilitated by networking and collaborations. In many respects, health care functions like political advocacy where you get to know people (networking) and learn to work together on common goals (collaboration). Psychologists pride themselves on their independent thinking, which incorporates an attitude of skepticism and a willingness (if not eagerness) to challenge others. It generates a philosophical orientation that needs to be explained in terms of psychological phenomena. I refer to this as "psychocentrism." This approach may be useful for academic debate, but alienates other health-care professionals in providing care.

Psychocentrism is a destructive attitude that must be overcome if practice and advocacy are to be successful. Since everyone considers one's own views as valid, psychocentrism places psychology in an adversarial position with conventional wisdom. On the other hand, if conventional wisdom and psychological findings agree, the expertise of psychologists is discounted by observing that they are merely providing the obvious, and everyone knows that already. The staff model developed by the APA Practice Directorate has greatly improved networking and collaboration with regard to psychology and the public. Its pragmatism has reduced psychocentrism and has established a presence on Capitol Hill and in state legislatures, building relationships with a variety of federal and state agencies. Nevertheless, the rapid turnover in the APA

Council membership results in a persistent view that all problems can be solved through more representation and better education of the public. This view fails to countenance the fact that it is the public and its legislative representatives that set the agenda, not psychology. Thus, networking and collaboration in executing APA functions must be valued, as must the role of psychologists as an independent and socially responsible group.

Summary

In summary, insurance reimbursement was one of a number of issues that dramatically shifted the membership of the APA from academe practice, to the applied from the theoretical. It changed much of the agenda of the association to more pragmatic issues in the health field without surrendering psychology's scientific values. It demonstrated the value of advocacy, and advocacy, in turn, created the necessity for a strong staff model for sustained and effective management of that agenda. Advocacy has shown that networking and collaboration are compatible with the goal of independence of a socially responsible profession and discipline. These are the legacies of the passionate and dedicated group called the Dirty Dozen *and* their many supporters and collaborators over nearly four decades.

Things Left Undone

It would be unthinkable for one as immersed in advocacy for our profession as I have been for so many years to complete such a chapter without making a pitch for tasks needing to be done and dreams to be fulfilled. Advocates are always looking to the future, and such is the case here. Up until now, fee-for-service insurance reimbursement has been a major stimulus to psychology's growth in the health field. If this is not to be the funding mechanism of the future, new mechanisms must be found.

In the current health-care market, there are at least two practice issues that need to be called to the attention of the reader. The issue of psychology as a primary health-care profession was initially raised 30 years ago in COHI and only now is becoming ripe for action. The second issue is that of psychopharmacology as a way for psychology to become a full service profession. These tasks are not mutually exclusive, but are separate and distinct. Both will be driven by economic factors in the marketplace. It is time to create a Department of Health Economics within the APA to forecast occupational opportunities and to match training opportunities with public needs.

The health-care field has continued to grow and has become more and more specialized as its knowledge base has expanded. Duties and services once reserved for physicians are now shared by many disciplines. Physicians in primary health care find that their scope of practice is stretching competence to the limit. More and more of these family physicians are complaining of the multiplicity of demands placed on them, while the advent of such medications as specialized serotonin reuptake inhibiting (SSRI) antidepressants has given them new tools with which to work and challenged them to provide care for conditions about which they have little knowledge. And this dilemma applies not only to family physicians, but to other medical specialties as well. Thus, a new opportunity has been created for collaboration between psychology and medicine because patient attitudes and emotions are being brought back into the healing equation. Medical technology is not enough for the American public. With access to health information readily available, the public is seeking its own solutions. It relies on physicians' opinions and seeks second, and even third, opinions, as well as alternative solutions, in the quest for health and comfort.

The U.S. Food and Drug Administration, in lifting the ban on the direct marketing of medications through the public media some three years ago, has intensified this situation. Pharmaceutical companies spend over $900 million on advertising to increase the demand for their products. This heightened awareness of and demand for medication, and the increasing numbers of nonphysicians prescribing such medication, is placing ever-greater pressure on psychologists to obtain prescriptive authority.

Today's tacit acceptance by the health field of Engle's 1978 recommendation of the biopsychosocial model leaves psychology little choice but to rethink its position in the health-care market. Psychology must organize its training objectives to meet biopsychosocial demands as a full-service health profession. The psychological aspects of various health problems, including the disabling effects of depression generated by chronic disease and injury, create a myriad of specialized niche markets in which to expand the delivery of psychological services. Psychology is a *primary-care* health profession whose function is to remove or alleviate the disabling effects of illness and injury. Thus, psychology is uniquely qualified to help individuals retain as much functionality as possible throughout the process of prevention, detection, diagnosis, treatment, and rehabilitation. Proficiency training and documentation of that training are required to meet this challenge. The psychologist's familiarity with specific diseases is leading to the development of proficiencies beyond generic licensing. And there is still a major unfilled niche in the mental health arena for psychologists who wish to prescribe.

Psychotherapy and counseling have become commodities. The mental health field is saturated with lesser-trained practitioners who will work for less money. In order to distinguish ourselves from our rivals in the commercial marketing of psychological expertise, the APA will have to increase its budget for advocacy and defend the discipline of psychology against imitators. It will have to spend more money on public education. This will lead inevitably to dues increases and further strains on academic/practitioner ties. New sources of income must be found and individual psychologists must play a more active role in advocating for their discipline.

Students seeking graduate training in psychology expect to be trained to practice in the field that is emerging rather than in the scientist/practitioner model of the 1940s. Current APA accreditation guidelines explicitly encourage "vanity" training programs by allowing them to define their own objectives. The vanity involved in such self-determined and self-fulfilling programs no longer can be tolerated as public policy. These self-styled programs must give way to more socially conscious, centrally described training programs designed to meet identified societal needs. It will be interesting to see how soon psychology will become an appropriately trained full-service health-care discipline.

JACK G. WIGGINS, PH.D., PSY.D.

CHAPTER 8

Heirs to the Dirty Dozen

The Dirty Dozen taught psychologists a valuable lesson, that in order to advance the profession, doing good work in our offices is necessary, but not sufficient. Political activity is an important adjunct to our usual roles as psychotherapists, consultants, educators, and researchers. The Dirty Dozen demonstrated that motivating practitioners to become involved in the political process, getting the vote out, and having our leaders seek governance positions within the APA all required more sophisticated methods than we habitually employed.

Association of Practicing Psychologists

We, the heirs to the legacy of the Dirty Dozen, have fine-tuned the process by creating the Association of Practicing Psychologists (APP). The membership comes, first, from the APA Council of Representatives, where the APP is the prominent practitioner caucus. Membership requires that the applicant hold a valid license for independent practice, as well as a position of governance in the APA or one of its Divisions, or in a state psychological association. There are currently 250 members, and the annual dues of $50 have yielded a treasury of $19,000 to date. The money has been used to cover APP expenses and to enable contributions to practice causes, including $5,000 to help finance a lawsuit against MCC, a managed-care company, brought by the New Jersey Psychological Association, and a fund that brought a group of psychologists together to craft a widely distributed health-care policy statement. This group was spearheaded by Arthur Kovacs and included, among others, Russ Newman, Dorothy Cantor, Pat Bricklin, and Wayne Sotile. There are plans to bring the work of the group to the attention of the APA Council of Representatives (C/R) in the hope that it will adopt a health-care-reform position.

The APP also gave money to support the "wild card plan," which added 48 seats to the Council of Representatives, enabling small states to have representatives there as Divisions and larger states do. Since not every state has a seat on the Council of Representatives, money has been advanced to ensure that every state without a representative at least has a liaison person present. What may occur in Montana, for example, affects every other state. Under the new plan, every state has the opportunity to participate in discussions of important policy issues, and this goal is close to being achieved. Other contributions were made to advance the practice agenda. Again, although the C/R serves as the main source for APP membership, state associations and practice Divisions are also a source.

The APP's primary goal is to enable practitioners to be elected to APA boards and committees, including the Board of Directors itself, and to influence the election of a practitioner to the APA Presidency. A second goal is to introduce motions to the C/R that advance professional issues. A platform committee of the APP identifies the issues to be addressed, the implementation committee translates the platform into motions to go before the C/R, and then the campaign coordinator rounds up the votes. The APP has been enormously successful in getting its members elected, so much so that this strategy is being emulated successfully by other caucuses in the Council. Even though name recognition still attracts votes, membership in the APP goes a long way toward producing a winner. Other Council caucuses include those of the state associations, the scientist/practitioner women and mi-

norities. In earlier days, membership in the APP was usually sufficient to guarantee election, but now the chances of being elected
are enhanced by belonging to more than one caucus.

The leadership of the APP reads like a virtual "who's who" of
the practitioner community, with the following on its roster of
past presidents: Rogers Wright, Bryant Welch, Pat DeLeon, Marvin
Metsky, Arthur Kovacs, Stan Moldawsky (two terms), George
Taylor, and Pat Bricklin. Stan Moldawsky, Dorothy Cantor,
Sandy Haber, and George Taylor have been campaign coordinators. Past secretaries are Faith Tanney, Norine Johnson, and
Karen Zager, while past treasurers are Jay Benedict, Ron Levant,
and John Stuart Currie. Among prominent members of the board
were Stanley Graham (consultant), Terry Koller, Judith Stewart,
Kathy Nordahl, Nick Bisenius, and Asher Pacht.

The Dirty Dozen succeeded in getting Ted Blau elected president of the APA, the first practitioner to achieve that position. A
concerted effort to get out the practitioner vote throughout the
country was key to his election. People calling people and letters
(this was before e-mail) to organizations were the primary methods of energizing the practitioner constituency at that time. Now,
however, by using electronic methods, the members on various
lists can be mobilized rapidly.

The APP has attained a prestigious reputation as an efficient
"political party." The Dirty Dozen showed the way, and the
group's heirs have continued the tradition of supporting practitioners for elective offices in psychology.

Division 42: Psychologists in Independent Practice

Only two of the Dirty Dozen were involved in the formation of
Division 42: Marvin Metsky and Bob Weitz. Metsky orchestrated
the C/R vote that brought the Division into being, with the assistance of Weitz, Moldawsky, and Graham. This was difficult task,
as there was considerable opposition. Other members of the
Council were concerned that Divisions were proliferating too rapidly, although they may not have had any particular opposition to
this particular Division. In either case, many arms had to be

twisted. Metsky persuaded a prominent scientist member of Division 3 to speak in the new Division's favor, a matter of considerable importance since most of the proponents were practitioners. Florence Denmark, the APA President at the time (1980), skillfully brought the matter to conclusion in the C/R.

The history of Division 42 has been written by Evelyn Hill, a past president of the Division of Psychologists in Independent Practice, and will not be repeated here. However, it is important to point out that the founding president was Stanley Graham. The Division was conceived at a historic meeting at the late Herb Freudenberger's New York office. In addition to Freudenberger, also in attendance were Stanley Graham, Stan Moldawsky, Richard Samuels, Leah Gold Fein, John Vayhinger, and Bob Weitz. The nucleus and immediate predecessor of Division 42 was the Society of Psychologists in Private Practice (SPPP). It was clear to that group that practitioners needed a forum at which to present their interests, to provide a venue in which to meet and discuss private-practice issues, and to be a political force in the APA. Although private-practice issues were given attention in Division 29 (Psychotherapy), Division 42 was to devote itself exclusively to promoting, protecting, and defining the issues in independent practice. Division 42 is thus the heir of the Dirty Dozen.

With 8,000 members, Division 42 is now the largest Division in the APA, which gives it seven representatives on the C/R, and makes it an active force in the promotion of private-practice concerns. In its two decades, it has been in the forefront of a number of changes within the APA: (1) It led the way in the creation of the Practice Directorate that is a strong presence in the APA central office. (2) It introduced a plethora of successful motions, most of which were initiated by Arthur Kovacs, in the C/R that made it a more efficient body. (3) It was a strong proponent of the APA's public education campaign as originally introduced by its representative, Stan Moldawsky. (4) Under the leadership of Sandy Haber, Elaine Rodino, and Peter Sheras, it created eight brochures that promote private practice. (5) In concert with Divisions 29 and 39, and through a special task force, it publicized the abuses of managed care. (6) It helped to create the AOPA task force on rural health, which was actually a spin-off of Division 42's own task force as led by Mike Enright. (7) It played an important role in electing five APA presidents: Jack Wiggins, Stanley Graham, Dorothy Cantor, Ron Fox, and Norine Johnson.

In two ceremonies at the APA's 1999 Convention in Boston, Division 42 joined the APP in honoring the Dirty Dozen for their pioneering work in furthering practice issues in the APA. It was the 30th anniversary of the Dirty Dozen, and the honorees in attendance were Rogers Wright (the spiritual leader of the Dirty Dozen), Nick Cummings, Bob Weitz, Gene Shapiro, Ray Fowler, Marv Metsky, Mel Gravitz, Ted Blau, and Jack Wiggins. Ernie Lawrence and Frank Young were unable to attend. Honored in memorium were Max Siegel, C. J. Rosecrans, and Don Schultz. The honors were significant in that they were extended by the heirs to the Dirty Dozen.

A proclamation by the chair of CAPP, Ron Fox, was read, and special lapel pins were distributed by Ray Fowler on behalf of the APA. (These documents are included in Appendix I.) It was noted that six members of the Dirty Dozen had been elected to the presidency of the APA, two others had been elected to the APA Board of Directors, and all had toiled aggressively for many years to advance practice within the APA, the nation, and throughout the world. Gratitude was expressed to these activists for their boldness and dedication, which earned them the appellation "Dirty Dozen." It is noteworthy that many of their heirs to the Dirty Dozen were in attendance, and gave the honorees a standing ovation.

STANLEY MOLDAWSKY, PH.D.

From the *APA Monitor*, From the *National Psychologist*:

Citations Honoring the Dirty Dozen

Kudos to the "Dirty Dozen"

Thirty-five years ago, a group of practitioners sometimes referred to as the "Dirty Dozen" began a quiet revolution that, after all was over, transformed APA and organized psychology.

During APA's 1999 Annual Convention in Boston, the work of the Dirty Dozen—and the hundreds of other practitioners who worked to achieve equal representation in APA—was honored at a reception of the Association of Practicing Psychologists (APP), at a business meeting of APA's Div. 42 (Independent Practice) and by the Association for the Advancement of Psychology.

The practitioner movement goes back to the earliest days of APA, but it greatly accelerated after World War II. At that time, the practice of psychology was relatively new and APA was primarily an organization for academic psychologists. But by the 1950s, practitioners became a larger proportion of the association's membership and sought greater representation and more membership services.

Practitioners and others sympathetic to their cause began to organize, seeking better representation. Many drummed up support at the state level, while the group that came to be called the Dirty Dozen focused on the heart of political power in APA.

"At that time, practitioners didn't have much say in APA's governance," said Rogers H. Wright, Ph.D, a Dirty Dozen founder who brought together concerned practitioners from around the country. "We needed support at the national level to address our concerns. Primarily, we wanted better training for practitioners and stronger advocacy on Capitol Hill on behalf of psychology."

By the late 60s, the Dirty Dozen—who actually numbered 14 but liked the sound of the moniker—decided that the best way to advance their cause was to get practitioners elected to APA's Council of Representatives and Board of Directors. The Dirty Dozen and their allies spent hundreds of hours telephoning members, urging them to support practitioner candidates.

Their first major victory was in 1973 when Wright was elected to APA's Board of Directors. Then in 1977, Theodore H. Blau, Ph.D., a practitioner from Tampa, FL, became APA president.

"You have to realize how difficult it was to get a practitioner elected at that time," explains Stan Moldawsky, Ph.D., a private practitioner in Chatham, NJ, who has continued the work started by the Dirty Dozen. "The academicians were famous for their books or their research. Practitioners were unknowns."

"We were never interested in throwing the scientists out," adds Nicholas Cummings, Ph.D., Dirty Dozen member from Reno, NV. "We just wanted equal representation and for them to take us seriously."

As the proportion of practitioners in APA leadership began to increase, the association's agenda shifted. An external group was established to advocate on psychology's behalf on Capitol Hill, and APA strengthened its ties with state psychological associations. In 1985, APA's council approved a special assessment from practitioners to promote the practice agenda, and created the APA Committee for the Advancement of Professional Practice (CAPP) to manage the funds.

Individually, the Dirty Dozen have also done well in APA. Among them, eight have served on the Board of Directors, one as chief executive officer and five as APA presidents.

They are Theodore H. Blau, Ph.D., Nicholas A. Cummings, Ph.D., Raymond D. Fowler, Ph.D., Melvin A. Gravitz, Ph.D., Ernest S. Lawrence, Ph.D., Marvin Metsky, Ph.D., Clarence J. Rosecrans, Jr., Ph.D. (deceased), Donald Schultz, Ph.D. (deceased), Max Siegel, Ph.D. (deceased), A. Eugene Shapiro, Ph.D., Robert D. Weitz, Ph.D., Jack G. Wiggins, Ph.D., Rogers H. Wright, Ph.D., and Francis A. Young, Ph.D.

During the convention, CAPP and APP presented a resolution honoring the group for "transforming the face of organized psychology to the benefit of all practitioners."

— *S. Martin*
APA Monitor, October 1999

"Dirty Dozen" Transformed Psychology
From Academic to Practice Profession

In 1965, when Medicare was high on America's political agenda, three plucky psychologists, Nicholas Cummings, Ph.D., Melvin Gravitz, Ph.D., and Rogers Wright, Ph.D., marched to the office of Wilbur Cohen, the Assistant Secretary for Legislation in the Department of Health, Education and Welfare (HEW) in Washington.

Medicare was about to become law and the Health Care Financing Administration (HCFA) would be responsible for administering the program. The three psychologists sought the inclusion of psychologists for reimbursement in the treatment of elderly Americans.

§

Psychology was then still a largely academic profession and APA was apathetic toward legislative issues except funding for research. So it wasn't surprising that APA would absent itself from the negotiating table during the Medicare debate. This was also a time when no practitioner had yet been elected APA president and when the practice sector was not represented on APA's major boards. In their dialogues, academicians and practitioners often held one another in contempt, resisting the "business" agenda that practitioners were known to espouse.

But academicians controlled the votes on APA committees and on the Council of Representatives, enabling them to veto unwanted changes and repressing the practitioners who were growing in numbers that made change ultimately inevitable.

The discussion that afternoon with HEW's Cohen was surprisingly productive. Cohen assured his visitors that inclusion in Medicare was theirs for the asking if they could secure a letter of support from the American Psychological Association. But the deadline for submitting the letter would be within 48 hours because a final public hearing in Congress on the Medicare legislation was scheduled imminently.

§

By coincidence, the APA Board of Directors was meeting in Washington that weekend. As soon as the three left the HEW Secretary, they rushed to APA's executive offices where the directors were meeting.

After initially resisting, the APA Board of Directors granted a 20-minute presentation and then approved the request, according to Cummings. Wheels were set in motion to assure that the letter would be in the Executive Director's office, ready for delivery to Capitol Hill before the Monday deadline.

Cummings said he and his colleagues retreated to the Gramercy Hotel, less than a block from the APA building. Cummings was chosen to draft the letter. When he finished his handwritten draft late that night, he returned to the APA building to type the letter which he said he placed on the desk of Arthur Brayfield, Ph.D., the executive officer.

His task completed, he headed for Dulles Airport to return to San Francisco, his home.

Two months later, Cummings remembers receiving a call from the secretary of Jerome Bruner, Ph.D. of Harvard University, then president of APA, stating that "Dr. Bruner is in Europe. I found this letter. What do you want me to do with it?"

Recalling the story, Cummings said: "I almost went through the floor."

§

It would be another 24 years after the bungled opportunity before psychology would be included in Medicare, the breakthrough occurring only after American psychiatry had established Medicare as its turf and resolved to try to prevent psychology's participation in territory they had now owned for a quarter century.

By then, in 1989, the Practice Directorate had been created, and a lobbying force at state and national levels was in place to counter psychiatry's onslaught. Behind the leadership of Bryant Welch, Ph.D., the first head of the APA Practice Directorate, and critical support from Sen. Jay Rockefeller (D–W. VA) in the Senate, psychology won a major victory. Ironically, in 1989, Cummings was the APA spokesperson before California Rep. Pete Stark's House Medicare Committee as he had been one of the activists two decades earlier.

§

Whether the 1965 incident in Washington was an oversight by an absent-minded professor or another example of the academic sector stifling practitioners still remains unclear and uncorroborated today.

However, it illustrates the skirmishes between academia and practice which pervaded the 1960s and led to the creation and success of a group that came to be known as the "Dirty Dozen."

They started with the designation "AHCIRSD" (pronounced "accursed"), eventually became "COHI" and then "CAPPS." Their achievements have become legendary.

They worked largely without APA's imprimatur. According to Cummings, they became a "roll up your sleeves" organization, raising money for their operation; lobbying more intently on Capitol Hill during their first year of existence than APA had in its previous history; advocating for Medicare; suing the U.S. Civil Service Commission which had rejected including psychologists in Federal Employment Benefits programs; and helping state psychological associations ease the path to Freedom of Choice (insurance reimbursement) legislation.

They fought as perhaps no other psychology organization before or since. Academicians had ruled psychology during the first 70 years of the organization's existence. Suddenly, this dauntless, resolute group of practitioners began to challenge them, winning the battles and finally the war.

The conflicts between academicians and practitioners dealt not only with issues before Congress and federal agencies but equally within APA because the powerful academicians rejected endorsing advocacy as demanded by the fledgling practitioners.

Already Ted Blau, Ph.D. of Tampa, FL, had tried vainly on

three occasions to become the first practitioner president of APA. He was finally supported by the Dirty Dozen and elected on his fourth try, a victory attributable largely to the creation of Division 31 — the Division of State Psychological Affairs, Cummings said. Working hand-in-hand with Division 31, the militants were able to gain membership on both the APA Council and Board of Directors.

Indeed, a string of practitioners, Cummings, the late Max Siegel, Ph.D., Raymond Fowler, Ph.D., and Jack Wiggins, Ph.D., were elected, and the election of practitioners continues today. Cummings attributes the creation of Division 31 to the work and influence of Francis Young, Ph.D., an academician who sided with the practitioners. "He was our technician," Cummings said. "He kept tabs on who should run for office and who was electable. He was the funnel to help get our council members elected." Young, now blind, formerly a professor at Washington State University in Pullman, WA, in now retired.

§

Historically, the opening salvo in the clash between practitioners and academicians may have been fired 20 years earlier when Connecticut — during the presidency of Karl Heiser, Ph.D., for whom an annual APA award to state psychological association leaders was named — became the first state in 1944 to license psychologists. This legislative process continued ever so slowly for 30 years until Missouri became the 50th state in 1974 to license psychologists. As psychologists gained licensing, many began to switch from academia to practice.

§

As the Dirty Dozen's first function, a few of its members called on insurance companies to persuade them to reimburse psychologists much as they were reimbursing psychiatrists.

They found this to be a thankless task. After several years, the committee reported that it had succeeded with only two small insurance firms who were willing to reimburse psychologists. "It represented two-tenths of 1% of the insured population of the world," Cummings said. "We decided that, unless we changed strategy, it would be the year 3000 before psychologists got reimbursement."

§

The new strategy was developed at a marathon weekend meeting at the home of Rogers Wright in Long Beach, CA, attended by Ernest Lawrence, Ph.D. and Cummings. The trio vowed not to leave Wright's home until they formed a fundraising organization. Attesting to that urgency, they founded an organization within 24 hours which they called the "Council for the Advancement of Psychological Professions and Sciences" (CAPPS).

Then came the difficult part: engaging members. They divided a large roster of psychologists, whom they telephoned to ask them to join as members of a Board of Governors at a cost of $500.

The result was incredible, Cummings reminisced. "We got 500 people to cough up $500 apiece which gave us a quarter of a million dollars. In 1970, that was a lot of money."

The group hired Jack Donahue as their executive director. Donahue later joined the APA as executive assistant to the Executive Director. He died about a decade ago. With the bounty the group had gained during that single memorable weekend, they were off to a running start.

By the late 1960s, APA appointed the "Committee on Health Insurance" (COHI) which was to devise strategy for the upcoming battle to gain insurance reimbursement nationwide. COHI called a meeting of state psychological association insurance chairs in San Francisco. About 42 states sent delegates. Cummings asked two major insurance barons, who were sympathetic, to attend. They recommended that the advocates avoid requesting that mental health coverage be mandated. Better strategy would be, they recommended, to request that insurance plans which reimbursed psychiatrists would similarly reimburse psychologists. The plan was accepted.

Cummings credited Jack Wiggins, Ph.D. formerly of Cleveland, with "a stroke of genius" by changing the "insurance reimbursement" title to "freedom of choice" legislation. The euphemistic phrasing worked and results were quick to follow. New Jersey became the first state to enact the reimbursement legislation in 1968 with California not far behind. However, then-Gov. Pat Brown pocket-vetoed the California bill which had to be reintroduced the following year.

All of it was accomplished without APA endorsement, according to Cummings. He said that six more states enacted freedom of choice laws before APA's Council recognized and endorsed freedom of choice laws as APA policy.

Cummings stepped down as chair of COHI to assume the role of founder of California's four Schools of Professional Psychology.

His ascendancy to the California professional school program soon raised a new issue of interest to those advocating the practitioners' model, a cause for the Dirty Dozen. The group had become increasingly disenchanted with clinical training provided in America's accredited Ph.D. programs. "Students were being trained by faculty who never saw a patient, who were filled with contempt for private practice," Cummings said. "In those days, the fastest way to fail in clinical training programs was to let it be known that the student intended to go into independent practice upon graduation."

The advent of professional schools — there are now about 100 in the country — opened the way to hire clinical faculty even when such individuals lacked the requisite number of publications, Cummings noted.

As APA and the practice activists increasingly headed in separate directions, it raised concerns that psychology was speaking with two voices on Capitol Hill, one representing APA, the other representing the Dirty Dozen.

This dilemma eventually led to APA asking CAPPS to disband. CAPPS agreed if APA would form an advocacy organization. This was done and the new organization became known as APP, the Association for the Advancement of Psychology. Cummings said CAPPS members were pleased with the outcome because they wanted to continue being part of APA, notwithstanding the conflicts of the past.

§

During the intervening years, the pendulum in APA membership swung markedly. The once dominant academic majority became a minority while the practice sector grew and added a new structure with the Practice Directorate, created in 1986 to be supported by a special assessment of practitioners. Meanwhile, dissatisfaction among the academic sector was spreading and led to a split that created the American Psychological Society, now numbering 15,000 members. Despite the stress and distress, APA today claims 88,500 members (which includes members, associate members and fellows), an increase from 72,000 in 1989, and from 37,000 in 1974.

— Henry Saeman
The National Psychologist, November/December 1999

Reactions from Some "Dirty Dozen" Members

At my first meeting with other Dirty Dozen founders in Washington, I had agreed to participate without really knowing what was intended. The meeting began after breakfast, lasted through lunch, broke briefly for dinner, then resumed. We deliberated well into the night.

About 2 A.M., as I lay on the carpet trying to get some rest while participating at the same time (and just before I dropped off into sleep), I remember asking myself: "What have I gotten myself into?" Several participants had come from the West Coast, so they were three hours behind DC time.

What I soon learned to my delight and satisfaction was that we were planning nothing less than the creation of a new professional of practicing psychology. The rest is history.

— *Melvin Gravitz, Ph.D.*

The most amazing dynamic about the "Dirty Dozen" was the unusual extent to which a group of strong-willed, highly opinionated, independent leaders were able to sublimate personal agendas in the interest of working toward a common goal that we never lost sight of. What an experience! And it went on for years.

— *Melvin Metsky, Ph.D.*

The "Dirty Dozen" changed the course of professional psychology and the course of my life. It provided a voice of pride in the practice of psychology. Scope of practice was a state issue but increasingly federal policies were shaping health practices. Without a strong APA that would advocate for practice, our training in clinical psychology was for naught. We developed empowering structures within APA and within state psychological associations to serve the public through psychological practice.

The task is not yet done. Ted Blau, Mel Gravitz and I still sit on APA Council representing practice issues and Ray Fowler is our Executive Officer. Prescriptive authority, a key issue to the future of practice in health care, still gets me off golf courses and into legislators' offices.

— *Jack G. Wiggins, Ph.D.*

ʀesolutioɴ

Honoring

The Dirty Dozen

In anticipation of the 30th anniversary of the creation of the so-called "Dirty Dozen", the Association of Practicing Psychologists and the Committee for the Advancement of Professional Practice have unanimously voted the following resolution.

Whereas the "Dirty Dozen" has transformed the face of organized psychology to the benefit of all practitioners in a span of only three decades, and

Whereas, the organizing group founded the first active caucus of the APA Council of Representatives which is now known as the Association of Practicing Psychologists, and

Whereas, their efforts led to many actions of considerable benefit to practitioners including the formation of a psychology political action committee, strong legislative and regulatory advocacy programs, strengthening state psychological associations as bases for support of practice, the regulation and promotion of psychological practice on state and national levels, establishment of special assessment and the creation of the Committee for the Advancement of Professional Practice, and

Whereas, the political acumen and leadership qualities of the group is demonstrated by the fact that it has produced 8 members of the Board of Directors, 1 Chief Executive Officer and 5 presidents of the American Psychological Association, and

Whereas, there is scarcely any governance unit, structure, policy or action of APA related to practice over the past 3 decades that does not bear the imprimatur of the "Dirty Dozen" or their immediate successors, and

Whereas members of the group have been mentors, role models and motivators to more practitioners than any other single individual or group in the history of the profession,

Now therefore be it resolved that we gratefully acknowledge the numerous contributions of the "Dirty Dozen" (despite the fact they never learned to count) and hereby vow to faithfully protect the profession they did so much to create:

Theodore H. Blau, PhD
Nicholas A. Cummings, PhD
Raymond D. Fowler, PhD
Melvin A. Gravitz, PhD
Ernest S. Lawrence, PhD
Marvin Metsky, PhD
A. Eugene Shapiro, PhD
Robert D. Weitz, PhD
Jack G. Wiggins, PhD

Rogers H. Wright, PhD
Francis A. Young, PhD

Deceased

Clarence J. Rosecrans, Jr., PhD
Donald Schultz, PhD
Max Siegel, PhD

In witness whereof, we affix our signatures on the 19th of August, 1999 at the annual convention of the American Psychological Association in Boston, Massachusetts.

Ronald E. Fox, PhD, Chair
CAPP

Patricia M. Bricklin, PhD, Chair
APP

Citations presented to the Dirty Dozen on the occasion of their 30th anniversary by the Association for the Advancement of Psychology (AAP) and the Association of Practicing Psychologists (APP). The presentation was made in a special ceremony at the 1999 APA Convention in Boston.

The Association for the Advancement of Psychology

AAP

Honors

THE DIRTY DOZEN

THEODORE F. BLAU, PH.D.	NICHOLAS A. CUMMINGS, PH.D.
RAYMOND D. FOWLER, PH.D.	MELVIN A. GRAVITZ, PH.D.
MARVIN METSKY, PH.D.	A. EUGENE SHAPIRO, PH.D.
ROBERT D. WEITZ, PH.D.	JACK G. WIGGINS, PH.D.
ERNEST S. LAWRENCE, PH.D.	FRANCIS A. YOUNG, PH.D.

ROGERS H. WRIGHT, PH.D., CHAIR

IN MEMORIUM

C.J. ROSECRANS, JR., PH.D.
S. DON SCHULTZ, PH.D.
MAX SIEGEL, PH.D.

For Their Unparalleled Leadership In The Advancement Of Professional Psychology
For Their Vision In Creating The First Political Action Committee For Psychology
And For Their Unfaltering Dedication And Service Which Has Permeated
Every Aspect Of The Profession For The Past 30 Years.

American Psychological Association Convention

30th Anniversary – "Dirty Dozen"

Boston, Massachusetts – August 21, 1999

The Honorable Order of

The Dirty Dozen

Once scorned, and confronted by seemingly insurmountable odds,
the following fourteen professional psychologists, affectionately
called The Dirty Dozen, changed for all time the face of the

American Psychological Association

Theodore H. Blau, Ph.D.
Nicholas A. Cummings, Ph.D
Raymond D. Fowler, Ph.D.
Melvin Gravitz, Ph.D.
Ernest Lawrence, Ph.D.
Marvin Metsky, Ph.D.
A. Eugene Shapiro, Ph.D.
Robert Weitz, Ph.D.
Jack G. Wiggins, Ph.D.
Rogers H. Wright, Ph.D.
Francis Young, Ph.D.

In Memoriam

C. J. Rosecrans, Ph.D.
S. Don Schultz, Ph.D.
Max Siegel, Ph.D.

Presented on the occasion of the 30th Anniversary of the beginning
of its successful and unrelenting activities to change
organized psychology.

August 19, 1999
Boston, Massachusetts

California School of Professional Psychology president Nick Cummings with his four campus deans: Abou Ghorra (Fresno), Art Kovacs (Los Angeles), Don Schultz (San Francisco), and Maury Zemlick (San Diego). The occasion was the 1974 CSPP retreat at the Highlands Inn, Carmel, California. All are wearing the Scotish tam, CSPP's badge of leadership.

Ted Blau, the first Dirty Dozen member elected to the
presidency of the APA, presided over the APA Board of Directors in 1977.

Dirty Dozen member Ray Fowler
during his term as president of the APA.

Marvin Metsky when he first became
a member of the Dirty Dozen in 1966.

Dirty Dozen member Jack Wiggins
during his term as president of the APA.

The late Dirty Dozen member Max Siegel
during his term as president of the APA.

APA president Nick Cummings announces his appointment of
Rachel Hare-Mustin, Ph.D., as the APA parliamentarian in 1979.
Hare-Mustin was the first woman and the first certified parliamentarian
to serve in that capacity.

Rogers Wright "making his pact with the devil" (circa 1978).
This statue adorned the foyer of the Devil's Pitchfork Restaurant in the
Gramercy Inn, Washington, DC, a favorite meeting place
of the Dirty Dozen in the years beginning with the early 1960s.

Dirty Dozen members and Arkansas buddies Rogers Wright and the late C. J. Rosecrans at an AAP cocktail party.

The historic 1978 APA Board of Directors meeting in which four of the Dirty Dozen, three of whom became APA presidents, were members: Second, back row: Nick Cummings. Center front row, left to right: Max Siegel, Ted Blau, and Rogers Wright. At the very end is Charles Kiesler, the first APA executive officer chosen with Dirty Dozen participation (Wright and Cummings were on the selection committee).

APA president Nick Cummings presiding over the APA Board of Directors in 1979. Seated next to him is past president and Dirty Dozen member Ted Blau, and above Ted is Dirty Dozen board member Don Schultz.

Dirty Dozen stalwart Rogers Wright representing Division 12 (Clinical Psychology) at the 1982 Council of Representatives.

Dirty Dozen member A. Eugene Shapiro with U.S. Senator Harrison "Pete" Williams, March 28, 1979. Gene had just testified before the Senate Committee on Labor and Human Resources on behalf of the Association for the Advancement of Psychology (AAP). As a result of this testimony, psychologists were included as providers under worker compensation law. This was the first reference to psychologists, as reimbursable providers, under federal law.

Max Siegel presenting a plaque to Eugene Shapiro on completion of his term serving on the APA Board of Directors in January 1984. Kitty Katzell is in the background.

Surgeon General Koop with Dirty Dozen members Ray Fowler and Jack Wiggins, who was then APA president. Photo taken circa 1989.

Nick Cummings addressing the Ph.D. graduates at the
first commencement of the California Schools of Professional Psychology.

INDEX

ROGERS J. WRIGHT, PH.D., LITT.D. Recently retired from several decades of practice in Long Beach, California, he was one of the pioneering psychologists who entered practice long before the advent of licensure and the recognition of psychology as an autonomous profession. He was the second practitioner elected to the APA Board of Directors, and he remained for 30 years the acknowledged leader for professional advocacy. Dr. Wright's career culminated in his serving as Executive Director of the Association for the Advancement of Psychology (AAP).

NICHOLAS A. CUMMINGS, PH.D., SC.D. President, Foundation for Behavioral Health, and Chairman, The Nicholas & Dorothy Cummings Foundation, Inc. Founding CEO, American Biodyne (MedCo/Merck, then Merit, now Magellan Behavioral Care). Former President, American Psychological Association. Founder of the four campuses of the California School of Professional Psychology. Chief Psychologist (Retired), Kaiser Permanente. Founder, National Academies of Practice. Founder, American Managed Behavioral Healthcare Association. Founder, National Professional Schools of Psychology. Former Executive Director, Mental Research Institute, Palo Alto, California. Currently, Distinguished Professor, University of Nevada, Reno.

The practice of psychology